Praise for *Thinking Strategically*

"Machiavelli is brought up-to-date in this book by Dixit and Nalebuff. They make strategic tools humorous, human, and effective."
> —Elizabeth Bailey, former dean, Graduate School of
> Industrial Administration, Carnegie Mellon University

"I confess that I have never thought of monetary policy or government as a game, but Professors Dixit and Nalebuff succeed brilliantly in clarifying questions we all face in decision-making, elevated or mundane."   —Paul A. Volcker

"*Thinking Strategically* gives you the vital components for good and effective negotiating."
> —Bob Woolf, author of *Friendly Persuasion*

"To be literate in the modern age, you need to have a general understanding of game theory. Dixit and Nalebuff provide the skeleton key. You'll benefit from *Thinking Strategically* and enjoy the book."   —Paul Samuelson

t © 1991 by Avinash K. Dixit and Barry J. Nalebuff
All rights reserved.
Printed in the United States of America.
ypeset by Barry J. Nalebuff using Textures.

ion credit: Chapter 2: Cartoon by Charles Schulz.
d with permission of United Feature Syndicate, Inc.

Reissued in Norton Paperback 1993

ary of Congress Cataloging in Publication Data

strategically: the competitive edge in business, politics,
life / by Avinash K. Dixit and Barry J. Nalebuff.

s Index
neory   2. Management   3. Competition
arry, 1958 – .   II. Title.
1991
20   90-33760

ISBN 0-393-31035-3

& Company, Inc., 500 Fifth Avenue, New York, N.Y. 10110
& Company Ltd, 10 Coptic Street, London WC1A 1PU

7 8 9 0

About the authors

AVINASH K. DIXIT is John J. F. Sherrerd University Professor of Economics at Princeton University. He has taught courses on games of strategy and has done research into strategic behavior in international trade policy. He earned his Ph.D. at the Massachusetts Institute of Technology and has taught previously at Warwick University (U.K.), Berkeley, and Oxford.

BARRY J. NALEBUFF is Professor of Economics and Management at the Yale School of Organization and Management. He teaches courses on strategy, politics, and decision-making. A frequent contributor on questions of strategy, his work has appeared in the *New York Times* and the *Washington Post,* among other widely read publications. He has also applied the tools of thinking strategically for Chemical Bank, McKinsey & Co., and the Sawyer-Miller Group. A Rhodes Scholar, he earned his doctorate at Oxford University.

Thinkin

The Compe
Politics,

Avinash K. Di

W. W.

Ne

Copyri

Illust
Reprin

Li

Dixit, Avinash
Thinkin
and everyd
p. c
Inclu
1. Game
I. Nalebuff,
HD30.28.D
658.4'012–

W. W. Nort
W. W. Nort

For Kusum and Marcia

Contents

Preface

Strategic thinking is the art of outdoing an adversary, knowing that the adversary is trying to do the same to you. All of us must practice strategic thinking at work as well as at home. Businessmen and corporations must use good competitive strategies to survive. Politicians have to devise campaign strategies to get elected, and legislative strategies to implement their visions. Football coaches plan strategies for the players to execute on the field. Parents trying to elicit good behavior from children must become amateur strategists (the children are the pros). For forty years, superpowers' nuclear strategies have governed the survival of the human race.

Good strategic thinking in such numerous diverse contexts remains an art. But its foundations consist of some simple basic principles — an emerging science of strategy. Our premise in writing this book is that readers from a variety of backgrounds and occupations can become better strategists if they know these principles.

The science of strategic thinking is called game theory. This is a relatively young science — less than fifty years old. It has already provided many useful insights for practical strategists. But, like all sciences, it has become shrouded in jargon and mathematics. These are essential research tools, but they prevent all but the specialists from understanding the basic ideas. We have attempted a translation of many important insights for the intelligent general reader. We have replaced theoretical arguments with illustrative examples and case studies. We have removed all the mathematics and most of the jargon. The book should be accessible to all readers who are willing to follow a little bit of arithmetic, charts, and tables.

Many books have already attempted to develop ideas of strategic thinking for particular applications. Tom Schelling's writings on nuclear strategies, particularly *The Strategy of Conflict* and *Arms and Influence*, are justly famous. In fact, Schelling pioneered a lot of game theory in the process of applying it to nuclear conflict. Michael Porter's *Competitive Strategy*, drawing on the lessons of game theory for business strategy, is equally famous. Steven Brams has written several books, the most notable being *Game Theory and Politics*.

In this book we do not confine the ideas to any particular context. Instead, we offer a very wide range of illustrations for each basic principle. Thus readers from many different backgrounds will all find something familiar here. They will also see how the same principles bear on strategies in less familiar circumstances; we hope this gives them a new perspective on many events in news as well as history. We also draw on the shared experience of most American readers, with illustrations from, for example, literature, movies, and sports. Serious scientists may think this trivializes strategy, but we believe that familiar examples from movies and sports are a very effective vehicle for conveying the important ideas.

Like Tolkien's *Lord of the Rings*, this book grew in the telling. Its ancient origins are a course on "games of strategy" that Avinash Dixit developed and taught at Princeton's Woodrow Wilson School of Public and International Affairs. Barry Nalebuff later taught this course, and a similar one at Yale University's Political Science Department and then at Yale's School of Organization and Management (SOM). We thank many students from these courses for their enthusiasm and ideas. Particular mention should be made of Anne Case, Jonathan Flemming, Heather Hazard, Dani Rodrik, and Jonathan Shimshoni. Takashi Kanno and Yuichi Shimazu undertook the task of translating our words and ideas into Japanese; in the process, they improved the English version.

Thinking Strategically

The idea of writing a book at a more popular level than that of a course text came from Hal Varian of the University of Michigan. He also gave us many useful ideas and comments on earlier drafts. Drake McFeely at W. W. Norton was an excellent if exacting editor. He made extraordinary efforts to fashion our academic writing into a lively text. If the book still retains some traces of its teaching origins, that is because we did not listen to all of his advice.

Many colleagues and friends read earlier drafts with care and gave us numerous detailed and excellent suggestions for improvement. At the risk of omitting some, we should make particular mention of David Austen-Smith (Rochester), Alan Blinder (Princeton), Seth Masters (S. Bernstein), Carl Shapiro (Princeton), Louis Taylor (MITRE Corporation), Thomas Trendell (ATT-Paradyne), Terry Vaughn (MIT Press), and Robert Willig (Princeton). As manuscript editors, Stacey Mandelbaum and Laura Kang Ward were generous to our faults — each time you don't find a mistake, you should thank them.

We also want to give credit to those who have helped us find a title for this book. Hal Varian started us off with *Thinking Strategically*. Yale SOM students gave us many more choices. Our favorite was Deborah Halpern's *Beyond the Playground* and an advertising campaign written by William Barnes:
"Thinking Strategically — Don't Compete Without It."*

> Avinash Dixit
> Barry Nalebuff
> October 1990

---

* There were also some pretty amusing suggestions, including *Strategy and You*.

Introduction

What Is Strategic Behavior?

How should people behave in society?

Our answer does not deal with ethics or etiquette. Nor do we aim to compete with philosophers, preachers, or even Emily Post. Our theme, although less lofty, affects the lives of all of us just as much as do morality and manners. This book is about strategic behavior. All of us are strategists, whether we like it or not. It is better to be a good strategist than a bad one, and this book aims to help you improve your skills at discovering and using effective strategies.

Work, even social life, is a constant stream of decisions. What career to follow, how to manage a business, whom to marry, how to bring up children, whether to run for president, are just some examples of such fateful choices. The common element in these situations is that you do not act in a vacuum. Instead, you are surrounded by active decision-makers whose choices interact with yours. This interaction has an important effect on your thinking and actions.

To illustrate the point, think of the difference between the decisions of a lumberjack and those of a general. When the lumberjack decides how to chop wood, he does not expect the wood to fight back; his environment is neutral. But when the general tries to cut down the enemy's army, he must anticipate and overcome resistance to his plans. Like the general, you must recognize that your business rivals, prospective spouse, and even your child are intelligent and purposive people. Their aims often conflict with yours, but they include some potential allies. Your own choice must allow for the conflict, and utilize the cooperation. Such interactive decisions are called strategic, and the plan of action appropriate to them is called a strategy. This book aims to help you think strategically, and then translate these thoughts into action.

The branch of social science that studies strategic decision-making is called *game theory*. The games in this theory range from chess to child-rearing, from tennis to takeovers, and from advertising to arms control. As the Hungarian humorist George Mikes expressed it, "Many continentals think life is a game; the English think cricket is a game." We think both are right.

Playing these games requires many different kinds of skills. Basic skills, such as shooting ability in basketball, knowledge of precedents in law, or a blank face in poker, are one kind; strategic thinking is another. Strategic thinking starts with your basic skills, and considers how best to use them. Knowing the law, you must decide the strategy for defending your client. Knowing *how well* your football team can pass or run, and how well the other team can defend against each choice, your decision as the coach is *whether* to pass or to run. Sometimes, as in the case of superpowers contemplating an adventure that risks nuclear war, strategic thinking also means knowing when not to play.

Our aim is to improve your strategy I.Q. But we have not tried to provide a book of recipes for strategies. We develop the ideas and principles of strategic thinking; to apply them to a specific situation you face and to find the right choice there, you will have to do some more work. This is because the specifics of each situation are likely to differ in some significant aspects, and any general prescriptions for action we might give could be misleading. In each situation, you will have to pull together principles of good strategy we have discussed, and also other principles from other considerations. You must combine them and, where they conflict with each other, evaluate the relative strengths of the different arguments. We do not promise to solve every question you might have. The science of game theory is far from being complete, and in some ways strategic thinking remains an art.

We do provide guidance for translating the ideas into action. Chapter 1 offers several examples showing how strategic issues arise in a variety of decisions. We point out some effective strategies, some less effective ones, and even some downright bad ones. The subsequent chapters proceed to build these examples into a system or a framework of thought. In the later chapters, we take up several broad classes of strategic situations — brinkmanship, voting, incentives, and bargaining — where you can see the principles in action.

The examples range from the familiar, trivial, or amusing — usually drawn from literature, sports, or movies — to the frightening — nuclear confrontation. The former are merely a nice and palatable vehicle for the game-theoretic ideas. As to the latter, at one point many readers would have thought the subject of nuclear war too horrible to permit rational analysis. But as the cold war winds down and the world is generally perceived to be a safer place, we hope that the game-theoretic aspects of the arms race and the Cuban missile crisis can be examined for their strategic logic in some detachment from their emotional content.

The chapters are full of examples, but these serve primarily to develop or illustrate the particular principle being discussed, and many other details of reality that pertain to the example are set aside. At the end of each chapter, we present a "case study," similar to one you might come across in a business-school class. Each case sets out a particular set of circumstances and invites you to apply the principles discussed in that chapter to find the right strategy for that situation. Some cases are open-ended; but that is also a feature of life. At times there is no clearly correct solution, only imperfect ways to cope with the problem. A serious effort to think each case through before reading our discussion is a better way to understand the ideas than any amount of reading of the text alone. For more practice, the final chapter is a collection of twenty three more cases, in roughly increasing order of difficulty.

By the end of the book, we hope that you will emerge a more effective manager, negotiator, athlete, politician, or parent. We warn you that some of the strategies that are good for achieving these goals may not earn you the love of your defeated rivals. If you want to be fair, tell them about our book.

Part I

1

Ten Tales of Strategy

We begin with ten tales of strategy from different aspects of life and offer preliminary thoughts on how best to play. Many of you will have faced similar problems in everyday life, and will have reached the correct solution after some thought or trial and error. For others, some of the answers may be surprising, but surprise is not the primary purpose of the examples. Our aim is to show that such situations are pervasive, that they amount to a coherent set of questions, and that methodical thinking about them is likely to be fruitful. In later chapters, we develop these systems of thought into prescriptions for effective strategy. Think of these tales as a taste of dessert before the main course. They are designed to whet your appetite, not fill you up.

1. THE HOT HAND

Do athletes ever have a "hot hand"? Sometimes it seems that Larry Bird cannot miss a basket, or Wayne Gretzky or Diego Maradona a shot on goal. Sports announcers see these long streaks of consecutive successes and proclaim that the athlete has a "hot hand." Yet according to psychology professors Thomas Gilovich, Robert Vallone, and Amos Tversky, this is a misperception of reality.[1] They point out that if you flip a coin long enough, you will find some very long series of consecutive heads. The psychologists suspect that sports commentators, short on insightful things to say, are just finding patterns in what amounts to a long series of coin tosses over a long playing season. They propose a more rigorous test. In basketball, they look at all the instances of a player's baskets, and observe the percentage of times that player's next shot is also a basket. A similar calculation is made for the shots immediately following misses. If a basket is more likely to follow a basket than to follow a miss, then there really is something to the theory of the hot hand.

They conducted this test on the Philadelphia 76ers basketball team. The results contradicted the "hot hand" view. When a player made his last shot, he was less likely to make his next; when he missed his previous attempt, he was more likely to make his next. This was true even for Andrew Toney, a player with the reputation for being a streak shooter. Does this mean we should be talking of the "stroboscopic hand," like the strobe light that alternates between on and off?

Game theory suggests a different interpretation. While the statistical evidence denies the presence of streak shooting, it does not refute the possibility that a "hot" player might warm up the game in some other way. The difference between streak shooting and a hot hand arises because of the interaction between the offensive and the defensive strategies. Suppose Andrew Toney does have a truly hot hand. Surely the other side would start to crowd him. This could easily lower his shooting percentage.

That is not all. When the defense focuses on Toney, one of his teammates is left unguarded and is more likely to shoot successfully. In other words, Toney's hot hand leads to an improvement in the 76ers' *team* performance, although there may be a deterioration in Toney's *individual* performance. Thus we might test for hot hands by looking for streaks in team success.

Similar phenomena are observed in many other team sports. A brilliant running-back on a football team improves its passing game and a great pass-receiver helps the running game, as the opposition is forced to allocate more of its defensive resources to guard the stars. In the 1986 soccer World Cup final, the Argentine star Diego Maradona did not score a goal, but his passes through a ring of West German defenders led to two Argentine goals. The value of a star cannot be assessed by looking only at his scoring performance; his contribution to his teammates' performance is crucial, and assist statistics help measure this contribution. In ice hockey, assists and goals are given equal weight for ranking individual performance.

A player may even assist himself when one hot hand warms up the other. The Boston Celtics star, Larry Bird, prefers shooting with his right hand (though his left hand is still better than most). The defense knows that Bird is right-handed, so they concentrate on defending against right-handed shots. But they do not do so exclusively, since Bird's left-handed shots are too effective to be left unguarded.

What happens when Bird spends his off season working to improve his left-handed shooting? The defense responds by spending more time covering his left-handed shots. The result is that this frees his right hand more often. A better left-handed shot results in a more effective right-handed shot. In this case not only does the left hand know what the right hand is doing, it's helping it out.

Going one step further, in Chapter 7 we show that when the left hand is stronger it may even be used *less* often. Many of you will have experienced this seemingly strange phenomenon when playing tennis. If your backhand is much weaker than your forehand, your opponents will learn to play to your backhand. Eventually, as a result of all this backhand practice, your backhand will improve. As your two strokes become more equal, opponents can no longer exploit your weak backhand. They will play more evenly between forehands and backhands. You get to use your better forehand more often; this could be the real advantage of improving your backhand.

2. TO LEAD OR NOT TO LEAD

After the first four races in the 1983 America's Cup finals, Dennis Conner's *Liberty* led 3–1 in a best-of-seven series. On the morning of the fifth race, "cases of champagne had been delivered to *Liberty*'s dock. And on their spectator yacht, the wives of the crew were wearing red-white-and-blue tops and shorts, in anticipation of having their picture taken after their husbands had prolonged the United States' winning streak to 132 years."[2] It was not to be.

At the start, *Liberty* got off to a 37-second lead when *Australia II* jumped the gun and had to recross the starting line. The Australian skipper, John Bertrand, tried to catch up by sailing way over to the left of the course in the hopes of catching a wind shift. Dennis Conner chose to keep *Liberty* on the right-hand side of the course. Bertrand's gamble paid off. The wind shifted five degrees in *Australia II*'s favor and she won the race by one minute and forty-seven seconds. Conner was criticized for his strategic failure to follow *Australia II*'s path. Two races later, *Australia II* won the series.

Sailboat racing offers the chance to observe an interesting reversal of a "follow the leader" strategy. The leading sailboat usually copies the strategy of the trailing boat. When the follower tacks, so does the leader. The leader imitates the follower even when the follower is clearly pursuing a poor strategy. Why? Because in sailboat racing (unlike ballroom dancing) close doesn't count: only winning matters. If you have the lead, the surest way to stay ahead is to play monkey see, monkey do.*

Stock-market analysts and economic forecasters are not immune to this copycat strategy. The leading forecasters have an incentive to follow the pack and produce predictions similar to

---

* This strategy no longer applies once there are more than two competitors. Even with three boats, if one boat tacks right and the other tacks left, the leader has to choose which (if either) to follow.

everyone else's. This way people are unlikely to change their perception of these forecasters' abilities. On the other hand, newcomers take the risky strategies: they tend to predict boom or doom. Usually they are wrong and are never heard of again, but now and again they are proven correct and move to the ranks of the famous.

Industrial and technological competitions offer further evidence. In the personal-computer market, IBM is less known for its innovation than for its ability to bring standardized technology to the mass market. More new ideas have come from Apple, Sun, and other start-up companies. Risky innovations are their best and perhaps only chance of gaining market share. This is true not just of high-technology goods. Proctor and Gamble, the IBM of diapers, followed Kimberly Clark's innovation of resealable diaper tape, and recaptured its commanding market position.

There are two ways to move second. You can imitate as soon as the other has revealed his approach (as in sailboat racing) or wait longer until the success or failure of the approach is known (as in computers). The longer wait is more advantageous in business because, unlike sports, the competition is usually not winner-take-all. As a result, market leaders will not follow the upstarts unless they also believe in the merits of their course.

3. GO DIRECTLY TO JAIL

The conductor of an orchestra in the Soviet Union (during the Stalin era) was traveling by train to his next engagement and was looking over the score of the music he was to conduct that night. Two KGB officers saw what he was reading and, thinking that the musical notation was some secret code, arrested him as a spy. He protested that it was only Tchaikovsky's Violin Concerto, but to no avail. On the second day of his imprisonment, the interrogator walked in smugly and said, "You had better tell us all. We have caught your friend Tchaikovsky, and he is already talking."

So begins one telling of the prisoners' dilemma, perhaps the best-known strategic game. Let us develop the story to its logical conclusion. Suppose the KGB has actually arrested someone whose only offense is that he is called Tchaikovsky, and are separately subjecting him to the same kind of interrogation. If the two innocents withstand this treatment, each will be sentenced to 3 years' imprisonment.* If the conductor makes a false confession that implicates the unknown "collaborator," while Tchaikovsky holds out, then the conductor will get away with 1 year (and the KGB's gratitude), while Tchaikovsky gets the harsh sentence of 25 years for his recalcitrance. Of course, the tables will be turned if the conductor stands firm while Tchaikovsky gives in and implicates him. If both confess, then both will receive the standard sentence of 10 years.†

Now consider the conductor's thinking. He knows that Tchaikovsky is either confessing or holding out. If Tchaikovsky confesses, the conductor gets 25 years by holding out and 10 years by confessing, so it is better for him to confess. If Tchaikovsky holds out, the conductor gets 3 years if he holds out, and only 1 if he confesses; again it is better for him to confess. Thus confession is clearly the conductor's best action.

In a separate cell in Dzerzhinsky Square, Tchaikovsky is doing a similar mental calculation and reaching the same conclusion. The result, of course, is that both of them confess. Later, when they meet in the Gulag Archipelago, they com-

---

* There is the story of the newcomer to the Gulag who was asked by the residents, "How long is your sentence?" The answer was "Ten years." "What did you do?" "Nothing." "No, there must be some mistake. The sentence for that is only three years."

† This actually meant 3,653 days: "The three extra days were for leap years." (A. Solzhenitsyn, *One Day in the Life of Ivan Denisovitch*, 1962.)

pare stories and realize that they have been had. If they both had stood firm, they both would have gotten away with much shorter sentences.

If only they had had an opportunity to meet and talk things over before they were interrogated, they could have agreed that neither would give in. But they are quick to realize that in all probability such an agreement would not have done much good. Once they were separated and the interrogations began, each person's private incentive to get a better deal by double-crossing the other would have been quite powerful. Once again they would have met in the Gulag, there perhaps to settle the score of the betrayals (not of the concerto). Can the two achieve enough mutual credibility to reach their jointly preferred solution?

Many people, firms, and even nations have been gored on the horns of the prisoners' dilemma. Look at the life-or-death issue of nuclear arms control. Each superpower liked best the outcome in which the other disarmed, while it kept its own arsenal "just in case." Disarming yourself while the other remains armed was the worst prospect. Therefore no matter what the other side did, each preferred to stay armed. However, they could join in agreeing that the outcome in which both disarm is better than the one in which both are armed. The problem is the interdependence of decisions: the *jointly* preferred outcome arises when each chooses its *individually* worse strategy. Could the jointly preferred outcome be achieved given each side's clear incentive to break the agreement and to arm itself secretly? In this case it needed a fundamental change in Soviet thinking to get the world started on the road to nuclear disarmament.

For one's comfort, safety, or even life itself, one needs to know the ways to get out of the prisoners' dilemma. In Chapter 4 we look at some such avenues, and see when and how well they are likely to work.

The story of the prisoners' dilemma also carries a useful

general point: most economic, political, or social games are different from games such as football or poker. Football and poker are *zero-sum games*: one person's gain is another person's loss. But in the prisoners' dilemma, there are possibilities for mutual advantage as well as conflict of interest; both prisoners prefer the no-confession result to its opposite. Similarly, in employer-union bargaining, there is an opposition of interests in that one side prefers low wages and the other high ones, but there is agreement that a breakdown of negotiations leading to a strike would be more damaging for both sides. In fact such situations are the rule rather than the exception. Any useful analysis of games should be able to handle a mixture of conflict and concurrence of interests. We usually refer to the players in a game as "opponents," but you should remember that on occasion, strategy makes strange bedfellows.

4. HERE I STAND

When the Catholic Church demanded that Martin Luther repudiate his attack on the authority of popes and councils, he refused to recant: "I will not recant anything, for to go against conscience is neither right nor safe." Nor would he compromise: "Here I stand, I cannot do otherwise."[3] Luther's intransigence was based on the divinity of his positions. When defining what was right, there was no room for compromise. His firmness had profound long-term consequences; his attacks led to the Protestant Reformation and substantially altered the medieval Catholic Church.*

Similarly, Charles de Gaulle used the power of intransigence to become a powerful player in the arena of interna-

---

* Luther's reputation extends beyond the Church and behind the Iron Curtain. The Wartburg, East Germany's domestically produced car, is jokingly referred to as "The Luther": apparently it can be equally immobile.

tional relations. As his biographer Don Cook expressed it, "[De Gaulle] could create power for himself with nothing but his own rectitude, intelligence, personality and sense of destiny."[4] But above all, his was "the power of intransigence." During the Second World War, as the self-proclaimed leader in exile of a defeated and occupied nation, he held his own in negotiations with Roosevelt and Churchill. In the 1960s, his presidential "Non!" swung several decisions France's way in the European Economic Community.

In what way did his intransigence give him power in bargaining? When de Gaulle took a truly irrevocable position, the other parties in the negotiation were left with just two options — to take it or to leave it. For example, he single-handedly kept England out of the European Economic Community, once in 1963 and again in 1968; the other countries were forced either to accept de Gaulle's veto or to break up the EEC. De Gaulle judged his position carefully to ensure that it would be accepted. But that often left the larger (and unfair) division of the spoils to France. De Gaulle's intransigence denied the other party an opportunity to come back with a counteroffer that was acceptable.

In practice, this is easier said than done, for two kinds of reasons. The first kind stems from the fact that bargaining usually involves considerations beside the pie on today's table. The perception that you have been excessively greedy may make others less willing to negotiate with you in the future. Or, next time they may be more firm bargainers as they try to recapture some of their perceived losses. On a personal level, an unfair win may spoil business relations, or even personal relations. Indeed, biographer David Schoenbrun faulted de Gaulle's chauvinism: "In human relations, those who do not love are rarely loved: those who will not be friends end up by having none. De Gaulle's rejection of friendship thus hurt France."[5] A compromise in the short term may prove a better strategy over the long haul.

The second kind of problem lies in achieving the necessary degree of intransigence. Luther and de Gaulle achieved this through their personalities. But this entails a cost. An inflexible personality is not something you can just turn on and off. Although being inflexible can sometimes wear down an opponent and force him to make concessions, it can equally well allow small losses to grow into major disasters.

Ferdinand de Lesseps was a mildly competent engineer with extraordinary vision and determination. He is famous for building the Suez Canal in what seemed almost impossible conditions. He did not recognize the impossible and thereby accomplished it. Later, he tried using the same technique to build the Panama Canal. It ended in disaster.* Whereas the sands of the Nile yielded to his will, tropical malaria did not. The problem for de Lesseps was that his inflexible personality could not admit defeat even when the battle was lost.

How can one achieve selective inflexibility? Although there is no ideal solution, there are various means by which commitment can be achieved and sustained; this is the topic for Chapter 6.

5. BELLING THE CAT

In the children's story about belling the cat, the mice decide that life would be much safer if the cat were stuck with a bell around its neck. The problem is, who will risk his life to bell the cat?

This is a problem for both mice and men. How can rel-

___

* The Suez Canal is a sea-level passage. The digging was relatively easy since the land was already low-lying and desert. Panama involved much higher elevations, lakes along the way, and dense jungle. Lesseps' attempt to dig down to sea level failed. Much later, the U.S. Army Corps of Engineers succeeded using a very different method — a sequence of locks, using the lakes along the way.

atively small armies of occupying powers or tyrants control very large populations for long periods? Why is a planeload of people powerless before a single hijacker with a gun? In both cases, a simultaneous move by the masses stands a very good chance of success. But the communication and coordination required for such action is difficult, and the oppressors, knowing the power of the masses, take special steps to keep it difficult. When the people must act individually and hope that the momentum will build up, the question arises, "Who is going to be the first?" Such a leader will pay a very high cost — possibly his life. His reward may be posthumous glory or gratitude. There are people who are moved by considerations of duty or honor, but most find the costs exceed the benefits.

Khrushchev first denounced Stalin's purges at the Soviet Communist Party's 20th Congress. After his dramatic speech, someone in the audience shouted out, asking what Khrushchev had been doing at the time. Khrushchev responded by asking the questioner to please stand up and identify himself. The audience remained silent. Khrushchev replied: "That is what I did, too."

In a sense, we have seen these examples before. They are just a prisoners' dilemma with more than two people; one might call this the hostages' dilemma. Here we want to use this dilemma to make a different point — namely, the frequent superiority of punishment over reward. The dictator might keep the populace peaceful by providing it material and even spiritual comforts, but this can be a very costly proposition. Oppression and terror relying on the Hostages' Dilemma can be a much cheaper alternative.

There are many examples of this principle. In a large taxi fleet, cars are often assigned to drivers by a dispatcher. The fleet has some good cars and some clunkers. The dispatcher can use his assignment power to extract a small bribe from each of the drivers. Any driver who refuses to pay is sure to get a clunker, while those who cooperate are given the luck of the draw from the remainder.* The dispatcher gets rich, and the drivers as a group end up with the same set of cabs that they would have if no one used bribery. If the drivers acted in collusion, they probably could stop this practice. The problem lies in getting the movement organized. The point is not so much that the dispatcher can reward those who bribe him, but that he can punish severely those who don't.

A similar story can be told about evicting tenants from rent-controlled apartments. If someone buys such a building in New York, he has the right to evict one tenant so as to be able to live in his own building. But this translates into a power to clear the whole. A new landlord can try the following argument with the tenant in Apartment 1A: "I have the right to live in my building. Therefore, I plan to evict you and move into your apartment. However, if you cooperate and leave voluntarily, then I will reward you with $5,000." This is a token amount in relation to the value of the rent-controlled apartment (although it still buys a few subway tokens in New York). Faced with the choice of eviction with $5,000 or eviction without $5,000, the tenant takes the money and runs. The landlord then offers the same deal to the tenant in 1B, and so on.

The United Auto Workers have a similar advantage when they negotiate with the auto manufacturers sequentially. A strike against Ford alone puts it at particular disadvantage when General Motors and Chrysler continue to operate; therefore Ford is more likely to settle quickly on terms favorable to the Union. Such a strike is also less costly to the Union as only one third of their members are out. After winning against Ford, the Union takes on GM and then Chrysler, using each previous success as precedent and fuel for their fire. In contrast, Japanese union incentives work the other way,

---

* Even if everyone pays, some drivers will end up with a clunker. But if the clunkers are randomly assigned, no driver faces a great chance of the bad draw. In contrast, the first driver who refuses to pay can expect to drive the clunker quite regularly.

since they are organized by company and have more profit sharing. If the Toyota unions strike, their members' incomes suffer along with Toyota's profits and they gain nothing from the precedent effect.

We are not saying that any or all of these are good outcomes or desirable policies. In some cases there may be compelling arguments for trying to prevent the kinds of results we have described. But to do so effectively, one has to understand the mechanism by which the problem arose in the first place — namely, an " accordion effect," where each fold pushes or pulls the next. This phenomenon arises again and again; but it can be countered, and we will show you how in Chapter 9.

6. THE THIN END OF THE WEDGE

Most countries use tariffs, quotas, and other measures to restrict import competition and protect domestic industries. Such policies raise prices, and hurt all domestic users of the protected product. Economists have estimated that when import quotas are used to protect industries such as steel, textiles, or sugar, the rest of us pay higher prices amounting to roughly $100,000 for each job saved.[6] How is it that the gains to a few always get priority over the much larger aggregate losses to the many?

The trick is to bring up the cases one at a time. First, 10,000 jobs in the shoe industry are at risk. To save them would cost a billion dollars to the rest of us, or just over $4 each. Who wouldn't agree to pay $4 to save 10,000 jobs even for total strangers, especially when nasty foreigners can be blamed for their plight? Then along comes the garment industry, the steel industry, the auto industry, and so on. Before we know it, we have agreed to pay over $50 billion, which is more than $200 each, or nearly $1,000 per family. If we had foreseen the whole process, we might have thought the cost too high, and insisted that workers in each of these industries bear the risks of foreign trade just as they would have to bear any other economic risk. Decisions made case by case can lead to undesirable results overall. In fact, a sequence of majority votes can lead to an outcome that everyone regards as worse than the status quo.

The income tax reform of 1985–86 almost collapsed because the Senate initially took a case-by-case approach. In the first round of the Finance Committee's markup sessions, the amended Treasury proposal became so weighted down with special interest provisions that it sank to a merciful death. The senators realized that they were "powerless" to prevent any one organized lobby from getting special treatment. Yet the combination of these lobbyists could destroy the bill, and this would be worse than producing no legislation at all. So Senator Packwood, the committee chairman, made his own lobby: he persuaded a majority of the committee members to vote against *any* amendment to the tax bill, even those amendments that especially favored their own constituents. The reform was enacted. But special provisions are already staging a comeback, one or two at a time.

Along similar lines, the line-item veto would allow the president to veto legislation selectively. If a bill authorized money for school lunches and a new space shuttle, the president would have the option of neither, either, or both, instead of the current neither or both. Although a first reaction is that this allows the president greater control over legislation, the opposite might end up happening as Congress would be more selective about which bills it passes.* While the line-item veto is generally thought to be unconstitutional, this question may have to be resolved by the Supreme Court.

---

* Professor Douglas Holtz-Eakin of Columbia University has looked at the effects of line-item veto power at the state level. His results fail to detect any differences in spending when a line-item veto is available. This is discussed in greater detail in case study #10, following the chapter on voting.

These problems arise because myopic decision-makers fail to look ahead and see the whole picture. In the case of tax reform, the Senate recovered its vision just in time; the issue of protectionism still suffers. Chapter 2 develops a system for better long-range strategic vision.

7. LOOK BEFORE YOU LEAP

It is all too common for people to get themselves into situations that are difficult to get out of. Once you have a job in a particular city, it is expensive to resettle. Once you buy a computer and learn its operating system, it becomes costly to learn another one and rewrite all your programs. Travelers who join the frequent-flyer program of one airline thereby raise their cost of using another. And, of course, marriage is expensive to escape.

The problem is that once you make such a commitment, your bargaining position is weakened. Companies may take advantage of their workers' anticipated moving costs and give them fewer or smaller salary raises. Computer companies can charge higher prices for new, compatible peripheral equipment knowing that their customers cannot easily switch to a new, incompatible technology. Airlines, having established a large base of frequent flyers, will be less inclined to engage in fare wars. A couple's agreement that they will split the housework 50:50 may become subject to renegotiation once a child is born.

Strategists who foresee such consequences will use their bargaining power while it exists, namely, before they get into the commitment. Typically, this will take the form of a payment up front. Competition among the would-be exploiters can lead to the same result. Companies will have to offer more attractive initial salaries, computer manufacturers will have to charge sufficiently low prices for their central processing units (CPUs), and airline frequent-flyer programs will have to offer larger signing-on mileage bonuses. As for married couples, exploitation may be a game that two can play.

The same foresight is what prevents many curious but rational people from trying addictive drugs such as heroin. A Tom Lehrer song describes the drug dealer's ploy:

> "He gives the kids free samples
> Because he knows full well
> That today's young innocent faces
> Will be tomorrow's clientele."

Smart kids know it too, and turn down the free samples.

8. MIX YOUR PLAYS

Let us return for a moment to the world of sports. In football, before each snap of the ball the offense chooses between passing and running while the defense organizes itself to counter one of these plays. In tennis, the server might go to the forehand or the backhand of the receiver, while the receiver, in turn, can try to return crosscourt or down the line. In these examples, each side has an idea of its own strong points and of its opponent's weaknesses. It will have a preference for the choice that exploits these weaknesses, *but not exclusively*. It is well understood, by players and sports fans alike, that one should mix one's plays, randomly throwing in the unexpected move. The point is that if you do the same thing all the time, the opposition will be able to counter you more effectively by concentrating its resources on the best response to your one strategy.

Mixing your plays does not mean rotating your strategies in a predictable manner. Your opponent can observe and exploit any systematic pattern almost as easily as he can the unchanging repetition of a single strategy. It is *unpredictability* that is important when mixing.

Imagine what would happen if there were some known formula that determined who would be audited by the IRS. Before you submitted a tax return, you could apply the formula to see if you would be audited. If an audit was predicted, but you could see a way to "amend" your return until the formula no longer predicted an audit, you probably would do so. If an audit was unavoidable, you would choose to tell the truth. The result of the IRS being completely predictable is that it would audit exactly the wrong people. All those audited would have anticipated their fate and chosen to act honestly, while those spared an audit would have only their consciences to watch over them. When the IRS audit formula is somewhat fuzzy, everyone stands some risk of an audit; this gives an added incentive for honesty.

There are similar phenomena in the business world. Think of competition in the market for razors. Imagine that Gillette runs a coupon promotion on a regular schedule — say, the first Sunday of every other month. Bic can preempt Gillette by running a competing coupon promotion the week before. Of course, Bic's move is then predictable and Gillette can preempt the week before. This process leads to cutthroat competition and both make less profit. But if each uses an unpredictable or mixed strategy, together they might reduce the fierceness of the competition.

The importance of randomized strategies was one of the early insights of game theory. The idea is simple and intuitive but needs refinement if it is to be useful in practice. It is not enough for a tennis player to know that he should mix his shots between the opponent's forehand and backhand. He needs some idea of whether he should go to the forehand 30 percent or 64 percent of the time and how the answer depends on the relative strengths of the two sides. In Chapter 7 we develop methods to answer such questions.

9. NEVER GIVE A SUCKER AN EVEN BET

In *Guys and Dolls*, gambler Sky Masterson relates this valuable advice from his father:

> "Son, one of these days in your travels a guy is going to come to you and show you a nice brand-new deck of cards on which the seal is not yet broken, and this guy is going to offer to bet you that he can make the jack of spades jump out of the deck and squirt cider in your ear. But son, do not bet this man, for as sure as you stand there you are going to wind up with cider in your ear."

The context of the story is that Nathan Detroit had offered Sky Masterson a bet about whether Mindy's sold more strudel or cheesecake. Nathan had just discovered the answer (strudel) and was willing to bet if Sky would bet on cheesecake.

This example may sound somewhat extreme. Of course no one would take such a sucker bet. But look at the market for futures contracts on the Chicago Board of Exchange. If another speculator offers to sell you a futures contract, he will make money only if you lose money. This deal is a *zero-sum* game, just like sports competitions, in which one team's victory is the other's loss. Hence if someone is willing to sell a futures contract, you should not be willing to buy it. And vice versa.

The strategic insight is that other people's actions tell us something about what they know, and we should use such information to guide our own action. Of course, we should use this in conjunction with our own information concerning the matter and use all strategic devices to elicit more from others.

In the *Guys and Dolls* example, there is a simple device of this kind. Sky should ask Nathan at what odds he would be willing to take the cheesecake side of the bet. If the answer is "not at any odds," then Sky can infer that the answer must be strudel. If Nathan offers the same odds for both strudel and cheesecake, he is hiding his information at the cost of giving Sky the opportunity to take an advantageous gamble.

In stock markets, foreign exchange markets, and other financial markets, people are free to take either side of the bet in just this way. Indeed, in some organized exchanges, including the London stock market, when you ask for a quote on a stock the market-maker is required to state both the buying and selling prices *before* he knows which side of the transaction you want. Without such a safeguard, market-makers could stand to profit from private information, and the outside investors' fear of being suckered might cause the entire market to fold. The buy and sell prices are not quite the same; the difference is called the bid-ask spread. In liquid markets the spread is quite small, indicating that little information is contained in any buy or sell order. On the other hand, Nathan Detroit is willing to bet on strudel at any price and on cheesecake at no price; his bid-ask spread is infinity. Beware of such market-makers.

We should add that Sky had not really learned his father's teaching very well. A minute later he bet Nathan that Nathan did not know the color of his own bowtie. Sky cannot win: if Nathan knows the color, he takes the bet and wins; if he does not, he declines the bet and does not lose.

10. Game Theory Can Be Dangerous to Your Health

Late one night, after a conference in Jerusalem, two American economists found a licensed taxicab and gave the driver directions to their hotel. Immediately recognizing them as American tourists, the driver refused to turn on his meter; instead, he proclaimed his love for Americans and promised them a lower fare than the meter. Naturally, they were somewhat skeptical of this promise. Why should this stranger offer to charge less than the meter when they were willing to pay the metered fare? How would they even know whether or not they were being overcharged?*

On the other hand, they had not promised to pay the driver anything more than what would be on the meter. If they were to start bargaining and the negotiations broke down, they would have to find another taxi. Their theory was that once they arrived at the hotel, their bargaining position would be much stronger. And taxis were hard to find.

They arrived. The driver demanded 2,500 Israeli shekels ($2.75). Who knew what fare was fair? Because people generally bargain in Israel, they protested and counter-offered 2,200 shekels. The driver was outraged. He claimed that it would be impossible to get from there to here for that amount. Before negotiations could continue, he locked all the doors automatically and retraced the route at breakneck speed, ignoring traffic lights and pedestrians. Were they being kidnapped to Beirut? No. He returned to the original position and ungraciously kicked the two economists out of his cab, yelling, "See how far your 2,200 shekels will get you now."

They found another cab. This driver turned on his meter, and 2,200 shekels later they were home.

Certainly the extra time was not worth the 300 shekels to the economists. On the other hand, the story was well worth it. It illustrates the dangers of bargaining with those who have not yet read our book. More generally, pride and irrationality cannot be ignored. Sometimes, it may be better to be taken for a ride when it costs only two dimes.†

There is a second lesson to the story. Think of how much

---

* If the driver wanted to prove that he was going to charge less than the meter, he could have turned on the meter as asked and then charged 80 percent of the price. The fact that he did not should have told something about his intentions; see the Sky Masterson story just above.

† The two who learned this lesson in game theory, and lived to tell the tale, were John Geanakoplos of Yale University, and one of your authors, Barry Nalebuff.

stronger their bargaining position would have been if they had begun to discuss the price after getting out of the taxi. (Of course, for hiring a taxi, this logic should be reversed. If you tell the driver where you want to go before getting in, you may find your taxi chasing after some other customer. Get in first, then say where you want to go.)

11. THE SHAPE OF THINGS TO COME

The examples have given us glimpses of principles that guide strategic decisions. We can summarize these principles with a few "morals" from our tales.

The story of the hot hand told us that in strategy, no less than in physics, "For every action we take, there is a reaction." We do not live and act in a vacuum. Therefore, we cannot assume that when we change our behavior everything else will remain unchanged.

De Gaulle's success in negotiations suggests that "the stuck wheel gets the grease."* But being stubborn is not always easy, especially when one has to be more stubborn than an obstinate adversary.

The tale from the Gulag and the story of belling the cat demonstrate the difficulty of obtaining outcomes that require coordination and individual sacrifice. The example of trade policy highlights the danger of solving problems piece by piece. In technology races no less than in sailboat races, those who trail tend to employ more innovative strategies; the leaders tend to imitate the followers.

Tennis and tax audits point out the strategic advantage of being unpredictable. Such behavior may also have the added advantage that it makes life just a little more interesting.

---

* You may have heard this expression as the "squeaky wheel" — a stuck wheel needs even more grease. Of course, sometimes it gets replaced.

We could go on offering more examples and drawing morals from them, but this is not the best way to think methodically about strategic games. That is better done by approaching the subject from a different angle. We pick up the principles — for example, commitment, cooperation, and mixing — one at a time. In each instance, we select examples that bear centrally on that issue, until the principle is clear. Then you will have a chance to apply the principle in the case studies that end each chapter.

12. Case Study #1: Red I Win, Black You Lose

While we might never get the chance to skipper in an America's Cup race, one of us found himself with a very similar problem. At the end of his academic studies, Barry celebrated at one of Cambridge University's May Balls (the English equivalent of a college prom). Part of the festivities included a casino. Everyone was given $20 worth of chips, and the person who had amassed the greatest fortune by evening's end would win a free ticket to next year's ball. When it came time for the last spin of the roulette wheel, by a happy coincidence, Barry led with $700 worth of chips, and the next closest was a young Englishwoman with $300. The rest of the group had been effectively cleaned out. Just before the last bets were to be placed, the woman offered to split next year's ball ticket, but Barry refused. With his substantial lead, there was little reason to settle for half.

To better understand the next strategic move, we take a brief detour to the rules of roulette. The betting in roulette is based on where a ball will land when the spinning wheel stops. There are typically numbers 0 through 36 on the wheel. When the ball lands on zero, the house wins. The safest bet in roulette is to bet on even or odd (denoted by Black or Red). These bets pay even money — a one-dollar bet returns two dollars — while the chance of winning is only 18/37. Even betting her entire stake would not lead to victory at these odds; therefore, the woman was forced to take one of the more risky gambles. She bet her entire stake on the chance that the ball would land on a multiple of three. This bet pays two to one (so her $300 bet would return $900 if she won) but has only a 12/37 chance of winning. She placed her bet on the table. At that point it could not be withdrawn. What should Barry have done?

Case Discussion

Barry should have copied the woman's bet and placed $300 on the event that the ball landed on a multiple of three. This guarantees that he stays ahead of her by $400 and wins the ticket: either they both lose the bet and Barry wins $400 to $0, or they both win the bet and Barry ends up ahead $1,300 to $900. The woman had no other choice. If she did not bet, she would have lost anyway; whatever she bet on, Barry could follow her and stay ahead.*

Her only hope was that Barry would bet first. If Barry had been first to place $200 on Black, what should she have done? She should have bet her $300 on Red. Betting her stake on Black would do her no good, since she would win only when Barry wins (and she would place second with $600 compared with Barry's $900). Winning when Barry lost would be her only chance to take the lead, and that dictates a bet on Red.

The strategic moral is the opposite from that of our tale of Martin Luther and Charles de Gaulle. In this tale of roulette,

---

* If truth be told, this is what Barry wished he had done. It was 3:00 in the morning and much too much champagne had been drunk for him to have been thinking this clearly. He bet $200 on the even numbers figuring that he would end up in second place only in the event that he lost and she won, the odds of which were approximately 5:1 in his favor. Of course 5:1 events sometimes happen and this was one of those cases. She won.

the person who moved first was at a disadvantage. The woman, by betting first, allowed Barry to choose a strategy that would guarantee victory. If Barry had bet first, the woman could have chosen a response that offered an even chance of winning. The general point is that in games it is not always an advantage to seize the initiative and move first. This reveals your hand, and the other players can use this to their advantage and your cost. Second movers may be in the stronger strategic position.

2

Anticipating Your Rival's Response

1. It's Your Move, Charlie Brown

In a recurring theme in the cartoon strip "Peanuts," Lucy holds a football on the ground and invites Charlie Brown to run up and kick it. At the last moment, Lucy pulls the ball away. Charlie Brown, kicking air, lands on his back, and this gives Lucy great perverse pleasure.

Anyone could have told Charlie that he should refuse to play Lucy's game. Even if Lucy had not played this particular trick on him last year (and the year before and the year before that), he knows her character from other contexts and should be able to predict her action.

At the time when Charlie is deciding whether or not to accept Lucy's invitation, her action lies in the future. However, just because it lies in the future does not mean Charlie should regard it as uncertain. He should know that of the two possible outcomes — letting him kick and seeing him fall — Lucy's preference is for the latter. Therefore he should forecast that when the time comes, she is going to pull the ball away. The logical possibility that Lucy will let him kick the ball is realistically irrelevant. Reliance on it would be, to borrow Dr. Johnson's characterization of remarriage, a triumph of hope over experience. Charlie should disregard it, and forecast that acceptance will inevitably land him on his back. He should decline Lucy's invitation.

2. TWO KINDS OF STRATEGIC INTERACTION

The essence of a game of strategy is the interdependence of the players' decisions. These interactions arise in two ways. The first is *sequential*, as in the Charlie Brown story. The players make alternating moves. Each player, when it is his turn, must look ahead to how his current actions will affect the future actions of others, and his own future actions in turn.

The second kind of interaction is *simultaneous*, as in the prisoners' dilemma tale of Chapter 1. The players act at the same time, in ignorance of the others' current actions. However, each must be aware that there are other active players, who in turn are similarly aware, and so on. Therefore each must figuratively put himself in the shoes of all, and try to calculate the outcome. His own best action is an integral part of this overall calculation.

When you find yourself playing a strategic game, you must determine whether the interaction is simultaneous or sequential. Some games such as football have elements of both. Then you must fit your strategy to the context. In this chapter, we develop in a preliminary way ideas and rules that will help you play sequential games; simultaneous-move games are the subject of Chapter 3. We begin with really simple, sometimes contrived, examples, such as the Charlie Brown story. This is deliberate; the stories are not of great importance in themselves, and the right strategies are usually easy to see by simple intuition, so the underlying ideas stand out that much more clearly. The examples get increasingly realistic and more complex in the case studies and in the later chapters.

3. THE FIRST RULE OF STRATEGY

The general principle for sequential-move games is that each player should figure out the other players' future responses, and use them in calculating his own best current move. So important is this idea that it is worth codifying into a basic rule of strategic behavior:

Rule 1:   **Look ahead and reason back.**

Anticipate where your initial decisions will ultimately lead, and use this information to calculate your best choice.

In the Charlie Brown story, this was easy to do for anyone (except Charlie Brown). He had just two alternatives, and one of them led to Lucy's decision between two possible actions. Most strategic situations involve a longer sequence of decisions with several alternatives at each, and mere verbal reasoning cannot keep track of them. Successful application of the rule of looking ahead and reasoning back needs a better visual aid. A "tree diagram" of the choices in the game is one such aid. Let us show you how to use these trees.

4. DECISION TREES AND GAME TREES

A sequence of decisions, with the need to look ahead and reason back, can arise even for a solitary decision-maker not involved in a game of strategy with others. For Robert Frost in the yellow wood:

> Two roads diverged in a wood, and I
> I took the road less travelled by,
> And that has made all the difference.[1]

We can show this schematically.

This need not be the end of the choice. Each road might in turn have further branches. The road map becomes correspondingly complex. Here is an example from our own experience.

Travelers from Princeton to New York have several choices. The first decision point involves selecting the mode of travel: bus, train, or car. Those who drive then have to choose among the Verrazano Narrows Bridge, the Holland Tunnel, the Lincoln Tunnel, and the George Washington Bridge. Rail commuters must decide whether to switch to the PATH train at Newark or continue to Penn Station. Once in New York, rail and bus commuters must choose among going by foot, subway (local or express), bus, or taxi to get to their final destination. The best choice depends on many factors, including price, speed, expected congestion, the final destination in New York, and one's aversion to breathing the air on the Jersey Turnpike.

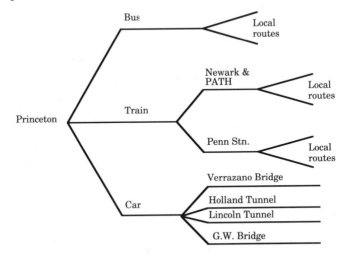

This road map, which describes one's options at each junction, looks like a tree with its successively emerging branches — hence the term "decision tree." The right way to use such a map or tree is not to take the route whose first branch looks best and then "cross the Verrazano Bridge when you get to it." Instead, you anticipate the future decisions and use them to make your earlier choices. For example, if you are commuting to the World Trade Center, the PATH train would be superior to driving because it offers a direct connection from Newark.

We can use just such a tree to depict the choices in a game of strategy, but one new element enters the picture. A game has two or more players. At various branching points along the tree, it may be the turn of different players to make the decision. A person making a choice at an earlier point must look ahead, not just to his own future choices, but to those of others. He must forecast what the others will do, by putting himself figuratively in their shoes, and thinking as they would think. To remind you of the difference, we will call a tree showing the decision sequence in a game of strategy a *game tree*, reserving the term *decision tree* for situations in which just one person is involved.

The story of Charlie Brown is absurdly simple, but you can become familiar with game trees by casting that story in such a picture. Start the game when Lucy has issued her invitation, and Charlie faces the decision of whether to accept. If Charlie refuses, that is the end of the game. If he accepts, Lucy has the choice between letting Charlie kick and pulling the ball away. We can show this by adding another fork along this road.

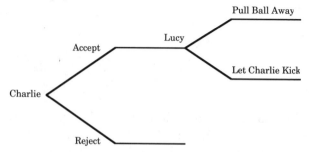

As we said earlier, Charlie should forecast that Lucy will choose the upper branch. Therefore he should figuratively prune the lower branch of her choice from the tree. Now if he chooses his own upper branch, it leads straight to a nasty fall. Therefore his better choice is to follow his own lower branch.

To fix the idea, consider a business example that has the same game tree. To avoid impugning any actual firms, and with apologies to Graham Greene, suppose the market for vacuum cleaners in pre-Castro Cuba is dominated by a brand called Fastcleaners, and a new firm, Newcleaners, is deciding whether to enter this market. If Newcleaners enters, Fastcleaners has two choices: accommodate Newcleaners by accepting a lower market share, or fight a price war.* Suppose that if Fastcleaners accommodates the entry, Newcleaners will make a profit of $100,000, but that if Fastcleaners starts a price war, this causes Newcleaners to lose $200,000. If Newcleaners stays away from this market, its profit is, of course, zero. We show the game tree and the profit amounts for each outcome:

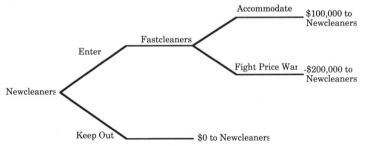

What should Newcleaners do? This is the kind of problem decision analysts solve, and business schools teach. They draw a very similar picture, but call it a decision tree. The

---

* In Greene's *Our Man in Havana*, the salesman for one of these two firms chose to fight — with poison rather than prices.

reason is that they often think of the outcomes "accommodation" and "price war" as alternatives that could arise by chance.
Therefore, they assign probabilities to the two. For example,
if accommodation and war are thought equally likely, each
gets a probability of 1/2. Then they can calculate the average profit that Newcleaners can expect from entry, multiplying each profit or loss figure by the corresponding probability
and adding. They get $(\frac{1}{2})\$100,000 - (\frac{1}{2})\$200,000 = -\$50,000$.
Since this is a loss, with these probabilities the business analysts' verdict would be that Newcleaners should keep away
from Cuba.

Where do the probability estimates come from? Game theory provides the answer: the probabilities come from Newcleaners' beliefs about Fastcleaners' profits in each of these
cases. In order to estimate what Fastcleaners will do, Newcleaners should first estimate Fastcleaners' profits in the different scenarios. Then the players can look forward and reason
backward to predict what the other side will do. To continue
this example, suppose that as a monopolist Fastcleaners is
able to make profits of \$300,000. Sharing the market with
Newcleaners reduces its profits to \$100,000. Fighting a price
war costs Fastcleaners \$100,000. Then we can fill out the tree,
adding in these payoffs.

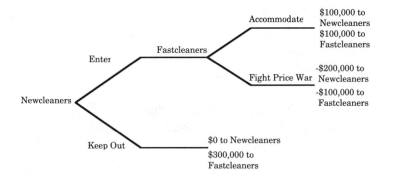

We use the information in the tree to predict all future moves. Since actions can be determined from the structure of the game, the tree is properly seen as a game tree, not a decision tree. For example, to predict Fastcleaners' response to entry, we recognize that it makes $100,000 under accommodation and loses $100,000 in the event of a price war; Newcleaners should forecast that Fastcleaners will choose accommodation. Looking ahead in this way, and reasoning back, Newcleaners should mentally cut off the price-war branch. They should enter, reckoning to make $100,000.

The decision might be different in other circumstances. For example, if there is a possibility that Newcleaners would go on to enter other islands where Fastcleaners has established markets, Fastcleaners may have an incentive to acquire a reputation for toughness, and may be willing to suffer losses in Cuba to this end. Newcleaners should reckon on a sure loss of $200,000, and therefore should keep out.

Newcleaners can see how any given payoffs translate into actions. But they may be unsure of Fastcleaners' rewards at the end of the tree. It is the uncertainty about profits that translates into an uncertainty about actions. For example, Newcleaners might believe that there is a 33.3 percent chance that Fastcleaners will lose $100,000 in a price war, a 33.3 percent chance that they will break even ($0 profits) in a price war, and a final 33.3 percent chance that Fastcleaners will make $120,000 in spite of a price war. In that event, "look forward and reason backward" says that in two of the three cases Fastcleaners will want to accommodate — $100,000 is better than losing $100,000 or breaking even but not as good as making $120,000. The chance of a price war is then 33.3 percent. The only way to find out what will actually happen is to enter. Given the odds, Newcleaners expects to make $100,000 in two out of three cases and lose $200,000 the other third of the time: its expected profits are exactly zero and so there is no point in entering.

In this example it was straightforward to translate New-cleaners' uncertainty about Fastcleaners' payoffs into a probability estimate of Fastcleaners' responses. But one must be careful about where to place the uncertainty. The right place is at the end of the tree. Look at what goes wrong if we look if we try to jump ahead in our estimation. On average, Fast-cleaners can make money in a price war [$(\frac{1}{3})$\$120,000$+(\frac{1}{3})$\$0$ - $(\frac{1}{3})$\$100,000 = \$6,667]. But that doesn't mean they will always want to fight. The probability is not 100 percent. Nor does the presence of uncertainty mean that one should guess a probability of 50 percent. The correct way to analyze the problem is for Newcleaners to start at the end of the game and figure out what Fastcleaners should do in each case.

5. More Complex Trees

In reality, the games you play are more complex than the ones we used above for illustrative purposes. But the same principles apply as these saplings develop into trees. Perhaps the best example is chess. While the rules of chess are relatively simple, they produce a game that lends itself to strategic reasoning. White opens with a move, Black responds with one, and so on in turns. Therefore the "purest" kind of strategic reasoning in chess involves looking ahead to the consequences of your move in just the way we saw. An example of such reasoning might be: "If I move that pawn now, my opponent will bring up his knight and threaten my rook. I should protect the square to which the knight wants to move with my bishop, before I move the pawn."

Since chess is a game with alternating moves, we can represent the game by a tree. White can open with any one of 20 moves.[2] In the picture below, we show White's first opportunity to move by the first decision point (or node) of the tree, labeled W1. The 20 moves he can make become 20 branches that emanate from this node. Each branch is labeled by the move it represents: pawn to king-4 (P-K4, or e4 in algebraic notation), pawn to queen-4, and so on. We want only to convey the general idea, and so to avoid cluttering the picture, we have not shown or labeled all branches. Each branch will lead to a node representing Black's first move, labeled B1. Black can also make any of 20 moves, so there will be 20 branches emanating from each such B1 node. After one move from both sides, we are already looking at a total of 400 possibilities. From here on, the number of branches will depend on the move previously made. For example, if White's first move is P-K4, he has numerous possible second moves because his queen and his king-side bishop can now venture out. You see how simply the tree is constructed in principle, and how complicated it quickly gets in practice.

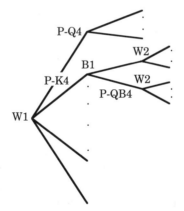

We can select a branch at each decision point (node) of the game tree, and follow a path down it. This will represent one particular way in which the game could evolve. Chess experts have examined many such paths in the early phases (openings) and speculated where they might lead. For example, the path we have labeled, where the first moves are P-K4 for White and

P-QB4 for Black, is the ominous-sounding Sicilian Defense.*

In many games, each such path ends after a finite number
of steps. In a sport or a board game, this might be when one
of the players wins or the game is a draw. More generally, the
end result of the game can be in the form of monetary or non-
monetary rewards or penalties for the players. For example,
a game of business rivalry might end with a sizable profit to
one firm and bankruptcy of the other. The "game" of the nuclear arms race might end in a successful treaty or in mutual
destruction.

If the game is going to end in a finite number of moves no
matter which path is followed, then we can in principle solve
the game completely. Solving the game means finding out who
wins and how. This is done by reasoning backward along the
tree. Once we have worked through the entire tree, we will
discover whether or not we can win, and if so what strategy
to use. *For any game with a finite number of sequential moves
there exists some best strategy.* Of course, just because a best
strategy exists doesn't mean that we can easily find it. Chess
is the prime example.

Chess experts have been very successful at characterizing
optimal strategies near the end of the game. Once the chess-
board has been reduced to three or four pieces, expert players
are able to see ahead to the end of the game and determine (by
working backward) whether one side has a guaranteed winning strategy or whether the other side can force a draw. They
can then use the desirability of different endgame positions to
evaluate the strategies in the middle game. The problem is
that nobody has ever been able to work through the tree all
the way back to the opening move.

Some simple games can be solved completely. For exam-

* The continuation, 2. N-KB3, P-Q3, 3. P-Q4, PxP, 4. NxP, N-KB3, 5.
N-QB3, P-QR3, 6. B-KN5, P-K3, 7. P-KB4, Q-N3, 8. Q-Q2, QxP, is called its
Poisoned Pawn Variation, which sounds as if it came from the palace of the
Borgias, or from Wall Street.

ple, in three-by-three tic-tac-toe, a draw can always be obtained.* That is why it is a game played by children rather than grownups. Even the game of checkers is in danger. It is believed, although not yet confirmed, that the second player can always achieve a tie. In order to maintain interest, checkers tournaments start the players at an intermediate position, where a winning or tying strategy is not known. The day it becomes possible to solve chess completely in this way, the rules may have to be changed.

In the meantime, what have chess players done? They do what we all should do when putting sequential strategies into practice: combine forward-looking analysis with value judgments. They ask, "Will this path after four or five moves lead to a generally good position or a bad one?" They assign a value to each of the possible outcomes, pretending that it is the end of the game. Then they look forward and reason backward toward a strategy that leads to the highest value five moves hence. Backward reasoning is the easy part. The hard problem is assigning a value to an intermediate position. The value of each piece must be quantified and trade-offs between material and positional advantage considered.

Paul Hoffman, in his book *Archimedes' Revenge*, describes the success of Hans Berliner's computer chess program. A postal chess world champion, Berliner has built a computer dedicated to chess that can examine thirty million options in the three minutes allocated to each move and has a good rule for valuing intermediate positions. Fewer than three hun-

* Although you may think tic-tac-toe is a simple game, don't try to draw the game tree. Note that no game can end before the fifth move, since that is the first time someone will have three pieces on the board. By this time, the number of branches is already up to $9 \times 8 \times 7 \times 6 \times 5 = 15,120$. Even so, the game can be solved easily as most of the branches are strategically identical. For example, although there are nine possible first moves, the symmetry of the game allows us to recognize that there are essentially only three moves: corner, side, or middle. It is tricks like this that help keep the game tree manageable.

dred human chess players can beat this computer program. In backgammon, Berliner has a program that has beaten the world champion.

The combination of explicit logic from backward reasoning and rules of thumb for valuing intermediate positions based on experience is a useful way to tackle complicated games other than chess.

6. BARGAINING

In business and in international politics, the parties often bargain or negotiate over the division of a total gain — the pie. We will examine this in more detail in Chapter 11. Here we use it as an illustration of how backward reasoning enables us to predict the outcome of games with alternating moves.

Most people follow social convention and predict that splitting the difference will be the outcome of a negotiation. This has the advantage of being "fair." We can demonstrate that for many common types of negotiations, a 50:50 split is the backward-reasoning solution, too.

There are two general features of bargaining that we must first take into account. We have to know who gets to make an offer to whom, i.e., the rules of the game. And then we have to know what happens if the parties fail to reach an agreement.

Different negotiations take place under differing rules. In most retail stores the sellers post a price and the buyers' only choice is to accept the price or to take their business elsewhere.* This is a simple "take-it-or-leave-it" rule. In the case of wage bargaining, a labor union makes a claim and then the company decides whether to accede. If it does not, it may make

---

* Some shoppers seem to be able to bargain anywhere (even including Sears). Herb Cohen's book, *You Can Negotiate Anything*, has many valuable tips in this regard.

a counteroffer, or wait for the union to adjust its demand. In some cases the sequencing is imposed by law or custom; in others it may have a strategic role of its own. Below, we will examine a bargaining problem in which the two parties take turns making offers.

An essential feature of negotiations is that time is money. When negotiations become protracted, the pie begins to shrink. Still, the parties may fail to agree, each hoping that the costs of negotiating will be outweighed by a more favorable settlement. Charles Dickens's *Bleak House* illustrates the extreme case; the dispute over the Jarndyce estate was so prolonged that the entire estate was swallowed up by lawyers' fees. In the same vein, if failure to reach a wage agreement leads to a labor strike, the firm loses profits and workers lose their wages. If nations enter into a prolonged round of negotiations to liberalize trade, they forgo the benefits of the enlarged trade while they are arguing about the division of the gains. The common thread is that all parties to the negotiations prefer to reach any given agreement sooner rather than later.

In reality the shrinkage occurs in complex ways and at different rates in different situations. But we can adequately illustrate the idea in a very simple way: suppose that the pie shrinks to zero in equal amounts at each step of offer or counteroffer. Think of it as an ice-cream pie, which melts as children argue over its division.

First suppose there is only one step involved. There is an ice-cream pie on the table; one child (Ali) proposes to the other (Baba) how to divide it. If Baba agrees, the division occurs as agreed; if not, the pie melts and neither gets anything.

Now Ali is in a powerful position: she is able to pose to Baba the stark choice between something and nothing. Even if she proposes to keep 100 percent of the pie for herself and just let Baba lick the knife at the end, the only thing Baba can do is to take that lick or get nothing.

Of course Baba may turn down the offer from sheer anger

at the unfairness of it. Or he may want to build or maintain a reputation for being a tough bargainer, to help him in future bargains, whether with Ali or with others who come to know of Baba's actions here. In practice Ali will have to think about such matters, and offer Baba just enough (perhaps a small slice?) to induce him to accept. To keep the exposition simple, we will leave these complications aside and suppose that Ali can get away with claiming 100 percent. In fact, we will forget about the lick for Baba and say that Ali can get the whole pie by being able to make a "take-it-or-leave-it" offer.*

Once there is a second round of negotiations, things come out much better for Baba. Again there is an ice-cream pie on the table but now it takes two rounds of bargaining before the entire pie melts. If Baba turns down Ali's offer, he can come back with a counteroffer, but at that point only half of the pie remains. If Ali turns down Baba's counteroffer, that half also melts and both sides are left with nothing.

Now Ali must look ahead to the consequences of her initial offer. She knows that Baba can turn down her offer and come back in the powerful position of making a take-it-or-leave-it offer in splitting the remaining half of the pie. This will give Baba essentially all of that half. Therefore he is not going to accept anything less from Ali's first-round offer. If Ali were to allow this second stage to come to pass, she would get nothing at all. Knowing this, she will open by offering Baba half, that is, just enough to induce acceptance while getting half for herself. They agree immediately to split the pie 50:50.

The principle is now clear, and we can easily add one more step. Again let the negotiations speed up or the pie melt more slowly. With each offer and counteroffer, the pie goes from whole to two-thirds to one-third to zero. If Ali makes the last offer, when the pie has shrunk to a third, she gets it all. Know-

---

* The same simplification will apply as we consider more rounds of offer and counteroffer. You can easily turn our account into a more realistic but messier calculation that allows for the complexities we are ignoring.

ing this, Baba will offer her a third when it is his turn and two-thirds of the pie remains. Thus the best Baba can expect is one-third, i.e., half of the remaining two-thirds. Knowing this, Ali will open the bargaining by offering him the one-third (just enough to induce acceptance) and get two-thirds for herself.

What happened to the 50:50 split? It reappears every time the number of steps is even. More importantly, even when the number of steps is odd, the two sides get closer and closer to 50:50 as the number of steps increases.

With four steps, Baba will make the last offer and get the quarter that is on the table at that point. Therefore Ali has to offer him a quarter at the last-but-one turn when there is half. Then at the turn before that, Baba can get Ali to accept only a quarter out of three-quarters. Therefore, looking ahead to all this, Ali opens the bargaining by offering Baba half and getting half herself.

With five steps, Ali will open by offering Baba two-fifths of the pie and keeping three-fifths to herself. With six the division is once again 50:50. With seven, Ali gets 4/7 and Baba 3/7. More generally, when the number of steps is even each side gets half. When the number of steps, n, is odd, Ali gets $(n+1)/(2n)$ and Baba gets $(n-1)/(2n)$. By the time the number of steps reaches 101, Ali's advantage from going first is that she gets 51/101 while Baba gets 50/101.

In the typical negotiation process, the pie shrinks slowly so that there will be time for many offers and counteroffers before the pie disappears. What this suggests is that it usually doesn't matter who gets to make the first offer given a long bargaining horizon. The split-the-difference solution seems pretty hard to escape unless the negotiations have been deadlocked for a long time and there is hardly anything left to win. It is true that the person who goes last can get everything that remains. But by the end of the negotiations process there is hardly anything left to win. Getting all of nothing is winning the battle and losing the war.

It is important to observe that even though we have considered many possible offers and counteroffers, the predicted outcome is for Ali's very first offer to be accepted. The later stages of the process are never called into play. However, the fact that those steps would be invoked if agreement were not reached on the first round is crucial in Ali's calculation of the just-acceptable first offer.

This observation in turn suggests another dimension of strategy in bargaining. The principle of looking ahead and reasoning back may determine the outcome of the process even before it starts. The time for strategic maneuvering may be earlier, when the rules of negotiation are being decided.

The same observation also leads to a puzzle. If the process of bargaining were exactly like that depicted here, there would be no labor strikes. Of course the prospect of a strike would affect the agreement reached, but the company — or the union, as the case may be — at its very first opportunity would make an offer that was minimally acceptable to the other party. The reality of strikes or, more generally, breakdowns of negotiations must arise from more subtle or complex features of reality that were excluded from the simple story above. We will touch upon some of these issues in Chapter 11.

7. WAR AND PEACE

A second illustration of backward reasoning comes from considering how peace can be maintained through a series of bilateral antagonisms.

Let us take an example that is only partly hypothetical. Sudan is a relatively weak country in danger of being attacked by its neighbor Libya. If these two countries were somehow in isolation there would be little to prevent Libya from attacking and defeating Sudan.

While two antagonistic neighbors may not maintain peace,

the presence of a third may provide the necessary deterrence. In the case of Libya and Sudan, this principle might be referred to as "My enemy's enemy is my friend." The danger for Libya if it enters a battle with Sudan is that this will draw troops away from its eastern border with Egypt. Although Egypt would not want to attack a full-strength Libya, if Libya were weakened through war with Sudan, this could provide a welcome opportunity for the Egyptians to dispose of a troublesome neighbor. Libya can (or at least should) reason backward and predict an attack by Egypt were they to go after Sudan. It appears that Sudan is safe. But stopping the chain of thought after three countries leads to a false sense of security.

If three enemies create stability, what about four? Enter Israel. Were Egypt to go after Libya this could open it up to an attack by Israel. Before Sadat and Begin normalized relations, this was a real threat for Egypt. In those pre-1978 years, Libya had less reason to fear an attack by Egypt because of the insecurity of Egypt with respect to Israel. As a result, Sudan could not count on Egypt to control Libya's expansionary interests.* With improved Israeli-Egyptian relations the backward chain stops at Egypt, and Sudan is safe, for the moment.

This example of deterrence is certainly stylized. Taken at face value it would suggest that whether or not a country will be attacked depends on whether there are an even or an odd number of links in the chain of potential predators. A more realistic scenario would take account of the complicated relationships between the countries and provide more detail about their willingness to attack each other. Yet, there is an important observation that carries forward: the outcome of games depends critically on how many people are playing. More may be better and then worse, even in the same game. The observation that two antagonistic countries make unstable neighbors but three antagonists restores stability does not imply that

---

* Thus we have "My enemy's enemy's enemy is not my friend."

four is even better; four in this case is the same as two.*

To develop this idea of deterrence further, we invite you to look at the "Three-Way Duel" in the collection of case studies at the end of the book. Three antagonists, each with a different level of ability, have to decide whom they should attack. You may find the answer surprising.

8. GAMES THE BRITISH PLAY

Throughout this chapter we have talked of games in which actions or moves followed one another in an orderly sequence. In fact, few games in life have well-specified rules that the players must obey. The players make their own rules. How can they look ahead and reason back, and indeed how can they know if there is any sequence to the game at all?

To illustrate this point, we use the setting of the British election campaign of 1987. The incumbent Conservative Party under Margaret Thatcher was being challenged by the Labor Party under the leadership of Neil Kinnock. In the campaign, each had to choose between the high road — a campaign based on issues — and the low road — a battle of personalities. A sufficiently large core of voters were satisfied with Mrs. Thatcher's performance to ensure that, if the two fought similarly oriented campaigns, the effects of the two would cancel and Mrs. Thatcher would win.

Mr. Kinnock's only hope was that he would make a sufficiently better impression in campaigns of contrasting styles; let us suppose his chances were the same when Mrs. Thatcher took the high road and he took the low road as they would be with the opposite choices. Suppose each of them preferred the

---

* In fact, if there is any odd number of countries in the chain, then A is safe. If the chain has an even length then B will attack A; after B's attack, the chain is reduced to an odd length and B is safe.

high road, but this consideration was subordinate to victory.

Which would be "the road less traveled"? The answer hangs critically on the order in which the two parties make their decisions. Let us look at some alternative possibilities.

Suppose Mrs. Thatcher chooses the campaign style first — because, say, it is traditional for the incumbent party to publicly launch its manifesto before the opposition. She can write down the following game tree.

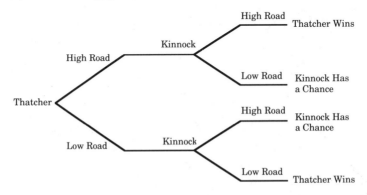

By looking forward and reasoning backward, Mrs. Thatcher can predict that if she takes the high road, then Mr. Kinnock will take the low, and vice versa.* Since the two alternatives give her the same chance of victory, she prefers taking the high road.

The fact that Mrs. Thatcher moves first is to her disadvantage, as it allows Mr. Kinnock to take the opposite tack. But the fact that she moves first does not in itself cause this problem. Let us ring a slight change on the scenario. Suppose Mrs. Thatcher has met with her Conservative Party advisors and the advertising campaign managers, and decided

---

* The refrain from the song *Loch Lomond* goes: "Oh, ye'll tak' the high road an' I'll tak' the low road, An' I'll be in Scotland afore ye." Therefore we should point out that the Labor Party won most of the seats in Scotland, although the Conservatives won the election in the United Kingdom as a whole by a very wide margin.

her strategy. But the choice is not made public. Mr. Kinnock is holding a similar meeting. What should he decide? Should he assume that, in making the first move, Mrs. Thatcher will reason in the way we just described? That would mean that she had chosen the high road, and therefore that Mr. Kinnock should choose the low. But if Mrs. Thatcher thought that Mr. Kinnock would think in this way, she should choose a low-road strategy of her own. Mr. Kinnock does not know her choice for sure, and he would be foolish to disregard the possibility of such a "second-level" thinking. Should he then choose the high road? Not necessarily, for Mrs. Thatcher can think at a third level, and so on. *The general point is that for the principle of looking ahead and reasoning back to apply, it is essential that earlier moves be observable to those who choose later.*

Even if Mrs. Thatcher moves first and her choice is observable, what if she could change her strategy during the course of the campaign? Suppose it is the final impression on the voters that matters most, and what Mrs. Thatcher said in her first announcement is irrelevant. Mr. Kinnock cannot take it as given when deciding his strategy. In turn, Mrs. Thatcher cannot rely on a fixed response by Mr. Kinnock when she thinks about her first move. So we have another condition for the validity of the principle of looking ahead and reasoning back: *strategies must be irreversible.*

What happens if one of these two conditions is not met? Even if the choices of the two parties are made at different times, so far as strategic thinking is concerned they might as well be simultaneous. This shift from sequential to simultaneous may be advantageous to either or both of the parties. In fact, in the 1987 British campaign there was at least one reversal of strategy by each side. Chapter 3 provides the rules for action in simultaneous games.

Athletic contests provide another view of the difference between sequential- and simultaneous-move games. A hundred-yard dash is simultaneous because there is no time for sequencing. In a butterfly-stroke swim race, there may be time to respond, but competitors find it difficult to see their opponent's position; hence it should be viewed as simultaneous. A marathon has the ingredients for a sequential structure: the runners can observe each other's positions (up to a point), and strategies are irreversible in that there is no going back and rerunning the earlier part of the race.

To end this chapter, we return to Charlie Brown's problem of whether or not to kick the football. This question became a real issue for football coach Tom Osborne in the final minutes of his championship game. We think he too got it wrong. Backward reasoning will reveal the mistake.

9. CASE STUDY #2: THE TALE OF TOM OSBORNE AND THE 1984 ORANGE BOWL

In the 1984 Orange Bowl the undefeated Nebraska Cornhuskers and the once-beaten Miami Hurricanes faced off. Because Nebraska came into the Bowl with the better record, it needed only a tie in order to finish the season with the number-one ranking.

But Nebraska fell behind by 31–17 in the fourth quarter. Then the Cornhuskers began a comeback. They scored a touchdown to make the score 31–23. Nebraska coach Tom Osborne had an important strategic decision to make.

In college football, a team that scores a touchdown then runs one play from a hash mark $2\frac{1}{2}$ yards from the goal line. The team has a choice between trying to run or pass the ball into the end zone, which scores two additional points, or trying the less risky strategy of kicking the ball through the goalposts, which scores one extra point.

Coach Osborne chose to play it safe, and Nebraska successfully kicked for the one extra point. Now the score was 31–24. The Cornhuskers continued their comeback. In the waning minutes of the game they scored a final touchdown, bringing the score to 31–30. A point conversion would have tied the game and landed them the title. But that would have been an unsatisfying victory. To win the championship with style, Osborne recognized that he had to go for the win.

The Cornhuskers went for the win with a two-point conversion attempt. Irving Fryer got the ball, but failed to score. Miami and Nebraska ended the year with equal records. Since Miami beat Nebraska, it was Miami that was awarded the top place in the standings.

Put yourself in the cleats of Coach Osborne. Could you have done better?

Case Discussion

Many Monday morning quarterbacks fault Osborne for going for the win rather than the tie. But that is not the bone of our contention. Given that Osborne was willing to take the additional risk for the win, he did it the wrong way. Tom Osborne would have done better to first try the two-point attempt, and then if it succeeded go for the one-point, while if it failed attempt a second two-pointer.

Let us look at this more carefully. When down by 14 points, he knew that he needed two touchdowns plus three extra points. He chose to go for the one and then the two. If both attempts were made, the order in which they were made becomes irrelevant. If the one-point conversion was missed but the two-point was successful, here too the order is irrelevant and the game ends up tied, with Nebraska getting the championship. The only difference occurs if Nebraska misses the two-point attempt. Under Osborne's plan, that results in the loss of the game and the championship. If, instead, they had tried the two-point conversion first, then if it failed they would not necessarily have lost the game. They would have been behind

31–23. When they scored their next touchdown this would have brought them to 31–29. A successful two-point attempt would tie the game and win the number-one ranking!*

We have heard the counterargument that if Osborne first went for the two-pointer and missed, his team would have been playing for the tie. This would have provided less inspiration and perhaps they might not have scored the second touchdown. Moreover, by waiting until the end and going for the desperation win-lose two-pointer his team would rise to the occasion knowing everything was on the line. This argument is wrong for several reasons. Remember that if Nebraska waits until the second touchdown and then misses the two-point attempt, they lose. If they miss the two-point attempt on their first try, there is still a chance for a tie. Even though the chance may be diminished, something is better than nothing. The momentum argument is also flawed. While Nebraska's offense may rise to the occasion in a single play for the championship, we expect the Hurricanes' defense to rise as well. The play is equally important for both sides. To the extent that there is a momentum effect, if Osborne makes the two-point attempt on the first touchdown, this should increase the chance of scoring another touchdown. It also allows him to tie the game with two field goals.

One of the general morals from this story is that if you have to take some risks, it is often better to do this as quickly as possible. This is obvious to those who play tennis: everyone knows to take risks on the first serve and hit the second serve more cautiously. That way, if you fail on your first attempt, the game won't be over. You may still have time to take some other options that can bring you back to or even ahead of where you were.

---

* Furthermore, this would be a tie that resulted from the failed attempt to win, so no one would criticize Osborne for playing to tie.

3

Seeing through
Your Rival's Strategy

Every week, *Time* and *Newsweek* compete to have the more
eye-catching cover story. A dramatic or interesting cover will
attract the attention of potential buyers at newsstands. Thus
every week the editors of *Time* meet behind closed doors to
select their cover story. They do so with the knowledge that
the editors of *Newsweek* are meeting elsewhere, also behind
closed doors, to select their cover. The editors of *Newsweek*
in turn know that the editors of *Time* are making a similar
decision, those of *Time* know that those of *Newsweek* know,
and so on.

The two newsmagazines are engaged in a strategic game,
but this game is quite different in nature from those we have
already examined. The games in Chapter 2 had a sequence of
alternating moves. Charlie Brown decided whether or not to
kick knowing that Lucy's decision whether or not to pull the
ball away lay in the future. In chess, White's moves alternated
with Black's. By contrast, the actions of *Time* and *Newsweek*
are simultaneous. Each must act in ignorance of the other's
choice. By the time each discovers what the other has done, it
is too late to change anything. Of course the loser for one week
might try to respond the next week, but in this fast-moving
world a whole new set of stories and a whole new game will
probably have emerged by then.

The nature of the strategic thinking and action needed for the two types of games differs markedly. For the sequential-move games discussed in Chapter 2, each player had to look ahead and anticipate his rival's future responses in order to reason back and decide his own current action. There was a linear chain of reasoning: "If I do this, the other player will do that — in which case, I will respond thus," and so on.

For the simultaneous-move games we consider in this chapter, neither player has the benefit of observing the other's completed move before making his own. Here, the interaction reasoning works not by seeing the other's strategy but by seeing *through* it. For this, it is not enough simply to put yourself in your opponent's shoes. What would you find if you did? You'd only discover that your opponent is doing the same thing, that is, thinking what it must be like to be wearing your shoes. Each person has to place himself simultaneously in *both* his own and the other guy's shoes and then figure out the best moves for both sides. Instead of a linear chain of reasoning, there is a circle that goes "If I think that he thinks that I think ..." The trick is to square this circle.

Not surprisingly, Sherlock Holmes and his arch-rival Professor Moriarty, the Napoleon of crime, were masters of this type of reasoning. As Holmes told Watson in *The Final Problem*:

"All that I have to say has already crossed your mind," said he.

"Then possibly my answer has crossed yours," I replied.

Like Dr. Watson, you may be wondering how Holmes does it. After hearing our explanation, we hope you will agree that it is rather elementary.

How do you see through all the interlocking but invisible strategies? First, you must not regard the unknown actions of the other players as being uncertain in an impersonal way like the weather. Before going to work, the editor of *Time* might listen to the weather forecast that predicts a 40 percent chance of rain, and he might use this information to decide whether or not to take an umbrella to work. The probability that *Newsweek* is using a particular cover theme is quite a different matter.

The difference is that the editor of *Time* has a very pertinent piece of information about *Newsweek*: unlike nature, the other magazine's editors are strategic game-players just as *Time*'s own editors are.* Even though one editor cannot actually observe the other magazine's decision, he can think the matter through from its perspective, and try to figure out what it *must* be doing.

In Chapter 2, we could offer a single, unifying principle to devise the best strategies for games with sequential moves. This was our Rule 1: look ahead and reason back. It won't be so simple in this chapter. But the thinking about thinking required for simultaneous moves can be summarized in three simple rules for action. These rules in turn rest on two simple ideas — dominant strategies and equilibrium. As in Chapter 2, we develop such ideas and rules through simple examples.

1. DOMINANT STRATEGIES

In baseball, when there are two outs and the count stands at three balls and two strikes, any forced base runners should run on the pitch. This can be seen by thinking through all possible cases. In most cases it does not matter what the runners do. If the pitch is not touched by the batter, either the pitch is the fourth ball and the runners advance, or it is the third strike

---

* Some people believe that nature, too, is a strategic game-player, and a malevolent one that takes pleasure at upsetting our best-laid plans. For example, when you hear that there is a forty percent chance of rain, that means six times out of ten you will remember to take your umbrella and it won't rain, while the other four times out of ten you'll forget your umbrella and there will be a downpour.

and the inning ends. If the pitch is fouled off, the runners simply return to their original bases. If it is foul-tipped and caught, the inning ends. But in one case running has a clear advantage: if the batter hits the pitch into fair territory, the runners have a better chance of advancing or scoring.

We say that running on the pitch is the *dominant strategy* in this situation; it is better in some eventualities, and not worse in any. In general, a player has a dominant strategy when he has one course of action that outperforms all others no matter what the other players do. If a player has such a strategy, his decision becomes very simple; he can choose the dominant strategy without worrying about the rival's moves. Therefore it is the first thing one should seek.

There are interesting examples of dominant strategies everywhere, detectable once you know what to look for. Consider the position of Indiana Jones in the climax of the movie *Indiana Jones and the Last Crusade*. Indiana Jones, his father, and the Nazis have all converged at the site of the Holy Grail. The two Joneses refuse to help the Nazis reach the last step. So the Nazis shoot Indiana's dad. Only the healing power of the Holy Grail can save the senior Dr. Jones from his mortal wound. Suitably motivated, Indiana leads the way to the Holy Grail. But there is one final challenge. He must choose between literally scores of chalices, only one of which is the cup of Christ. While the right cup brings eternal life, the wrong choice is fatal. The Nazi leader impatiently chooses a beautiful golden chalice, drinks the holy water, and dies the sudden death that follows from a wrong choice. Indiana picks a wooden chalice, the cup of a carpenter. Exclaiming "There's only one way to find out" he dips the chalice into the font and drinks what he hopes is the cup of life. Upon discovering that he has chosen wisely, Indiana brings the cup to his father and the water heals the mortal wound.

Although this scene adds excitement, it is somewhat embarrassing (to us) that such a distinguished professor as Dr.

Indiana Jones would overlook his dominant strategy. He should have given the water to his father without testing it first. If Indiana has chosen the right cup, his father is still saved. If Indiana has chosen the wrong cup, then his father dies but Indiana is spared. Testing the cup before giving it to his father doesn't help, since if Indiana has made the wrong choice, there is no second chance — Indiana dies from the water and his father dies from the wound.*

Finding dominant strategies is considerably easier than the search for the Holy Grail. Consider Alfred, Lord Tennyson's familiar line: "Tis better to have loved and lost than never to have loved at all."[1] In other words, love is a dominant strategy.

2. OVER-COVER WARFARE

In the competition between *Time* and *Newsweek*, think of a hypothetical week that produces two major news stories: there is an impasse between the House and the Senate on the budget, and a new drug is claimed to be effective against AIDS. The editors' choice of cover story is primarily based on what will attract the most newsstand buyers (subscribers buy the magazine no matter what the cover). Of these newsstand buyers, suppose 30 percent are interested in the budget story and 70 percent in the AIDS story. These people will buy the magazine only if the story that interests them appears on the cover; if both magazines have the same story, the group interested in it splits equally between them.

Now *Time*'s editor can reason as follows. "If *Newsweek* uses the AIDS story, then if I use the budget story I get the whole of the 'budget market' (30 percent of all readers), whereas if I use

---

* This example also points out one of the weaknesses of game theory. Acts are judged by their consequences alone. No moral value is placed on the act itself. Even though his father is already mortally wounded, Indiana might not want to take responsibility for the act that causes his death.

the AIDS story we share the 'AIDS market' (so I get 35 percent of all readers); so, the AIDS story yields me more sales than the budget story. If *Newsweek* uses the budget story, then I get 15 percent using the budget story, and 70 percent with the AIDS story; once again I do better using the latter. Therefore I have a dominant strategy, namely using the AIDS story. It works better for me than the other strategy regardless of which of the two courses my rival chooses."

We can see the logic of this reasoning much more quickly and clearly from a simple table. We show two columns corresponding to *Newsweek*'s choices, and two rows corresponding to *Time*'s choices. This produces four boxes; each corresponds to one combination of strategies. The entry in each box shows *Time*'s sales, measured in percentage of the total potential readership. The first row shows *Time*'s sales from choosing the AIDS story, as we range over *Newsweek*'s alternative choices. The second row shows *Time*'s sales from choosing the budget story, again as we range over *Newsweek*'s choices. For example, in the bottom left or south-west corner box, *Time* has the budget story and *Newsweek* has the AIDS story, and *Time* gets 30 percent of the market.

Time's Sales

Newsweek's Choices

		AIDS	Budget
Time's Choices	AIDS	35	70
	Budget	30	15

The dominant strategy is easy to see. The first row is uni-

formly better than the second row: each entry in the first row
is bigger than the entry immediately below it in the second
row. This is the criterion for dominance. With the table, you
can make a quick visual check of whether or not the criterion
is met. You can figuratively lift the first row and lay it over the
second, and each number in the second row will be covered by
a bigger number in the first. The visual advantage of the table over the verbal reasoning of the previous paragraph grows
in more complicated games, in which each side has several
strategies.

It so happens that in this game, both players have a dominant strategy. To see this, draw up a table for *Newsweek*'s
sales, shown below. The first column of numbers shows *Newsweek*'s sales if it uses the AIDS story, as we range over *Time*'s
choices. This column is uniformly better than the second column; once again you can perform the overlaying test in your
mind's eye. Therefore the AIDS story is the dominant strategy
for *Newsweek*, too.

Newsweek's Sales

Newsweek's Choices

		AIDS	Budget
Time's Choices	AIDS	35	30
	Budget	70	15

Games in which each side has a dominant strategy are the
simplest games from the strategic perspective. There is strategic interaction, but with a foregone conclusion. Each player's

choice is his dominant strategy, irrespective of what the other does. That does not make such games uninteresting, either to play or to think about. For example, in the hundred-yard dash, the dominant strategy is to run as fast as you can. But many people enjoy participating in and viewing such races. In Chapter 1's Prisoners' Dilemma, as played in Dzerzhinsky Square, both players have dominant strategies. Yet this compelling force takes them to a mutually disastrous outcome. This raises a very interesting question — how can the players cooperate to get a better result? We will have more confessions to make about this in our next chapter.

Sometimes one player has a dominant strategy but the other does not. We illustrate this with just a slight change in the cover story competition between *Time* and *Newsweek*. Suppose that the readership has a slight bias in favor of *Time*. When the two magazines have the same cover story, 60 percent of the potential buyers who like that story will pick *Time* and 40 percent will pick *Newsweek*. Now the table of *Time*'s sales is as follows:

Time's Sales

Newsweek's Choices

	AIDS	Budget
AIDS	42	70
Budget	30	18

Time's Choices

For *Time*, the AIDS story is still the dominant strategy. But *Newsweek*'s table becomes

Newsweek's Sales

Newsweek's Choices

AIDS   Budget

		AIDS	Budget
Time's Choices	AIDS	28	30
	Budget	70	12

If you lift the first column and lay it over the second, 30 gets covered by a smaller number (28), and 12 by a larger (70). Neither strategy dominates the other. In other words, *Newsweek*'s best choice is no longer independent of *Time*'s strategy. If *Time* chooses the AIDS story, *Newsweek* does better by choosing the budget story, and vice versa. For *Newsweek*, the whole of the budget market is now better than the smaller share of the larger AIDS market.

The editors of *Newsweek* do not observe what those of *Time* choose, but they can figure it out. Since *Time* has a dominant strategy, that must be their choice. So *Newsweek*'s editors can confidently assume that those of *Time* have chosen the AIDS story, and pick their own best response, namely the budget story.

Thus games in which only one side has a dominant strategy are also very simple. This side plays its dominant strategy, and the other chooses its best response to that strategy.

Now that we have introduced the idea of a dominant strategy, it is worth emphasizing two points about what a dominant strategy is not. It is easy to get confused about just what it is that a dominant strategy actually dominates.

In 1981, Leonard Silk, writing about the Congressional debate on the Economic Recovery Tax Act, concluded: "Mr. Reagan has sensed that the Republicans have what game theorists call a 'dominant strategy' — one that makes a player better off than his opponent, no matter what strategy his opponent uses."[2] We will look at this game more carefully in Chapter 5, but here we only want to point out that Silk's definition of a dominant strategy is incorrect. The dominance in "dominant strategy" is a dominance of one of your strategies over your other strategies, not of you over your opponent. A dominant strategy is one that makes a player better off than *he* would be *if he used any other strategy*, no matter what strategy his opponent uses. Recall that in the cover picture example, both *Time* and *Newsweek* have a dominant strategy; yet both cannot have higher sales than the other.

A second common misperception is that a dominant strategy requires that the worst possible outcome playing the dominant strategy be better than the best outcome of some other strategy. This happens to be true in the examples above. With the numbers in the original setup, the worst that could happen to *Time* when using the AIDS story was a 35 percent share; the best they could hope for with the budget story was 30 percent. However, this is not a general feature of dominant strategies.

Imagine a price war between *Time* and *Newsweek*. Suppose each issue costs $1 to produce, and there are just two possible pricing choices: $3 (implying a profit margin of $2 per copy) and $2 (implying a profit margin of $1 per copy). Suppose that customers will always buy the lower-priced magazine, and if the prices are equal, they will split equally between the two. The total readership is 5 million if the price is $3, and rises to 8 million if the price is only $2. You can easily calculate *Time*'s profits in the four possible pricing combinations, and produce the following table.

Time's Profits

Newsweek's Price

		$2	$3
Time's Price	$2	4	8
	$3	0	5

Time's dominant strategy is to charge $2 (and so is *Newsweek*'s). The worst that can happen to *Time* from following the dominant strategy is to net $4 million. But the best that can happen from following the other strategy is better, namely $5 million. The point is that the comparison of those two numbers is meaningless. The $5 million arises if both magazines charge $3; then *Time* would do even better ($8 million) by switching to $2.

We can sum up the lessons of these examples into a rule for behavior in games with simultaneous moves:

Rule 2: **If you have a dominant strategy, use it.**

Do not be concerned about your rival's choice. If you do not have a dominant strategy, but your rival does, then anticipate that he will use it, and choose your best response accordingly.

A word of caution. We developed the concept of a dominant strategy for games with simultaneous moves. Care must be taken in using it if moves are sequential. Because the nature of the strategic interaction is different, the idea of a dominant strategy is no longer the same. Suppose we say that you have a dominant strategy if for *each given* choice of the rival, you do better with this strategy than with any other. When moves are sequential and your rival moves first, you would always choose your dominant strategy. As we just said, it is your best response to *each* of your rival's moves, and therefore to the particular one he has chosen. But *if you move first*, your rival's move is not *given*. He will observe your choice when he makes his, and you have the opportunity to influence his behavior. In some circumstances this may best be done by choosing something other than your dominant strategy. We explain this fully in Chapter 6, when we discuss commitment.

3. DOMINATED STRATEGIES

Not all games have dominant strategies, even for one player. In fact, dominance is the exception rather than the rule. Although the presence of a dominant strategy leads to very simple rules for action, these rules are inapplicable to many actual games. Other principles must then be brought into action.

Just as a dominant strategy is uniformly better than every other strategy, a dominated strategy is uniformly worse than some other strategy. Just as you choose your dominant strategy if you have one, and can be sure that your rival will choose his if he has one, you should avoid your dominated strategies if you have any, and can be sure that your rival will avoid his, if he has any.

If you have just two alternative strategies, and one of them is dominated, then the other must be dominant. Therefore examples of avoiding dominated strategies that are genuinely different from those of choosing dominant strategies must be based on games in which at least one side has at least three strategies. Let us consider a simple example of this kind.

Think of a play in football in which the offense's sole concern is to gain as many yards as possible, and the defense's sole concern is to hold them to as few yards as possible. For example, with very little time left, the offense may want to improve its chances of kicking a winning field goal.

Suppose the offense has just two strategies, run and pass, while the defense has three strategies: counter the run, counter the pass, and blitz the quarterback. We can calculate the yards likely to be gained by the offensive team for each of the six strategy combinations. For example, take the case in which the defense blitzes and the offense tries a pass. Suppose there is a 10 percent chance that the quarterback will be sacked for a loss of 10 yards, a 70 percent chance of a quick 10-yard pass, and a 20 percent chance of a longer 20-yard pass. The average works out at

$$0.1 \times (-10) + 0.7 \times 10 + 0.2 \times 20 = -1 + 7 + 4 = 10.$$

The numbers obviously depend on the special skills (or lack thereof) of the two teams; we have chosen particular ones just for illustration.*

We show the outcomes of such calculations for all six possible combinations in the following table.

Offense's Expected Yardage Gain

		Defense's Strategies		
		Counter Run	Counter Pass	Blitz
Offense's Strategies	Run	3	7	15
	Pass	9	8	10

The offense tries to achieve the largest possible number in

---

* In our example the offensive team is strong at passing and weak at running. That is why the pass does better than the run even against a pass defense. The run does better against the blitz only because the defensive backs are not in position.

this table. The defense tries to secure the smallest possible number, so we do not need a separate table from which to determine their actions.*

Neither side has a dominant strategy: there is no row with numbers uniformly higher than those in the other row, and no column with numbers uniformly smaller than those in each of the other columns. But the defense does have a dominated strategy, namely the blitz. The result of a blitz is a yardage loss that is uniformly larger, and thus worse for the defense, than those possible with either of the other strategies. Therefore this defense should not blitz, and the offense can be confident that they will not.

The argument doesn't stop there. The blitz strategy might as well be removed from the defensive coach's playbook, and the game can be treated as if each side had two strategies. In this reduced game, the offense has a dominant strategy, namely pass. Its numbers, 9 and 8, are uniformly higher than those of the run strategy — 3 and 7, respectively. The reason pass was not dominant in the original game was that run had a better yield against the defense's blitz (as the ball-carrier might break into open field with the blitzing defensive safeties out of position), but that has now been removed from consideration. So the offense will choose the pass. The defense in turn should think this through, and choose its best response, namely the pass defense.

The general idea can be summed up into one more rule of behavior for games with simultaneous moves:

> *Rule 3*: **Eliminate any dominated strategies from consideration, and go on doing so successively.**

If, during the process, any dominant strategies emerge in the smaller games, they should be chosen successively. If this pro-

---

* This is so in all "zero-sum" games, in which one side's gain is exactly the other side's loss.

cedure ends in a unique outcome, you have found the prescriptions of action for the players and the outcome of the game. Even if the procedure does not end in a unique outcome, it will reduce the size and the complexity of the game.

We illustrate the idea of successively eliminating dominated strategies by making up a story of an impending naval engagement in the Persian Gulf.* The grid below shows the positions and the choices of the combatants. An Iraqi ship at the point I is about to fire a missile, intending to hit an American ship at A. The missile's path is programmed at the launch; it can travel in a straight line, or make sharp right-angled turns every 20 seconds. If the Iraqi missile flew in a straight line from I to A, American missile defenses could counter such a trajectory very easily. Therefore the Iraqis will try a path with some zigzags. All such paths that can reach A from I lie along the grid shown. Each length like IF equals the distance the missile can travel in 20 seconds.

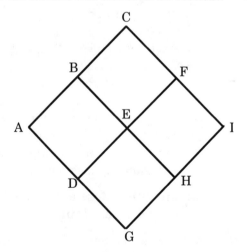

The American ship's radar will detect the launch of the in-

---

* This story is an updated version of the cat-and-mouse story in J. D. Williams, *The Compleat Strategyst*. Perhaps the cat was Persian.

coming Iraqi missile, and the computer will instantly launch an antimissile. The antimissile travels at the same speed as the Iraqi missile, and can make similar 90-degree turns. So the antimissile's path can also be set along the same grid starting at A. However, to allow for enough explosives to ensure a damaging open-air blast, the antimissile has only enough fuel to last one minute, so it can travel just three segments (e.g., A to B, B to C, and C to F, which we write as $ABCF$).

If, before or at the end of the minute, our antimissile meets the incoming missile, it will explode and neutralize the threat. Otherwise their missile will go on to hit our ship. The question is, How should the trajectories of the two missiles be chosen?

Only the first minute of travel is relevant for this game. Each side has to think ahead for three 20-second segments. Counting up all the alternatives at each segment, both sides have eight possible paths. We then examine all 64 combinations, and calculate which ones are hits and which are misses.

For example, consider the Iraqi strategy $IFCB$ of going in the straight line from I to F to C for the first two segments, and then making the right-angled turn to B for the last. Confront this with the American strategy of $ABCF$. The two missiles meet at C at the end of two segments (40 seconds); therefore this combination counts as a hit. If the same Iraqi strategy were countered by the American $ABEF$, this would be a miss. The trajectories seem to have the points B and F in common, but the two missiles reach these points at different times; for example the American missile is at B after 20 seconds and the Iraqi one gets to B after 60 seconds.

The table shows all such combinations. The eight Iraqi strategies are labeled $I1$ to $I8$, and the path for each is also shown — for example, $I1$ stands for $IFCB$. Similarly the American strategies are labeled $A1$ to $A8$. The hits are written H; the misses, O.

Table of Hits and Misses

Iraqi Strategies

		I 1 IFCB	I 2 IFEB	I 3 IFED	I 4 IFEH	I 5 IHGD	I 6 IHED	I 7 IHEB	I 8 IHEF
A m e r i c a n	A 1--ABCF	H	O	O	O	O	O	O	H
	A 2--ABEF	O	H	H	H	O	H	H	H
	A 3--ABEH	O	H	H	H	O	H	H	H
	A 4--ABED	O	H	H	H	H	H	H	H
S t r a t e g i e s	A 5--ADGH	O	O	O	H	H	O	O	O
	A6--ADEH	O	H	H	H	O	H	H	H
	A 7--ADEF	O	H	H	H	O	H	H	H
	A 8--ADEB	H	H	H	H	O	H	H	H

This looks complicated, but the rule of eliminating dominated strategies simplifies it very quickly. The American antimissile is trying to score a hit, so H is better for the Americans than O. Then it is easy to see that for the Americans, the strategy $A2$ is dominated by $A4$: if you lift the row $A4$ and lay it over $A2$, you will see that $A4$ has an H everywhere that $A2$ does, and in one more place — namely, in response to the Iraqi strategy $I5$. Doing such calculations for all the possibilities shows that the strategies $A2$, $A3$, $A6$, and $A7$ are dominated by both $A4$ and $A8$, $A1$ is dominated by $A8$, and $A5$ by $A4$. So the Iraqis will be sure that the Americans will not use anything other than $A4$ or $A8$. *Confining attention to these two rows*, the Iraqis are trying to achieve misses rather than hits, so for them $I2$, $I3$, $I4$, $I6$, $I7$, and $I8$ are dominated by $I1$ or $I5$. After we cross out the rows and columns of dominated strategies, the game is reduced to the following.

Table of Hits and Misses

Iraqi Strategies

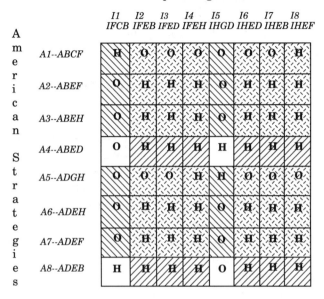

		I1 IFCB	I2 IFEB	I3 IFED	I4 IFEH	I5 IHGD	I6 IHED	I7 IHEB	I8 IHEF
American Strategies	A1--ABCF	H	O	O	O	O	O	O	H
	A2--ABEF	O	H	H	H	O	H	H	H
	A3--ABEH	O	H	H	H	O	H	H	H
	A4--ABED	O	H	H	H	H	H	H	H
	A5--ADGH	O	O	O	H	H	O	O	O
	A6--ADEH	O	H	H	H	O	H	H	H
	A7--ADEF	O	H	H	H	O	H	H	H
	A8--ADEB	H	H	H	H	O	H	H	H

Reduced Table of Missile Hits and Misses

Iraqi Strategies

American Strategies	I1--IFCB	I5--IHGD
A4--ABED	O	H
A8--ADEB	H	O

Our two rules cannot simplify it any further; there are no longer any dominant or dominated strategies. But we have achieved quite a lot. Looking at the remaining strategies in the map, we see that the Iraqi missile should travel along the outer edges of the grid, whereas the American antimissile should prowl in small loops. We shall soon see how to choose from the two alternatives that remain for each side.

4. Equilibrium Strategies

When all simplifications based on dominant and dominated strategies have been used, the game is at its irreducible minimum level of complexity and the problem of the circular reasoning must be confronted head-on. What is best for you depends on what is best for your opponent and vice versa. Here, we introduce the technique for squaring the circle, the way out of the circular reasoning.

For this, let us go back to the price war between *Time* and *Newsweek*, but instead of just two alternative prices of $2 and $3, allow a whole range of prices. Now the management of *Time* must think of its best response for every possible price that *Newsweek* might charge. Suppose each magazine has a core of loyal readers, but there is also a floating readership that can be attracted by price competition. If for some reason the management of *Newsweek* set a price of $1, the cost of production, then the management of *Time* would not follow them into this no-profit strategy, but would set a higher price, say $2, and make some profit from the sales to its loyal readers. As *Newsweek* charged a higher price, *Time* would raise its price, but by less, thus getting some competitive advantage. Suppose that for each $1 increase in the *Newsweek* price, *Time* does best to raise its price by 50 cents. This relationship of *Time*'s best response to all possible prices of *Newsweek* is shown in the chart below.

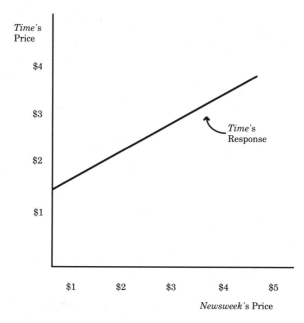

Suppose the two magazines are alike in having similar costs, equal pools of loyal readers, and similar drawing power over floating readers. Then the relationship of *Newsweek*'s best response to all possible prices of *Time* has an identical chart.

Now we can imagine the two managers separately engaged in a round of thinking. Thus *Time*'s manager says: "If he charges $1, I should charge $2. But he, knowing I am thinking in this way, will charge not $1, but his best response to my $2, namely $2.50. Then I should charge not $2, but my best response to his $2.50, namely $2.75. But then he ..." Where does this end?

It ends at $3. If the manager of *Time* thinks that the *Newsweek* price will be $3, then his best response is to charge $3 for *Time*. And vice versa. The circular reasoning has converged.

We can show this in another chart, where the two responses are juxtaposed in the same picture. The two lines meet at the point where each price is $3.

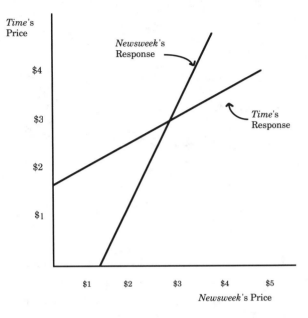

We have found a combination of strategies in which each player's action is the best response to that of the other. Given what the other is doing, neither wants to change his own move. Game theorists call such an outcome an *equilibrium*. This concept was developed by the Princeton mathematician John Nash and in his honor is often called a Nash equilibrium. Nash's idea underlies our final rule of behavior for simultaneous-move games:

> *Rule 4*: **Having exhausted the simple avenues of looking for dominant strategies or ruling out dominated ones, the next thing to do is to look for an equilibrium of the game.**

This must be the trick that Sherlock Holmes and Professor Moriarty were using in seeing through each other's mind.

This rule needs a little more explanation. Why should the players in a game be drawn to such an outcome? Several reasons can be given. No one of them is absolutely compelling on its own, but together they make a strong case.

First, there is the need to avoid circular reasoning, which gets nowhere. The equilibrium stays stable under successive rounds of "I think that he thinks ..." It makes the players' expectations about each other's action consistent. Each has correctly predicted the other's action, and has chosen his own best response.

A second virtue of the equilibrium strategy arises in zero-sum games, in which the players' interests are strictly opposed. In such a game, your opponents cannot gain by deceiving you into playing an equilibrium strategy. You have already taken into account their best response to what you are doing.

The third reason is pragmatic. The proof of the pudding is in the eating. Throughout this book, we discuss several games using the equilibrium approach. We ask you to examine the predictions of outcomes and the prescriptions for behavior that emerge from this way of thinking. We believe this will make our case better than any abstract discussion of its merits.[3]

Finally, there is a possible misinterpretation of the notion of equilibrium we urge you to avoid. When we say that an outcome is an equilibrium, there is no automatic presumption that it is best for all the players in the game, let alone for society as a whole. Such an evaluation is always a separate question, and the answer varies from one context to another. In Chapters 4 and 9 we will meet examples of both kinds.

5. Feast or Famine

Feast

Is the notion of equilibrium a complete solution to the problem of circular reasoning in simultaneous-move games? Alas, no. Some games have many such equilibria, others have none.

In still others, the notion of equilibrium must be made more subtle by admitting new kinds of strategies. We now illustrate and explain these points.

Which side of the road should you drive on? This question cannot be answered through the use of dominant or dominated strategies. Even so, the answer seems easy. If everyone else drives on the right-hand side, you too will want to drive on the right-hand side. To put it in the "If I think that he thinks" framework, if everybody thinks that everybody else thinks that everybody is going to drive on the right-hand side, then everybody will want to drive on the right-hand side and their expectations will all be confirmed. Driving on the right will be an equilibrium.

But so is driving on the left, as in England, Australia, and Japan. The game has two equilibria. Nothing in the notion of equilibrium tells us which (if either) does or should prevail. When a game has many equilibria, the players must have a common understanding of which one to pick. Otherwise there can be confusion.

In the driving example, an established rule gave you the answer. But what do you do when a phone call between Peter and Paula accidentally gets cut off? If Peter tries to call Paula, then Paula should stay off the phone (and not try to call Peter) so as to prevent her phone from being busy. On the other hand, if Paula is waiting for Peter to call, and Peter waits too, then their phone conversation will never be completed. What is best for one depends on what the other does. Again there are two equilibria, one in which Peter calls and Paula waits, and the other the other way around.

The two need a social convention to help them choose consistent strategies, that is, a common understanding of which equilibrium to attain. One solution is for the person who originally made the call to also make the callback. The person who answered the phone waits for the phone to ring again. The advantage of this is that the originator knows the other party's phone number, while the reverse may not always be true. Another possibility is that if one person can call for free and the other cannot (say Peter is in his office and Paula is at a pay phone), then the person with the free access should call again.

To test your ability to coordinate on an equilibrium, consider the following question: You are to meet someone in New York City sometime tomorrow. They are told to meet you. Neither you nor the other person is given any more instructions about where to meet or when. When and where do you go?

Thomas Schelling made this question famous in his *Strategy of Conflict*. There is no predetermined right answer other than the one most commonly given. Among our students, Grand Central Station at noon continues to be the most common answer. This is true even for Princeton students whose train arrives in New York at Penn Station.*

Famine

The other complication is that not all games have even a single equilibrium of the kind we described above. In the missile story, not one of the four remaining outcomes is an equilibrium. For example, look at the combination of Iraqi $I1$ and American $A4$. This produces a miss, and the Americans do better by switching to $A8$. But then the Iraqis should switch to $I5$, in turn the Americans should switch to $A4$, the Iraqis back to $I1$, and so on. The point is that if one side engages in any *determinate* behavior, the other can take advantage of it. The only sensible thing for each to do is to mix its moves randomly. This problem is so symmetric that the right mix

---

* Perhaps the most original alternative answer was offered by U.C.S.D. anthropology professor Tanya Luhrmann. She replied: "The New York Public Library main reading room." When told that this was an uncommon if not unique answer, she immediately defended her choice. She explained that although her probability of success might be low, she was much more interested in meeting the type of person who would pick the New York Public Library rather than the type of person who would pick Grand Central!

is obvious: the Americans should choose each of $A4$ and $A8$ with equal likelihood, and the Iraqis should likewise place a 50 percent probability on choosing each of $I1$ and $I5$.

This mixing strategy can arise even when parties are trying to cooperate. In the phone-call example, imagine that both parties flip a coin to determine whether or not they should be the one to return the call. This pair of random actions is a third equilibrium to the phone problem based on the criteria described above. If I try to call you, I have a 50 percent chance of getting through (when you are waiting for my call) and a 50 percent chance of finding your line busy. If I wait instead, then I also have a 50 percent chance of getting back in touch; the 50 percent comes from the one-half chance that you will be trying to call me. Each round, both parties are completely indifferent about what action to take: their responses are in fact optimal to each other. Since there is only a 50 percent chance of resuming our conversation, we expect that it will take two tries (on average) before we succeed.

In other games, the right proportions in which each player should mix his strategies is not so obvious. In Chapter 7 we develop a set of rules to determine when mixed strategies are needed and a method to find the right mixture.

Let us recapitulate briefly. We have three rules for action in games with simultaneous moves: first, look for and use dominant strategies; next, look for and avoid dominated strategies, in each case assuming similar behavior on the part of your rivals; and finally, look for and use an equilibrium. To conclude this chapter, we consider a case that shows how you can translate these thoughts into action.

6. CASE STUDY #3:
TOUGH GUY, TENDER OFFER

When Robert Campeau made his first bid for Federated Stores (and its crown jewel, Bloomingdales), he used the strategy of a *two-tiered* tender offer. This case study looks at the effectiveness of the two-tiered bid as a strategic move: does it give the raider an unfair advantage?

A two-tiered bid typically offers a high price to the first shares tendered and a lower price to the later shares tendered. To keep numbers simple, we look at a case in which the pretakeover price is $100 per share. The first tier of the bid offers a higher price, $105 per share to the first shareholders until half of the total shares are tendered. The next fifty percent of the shares tendered fall into the second tier; the price paid for these shares is only $90 per share. For fairness, shares are not placed in the different tiers based on the order in which they are tendered. Rather, everyone gets a blended price: all the shares tendered are placed on a prorated basis into the two-tiers. (Those who don't tender find all of their shares end up in the second tier if the bid succeeds.)* We can express the average payment for shares by a simple algebraic expression: if fewer than 50 percent tender, everyone gets $105 per share; if an amount $X\% \geq 50\%$ of the company's total stock gets tendered, then the average price paid per share is

$$\$105\frac{50}{X} + \$90\frac{X-50}{X} = 90 + 15\frac{50}{X}.$$

One thing to notice about the way the two-tiered offer is made is that it is unconditional; even if the raider does not get

---

* A raider who gains control of the company has a right to take the company private and thus buy out all remaining shareholders. By law, these shareholders must be given a "fair market" price for their stock. Typically, the lower tier of a two-tiered bid is still in the range of what might be accepted as fair market value.

control, the tendered shares are still purchased at the first-tier price. The second feature to note about the way this two-tiered offer works is that if *everyone* tenders, then the average price per share is only $97.50. This is less than the price before the offer. It's also worse than what they expect should the takeover fail; if the raider is defeated, shareholders expect the price to return to the $100 level. Hence they hope that the offer is defeated or that another raider comes along.

In fact another raider did come along, namely Macy's. Imagine that Macy's makes a conditional tender offer: it offers $102 per share *provided* that it gets a majority of the shares. To whom do you tender and which (if either) offer do you expect to succeed?

Case Discussion

Tendering to the two-tiered offer is a *dominant* strategy. To verify this, we consider all the possible cases. There are three possibilities to check.

The two-tiered offer attracts less than 50 percent of the total shares and fails.

The two-tiered offer attracts some amount above 50 percent and succeeds.

The two-tiered offer attracts exactly 50 percent. If you tender, the offer will succeed, and without you it fails.

In the first case, the two-tiered offer fails, so that the post-tender price is either $100 if both offers fail or $102 if the competing offer succeeds. But if you tender you get $105 per share, which is bigger than either alternative. In the second case, if you don't tender you get only $90 per share. Tendering gives you at worst $97.50. So again it is better to tender. In the third case, while other people are worse off if the offer succeeds, you are privately better off. The reason is that since there are exactly 50 percent tendered, you will be getting $105 per share. This is worthwhile. Thus you are willing to push the offer over.

Because tendering is a dominant strategy, we expect everyone to tender. When everyone tenders, the average blended price per share may be below the pre-bid price and even below the expected future price should the offer fail. Hence the two-tiered bid enables a raider to pay less than the company is worth. The fact that shareholders have a dominant strategy does not mean that they end up ahead. The raider uses the low price of the second tier to gain an unfair advantage. Usually the manipulative nature of the second tier is less stark than in our example because the coercion is partially hidden by the takeover premium. If the company is truly worth $110 after the takeover, then the raider can still gain an unfair advantage by using a second tier below $110 but above $100. Lawyers view the two-tiered bid as coercive and have successfully used this as an argument to fight the raider in court. In the battle for Bloomingdales, Robert Campeau eventually won, but with a modified offer that did not include any tiered structure.

We also see that a conditional bid is not an effective counterstrategy against an unconditional two-tiered bid. In our example, the bid by Macy's would be much more effective if its offer of $102 per share were made unconditionally. An unconditional bid by Macy's destroys the equilibrium in which the two-tiered bid succeeds. The reason is that if people thought that the two-tiered bid were certain to succeed, they would expect a blended price of $97.50, which is less than they would receive by tendering to Macy's. Hence it cannot be that shareholders expect the two-tiered bid to succeed and still tender to it.*

In late 1989, Campeau's operations unraveled because of excessive debt. Federated Stores filed for reorganization under

---

* Unfortunately, neither is it an equilibrium for the bid by Macy's to succeed, for in that case, the two-tiered bid would attract less than 50 percent of the shares and so the price per share offered would be above the bid by Macy's. Alas, this is one of those cases with no equilibrium. Finding a solution requires the use of randomized strategies, which is the topic of Chapter 7.

Chapter 11 of the bankruptcy law. When we say Campeau's strategy was successful, we merely mean that it achieved the aim of winning the takeover battle. Success in running the company was a different game.

Epilogue to Part I

In the first three chapters, we introduced several concepts and methods, using examples from business, sports, politics, etc., as vehicles. In the chapters to follow, we will put the ideas and techniques to work. Here we recapitulate and summarize them for ready reference.

A *game* is a situation of strategic interdependence: the outcome of your choices (strategies) depends upon the choices of another person or persons acting purposively. The decision-makers involved in a game are called players, and their choices are called *moves*. The interests of the players in a game may be in strict conflict; one person's gain is always another's loss. Such games are called *zero-sum*. But more typically, there are zones of commonality of interests as well as of conflict; there can be combinations of mutually gainful or mutually harmful strategies. Nevertheless, we usually refer to the other players in a game as one's rivals.

The moves in a game may be *sequential* or *simultaneous*. In a game of sequential moves, there is a linear chain of thinking: If I do this, my rival can do that, and in turn I can respond in the following way .... Such a game is studied by drawing the *game tree*. The best choices of moves can be found by applying *Rule 1: Look forward, and reason backward*.

In a game with simultaneous moves, there is a logical circle of reasoning: I think that he thinks that I think that .... This circle must be squared; one must see through the rival's action even though one cannot see it when making one's own move. To tackle such a game, construct a *table* that shows the outcomes corresponding to all conceivable combinations of choices. Then proceed in the following steps.

Begin by seeing if either side has a *dominant strategy* — one that outperforms all of that side's other strategies, irrespective of the rival's choice. This leads to *Rule 2: If you have a dominant strategy, use it.* If you don't have a dominant strategy, but your rival does, then count on his using it, and choose your best response accordingly.

Next, if neither side has a dominant strategy, see if either has a *dominated strategy* — one that is uniformly worse for the side playing it than another of its strategies. If so, apply *Rule 3: Eliminate dominated strategies from consideration.* Go on doing so successively. If during the process any dominant strategies emerge in the smaller games, they should be chosen successively. If this procedure ends in a unique outcome, you have found the prescriptions of action for the players and the outcome of the game. Even if the procedure does not lead to a unique outcome, it can reduce the size of the game to a more manageable level. Finally, if there are neither dominant nor dominated strategies, or after the game has been simplified as far as possible using the second step, apply *Rule 4: Look for an equilibrium, a pair of strategies in which each player's action is the best response to the other's.* If there is a unique equilibrium of this kind, there are good arguments why all players should choose it. If there are many such equilibria, one needs a commonly understood rule or convention for choosing one over the others. If there is no such equilibrium, that usually means that any systematic behavior can be exploited by one's rivals, and therefore indicates the need for *mixing one's plays.*

In practice, games can have some sequential moves and some simultaneous moves; then a combination of these techniques must be employed to think about and determine one's best choice of actions.

Part II

4

Resolving the
Prisoners' Dilemma

Throughout the 1970s, the Organization of Petroleum Exporting Countries (OPEC) colluded to raise the price of crude oil from under $3 per barrel in 1973 to over $30 per barrel in 1980. The world awaited the meeting of each OPEC price-setting meeting with anxiety. By the end of the 1970s, some energy experts were predicting that the price of oil would rise to over $100 per barrel by the end of the century. Then suddenly the cartel seemed to collapse. Prices moved down, briefly touching $10 per barrel in early 1986 before recovering to $18 per barrel in 1987.* As we write this, the Iraqi invasion of Kuwait has shot the price of oil up to $35 per barrel and experts are divided about the future of OPEC.

What governs the success or failure of such cartels? More generally, what governs the balance between cooperation and competition not just in business, but also in politics and social settings? This question can be answered, at least in part, using the prisoners' dilemma that we played out in KGB headquarters in Chapter 1.

The story of OPEC is just such a game. Of course we tell

---

* Of course it must be remembered that the dollar rose sharply against other currencies from 1981 to 1985, and fell almost equally fast from 1985 to 1987. Therefore neither the drop in oil prices in the first half of the 1980s, nor the recovery since then, were as dramatic in terms of an average of all currencies as they were in dollars alone.

it in a stylized way, highlighting the dilemma and leaving out many historical details. To start with, look at the production decisions of just two members, say Iran and Iraq. For further simplicity, allow each just two production levels, either 2 or 4 million barrels of crude oil a day. Depending on their decisions, the total output on the world market will be 4, 6, or 8 million barrels. Suppose the price will be $25, $15, and $10 per barrel, respectively. Extraction costs are $2 per barrel in Iran and $4 per barrel in Iraq. Then we can show the profits (measured in millions of dollars a day) of the two competitors in the usual table. In each box, the top right entry is Iraq's daily profit, the bottom left is Iran's.*

Table of Profits (Iran, Iraq)

Iraq's Output

		2	4
Iran's Output	·2	42 46	44 26
	4	22 52	24 32

Each country has a dominant strategy: produce at the higher of the two available levels. Iran, for example, sees that its profit row corresponding to the production level of 4, namely [$52 and $32], is uniformly higher than the one corre-

---

* This way of representing both players' payoffs in the same matrix is due to Thomas Schelling. With excessive modesty he writes, "If I am ever asked whether I ever made a contribution to game theory, I shall answer yes. Asked what it was, I shall say the invention of staggered payoffs in a matrix. ... I did not suppose that the invention was patentable, so I made it freely available and hardly anybody except my students takes advantage. I offer it to you free of charge."

sponding to the production level of 2, namely [$46 and $26].
When they both choose their dominant strategies, their profits
are $32 and $24 million a day, respectively. Nothing to sneeze
at, but cooperation would have gotten them more, $46 and $42.

This predicament is called the prisoners' dilemma. Its remarkable feature is that both sides play their dominant strategy, thus maximize their payoff, and yet the outcome is jointly
worse than if both followed the strategy of minimizing their
payoff. So why don't they follow the minimizing strategy?
Look back at the problem for Iran and Iraq. Even if Iran
were to follow the minimizing strategy of producing 2 million
barrels, Iraq still has an incentive to produce 4 million. Then
the outcome would be Iraq's ideal and Iran's worst. If Iran
doesn't cooperate and produces 4 million, then Iraq would be
foolish to sacrifice its own profits by producing 2 million. The
cartel's problem is to find a way to sustain the low-output,
high-price strategy that yields the highest joint profit, given
the temptation for each to cheat and gain at the expense of
the other.

Iran and Iraq's situation is analogous to that of the KGB's
prisoners. Each of them found it dominant to confess: if the
one held out, the other got a better deal by confessing; if one
confessed, the other would be foolish not to. Hence whatever
one does, the other wants to confess. But that's true for both.
And when both confess, each gets a harsh sentence. Again the
selfish pursuit of one's interests leads to an inferior outcome.
When neither confesses, the outcome is better for both. The
problem is how to attain such cooperation given the competition to obtain an especially good deal for oneself.

The same problem arises when there are several competing
firms in the industry. The problem plagues not just businesses,
but also students of business. A professor at Texas A&M University had his class of 27 students play a game that trapped
them in the prisoners' dilemma.[1] Each student owned a hypothetical firm and had to decide whether to produce 1 and help

keep the price high or produce 2 and gain at the expense of others. Depending on the total number of students producing 1, money would be paid to students according to the following table:

Number of Students Writing "1"	Payoff to Each Student Who Writes "1"	Payoff to Each Student who Writes "2"
0		$0.50
1	$0.04	$0.54
2	$0.08	$0.58
3	$0.12	$0.62
. . .	. . .	. . .
25	$1.00	$1.50
26	$1.04	$1.54
27	$1.08	

This is easier to see and more striking in a chart:

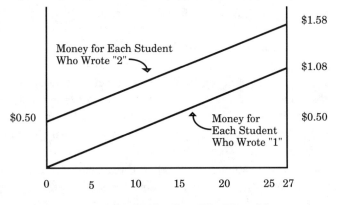

Number of Students Who Wrote "1"

The game is "rigged" so that students who write 2 always get 50 cents more than those who write 1, but the more of them that write 2, the less their collective gain. Suppose all 27 start planning to write 1, so each would get $1.08. Now one thinks of sneaking a switch to 2. There would be 26 1's, and each would get $1.04 (4 cents less than the original), but the switcher would get $1.54 (46 cents more). The same is true irrespective of the initial number of students thinking of writing 1 versus 2. Writing 2 is a dominant strategy. Each student who switches from writing 1 to writing 2 increases his own payout by 46 cents, but decreases that of each of his 26 colleagues by 4 cents — the group as a whole loses 58 cents. By the time everyone acts selfishly, each maximizing his own payoff, they each get 50 cents. If, instead, they conspired and acted so as to minimize their individual payoff, they would each receive $1.08. How would you play?

In some practice plays of this game, first without classroom discussion and then with some discussion to achieve a "conspiracy," the number of cooperative students writing 1 ranged from 3 to a maximum of 14. In a final binding play, the number was 4. The total payout was $15.82, which is $13.34 less than that from totally successful collusion. "I'll never trust anyone again as long as I live," muttered the conspiracy leader. And how did he vote? "Oh, I voted 2," he replied.

This situation reminds us of Yossarian's position in Joseph Heller's novel *Catch-22*. The Second World War was nearly won, and Yossarian did not want to be among the last to die. His commanding officer asks, "But suppose everyone on our side felt that way?" and Yossarian replies, "Then I'd certainly be a damned fool to feel any other way. Wouldn't I?"

Politicians, too, are prisoners of the same dilemma. In 1984, it was clear to most people that the U.S. federal budget deficit was too large. Expenditure cuts of the required magnitude were politically infeasible, and therefore a significant tax increase was inevitable. But who was going to exercise the political leadership necessary to bring this about? The Democratic presidential candidate, Walter Mondale, tried to

set the stage for such a policy change in his campaign, and
was soundly defeated by Ronald Reagan, who promised no tax
increase. In 1985, the issue got stalled. No matter how you
formed the political divisions — Democrats vs. Republicans,
the House of Representatives vs. the Senate, or the Administration vs. the Congress — each side preferred to leave the
initiative to the other.

For each, the best outcome was one in which the other proposed the tax increases and expenditure cuts, paying the political price. Conversely, proposing such policies oneself while
the other remained passive was the worst outcome. Both sides
agreed that the exercise of joint leadership, sharing the credit
and the blame, would be better for the country, and even for
themselves in the long run, than the combination in which
both were passive and the large deficit continued.

We can represent this as a game by drawing up the usual
table of strategies and outcomes. The two sides are the Republicans and the Democrats. To show who prefers what, let us
rank the outcomes from 1 to 4 from each side's point of view.
Low numbers mean better ranking. In each box the lower
left number is the Republicans' ranking; the upper right, the
Democrats'.

Rankings for Republicans and Democrats

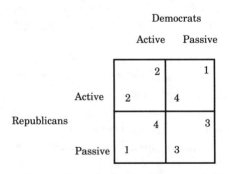

You can easily see that for each side, passivity is the dominant strategy. This is just what happened; there was no move

toward tax increase in the 99th Congress. The 99th Congress did pass the Gramm-Rudman-Hollings act, which mandated the deficit-reduction policies to be followed in *future* years. But that was merely a pretense of activity, in fact postponing the hard choices. Its targets are being met more by accounting tricks than by genuine fiscal restraint.

1. HOW TO ACHIEVE COOPERATION

Those who find themselves in a prisoners' dilemma will look for ways to escape and achieve the cooperative outcome they jointly prefer. Others may like to see the players remain trapped in the dilemma. For example, buyers benefit from lower prices when the prisoners' dilemma prevents firms in an industry from colluding. In this case society wants to thwart the industry's attempts to resolve the dilemma, and antitrust laws are part of this effort. In either case, whether we seek collusion or its opposite, we must first understand the ways in which the prisoners' dilemma might be averted. Then we can try to facilitate these ways, or to block them, as is appropriate in the case being considered.

The underlying problem is the players' incentive to cheat on any agreement. Therefore the central questions are, How can such cheating be detected? What prospect of punishment will deter it? Let us examine these in turn.

2. DETECTION OF CHEATING

A cartel has to find ways to discover if cheating has in fact occurred, and if so, then determine who has cheated. Recognizing that *someone* has cheated is often easy in the examples we have used. In the case of Iran and Iraq's oil production, the price will be $25 only if both countries cooperate and produce 2 million barrels daily; any price below $25 per barrel is a sure indicator of cheating. In reality, matters are more complicated. The price can be low either because of a fall in demand or because of cheating by a producer. Unless the cartel can sort out these separate influences and determine the truth, it might infer cheating and set in motion its punishment measures when no cheating has in fact occurred, or err the other way around.* This will reduce the accuracy and therefore the efficacy of the measures. A compromise solution is a critical or "trigger" price; if the price falls below this value, the cartel presumes that cheating has occurred and the punishment ensues.

There is yet another complication in reality. Games of this kind often have many dimensions of choice, and the possibility of observing cheating differs among them. For example, firms compete with one another in price, product quality, after-sales service, and many other aspects. The price is relatively easy to observe, although secret discounts or flexibility in pricing trade-ins can cause complications. There are many dimensions of quality that are hard to monitor. Therefore a cartel that tries to enforce collusive high prices finds competition continually breaking out in new dimensions. This happened in the airline industry. During the years of regulation, fares were fixed and entry of new competitors was effectively barred. This was as if the airlines formed a cartel with enforcement provided by the Civil Aeronautics Board. Airlines began to compete, or cheat on the cartel. While they couldn't lower prices, they could provide more valuable services through elaborate meals and beautiful stewardesses. When labor laws forced airlines to hire male stewards and not fire stewardesses over thirty, competition switched to nonstop schedules, seat width, and leg room.

---

* The statistical literature describes false positives as Type I errors and false negatives as Type II errors. Most common of all is the Type III error: not being able to remember which is which.

Another instance of this process occurred in the area of international trade policy. Tariffs are the most visible tools for restricting trade, and successive rounds of negotiations of the General Agreement on Tariffs and Trade (GATT) achieved large mutual reductions of tariff rates of all industrial countries. But each country still had its domestic political pressures from powerful special interests to restrict imports. Therefore countries gradually switched to other, less visible means, such as voluntary restraint agreements, customs valuation procedures, standards, administrative practices, and complicated quotas.*

The common theme of these examples is that collusion focuses on the more transparent dimensions of choice, and competition shifts to the less observable ones: we call this the Law of Increasing Opaqueness. Though you might not see it clearly, the collusion still hurts you. When quotas on Japanese auto imports went into effect in 1981, not only did the prices of all cars, Japanese and American, go up, but the low-end Japanese models disappeared from the market. Opaque competition was doubly bad: prices were higher, and the balance of the product mix was distorted.

Identifying the cheater may be even more difficult than detecting cheating. With just two players, an honest party knows that the other has cheated. There may still be a problem with getting him to admit his fault. With more than two players, we may know that someone has cheated, but no one (other than the cheater) knows who. In this case, the punishment to deter cheating must be blunt and affect the innocent and the guilty alike.

Finally, cheating may consist of remaining passive and may

* For example, quotas under the multifiber arrangement are levied by extremely complicated categories of garments and countries. This makes it very hard to see the effect of the quota in raising the price of any particular good. Economists have estimated these effects and found price increases as high as 100 percent; a tariff this high would surely arouse louder consumer protests.

thereby be difficult to isolate. This was so in our example of the exercise of leadership in proposing higher taxes. In such a case, it is far harder to infer or allege cheating. While positive action is there for all to see, there are numerous excuses for inaction: greater urgency of other issues, time needed to consolidate forces, and so on.

3. PUNISHMENT OF CHEATERS

Behind every good scheme to encourage cooperation is usually some mechanism to punish cheaters. A prisoner who confesses and implicates his collaborators may become the target of revenge by the others' friends. The prospect of getting out of prison more quickly may look less alluring given the knowledge of what waits outside. Police have been known to scare drug dealers into confessing by threatening to release them. The threat is that if they are released, their suppliers will assume they have squealed.

In the example of the Texas A&M classroom experiment, if the students could detect who had reneged on the conspiracy for all of them to write 1, they could ostracize the cheaters for the rest of the semester. Few students would risk that for the sake of fifty cents. In OPEC, because of the social and political cohesion of the Arab states in the 1970s, a country thinking of cheating may have been deterred by a fear of ostracism. These are examples of punishments that are added on to the original game, in order to reduce the incentive to cheat.

Other kinds of punishments arise within the structure of the game. Usually this happens because the game is repeated, and the gain from cheating in one play will lead to a loss in other plays. We illustrate this using the crude oil example with Iran and Iraq.

The possibility of punishment arises because the two countries are involved in this game day after day. Suppose they start on a basis of trust, each producing 2 million barrels a day and helping keep the price high. Each will constantly be tempted to sneak in a defection. Look again at the table of daily profits. A successful day of cheating while Iraq stays honest will raise Iran's profit from $46 million to $52 million, a gain of $6 million.

Table of Profits (Iran, Iraq)

Iraq's Output

		2	4
Iran's Output	2	42 46	44 26
	4	22 52	24 32

The question is what happens when Iraq recognizes what has gone on. A plausible scenario is that the mutual trust will collapse, and the two will settle down to a regime of high outputs and low prices from that day onward. Relative to the continuation of trust, this gets Iran $14 million a day (46 32) less profit. The short-term gain from cheating seems small in comparison with the subsequent cost: if it takes Iraq a month to detect Iran's cheating and respond, the month's extra profit to Iran ($180 million) would be wiped out if the period of collapsed trust lasts just 13 days. Of course time is money, and higher profits today are worth more than an equal reduction of profit in the future; but still this calculation looks distinctly unfavorable. For Iraq, breaking the cartel is even worse; the daily gain while its cheating goes undetected and unpunished is $2 million, whereas the daily cost once trust collapses is $18 million. It appears that in this instance, even a slight fear of the collapse of their mutual trust should be enough to keep the two competitors abiding by the agreement.

Trust can break down for all sorts of reasons. For example, the war between Iran and Iraq made it difficult for OPEC to impose production quotas on either country. Trust in maintaining cartel quotas is based on the subsequent ability to punish those who violate the agreement. But what additional punishments could be imposed on two countries already punishing each other with explosives and "human wave" assaults? With the war ended, there is once again a potential for cooperation because there is a potential for punishment.

To sum up, there is no solution that achieves reciprocal cooperation in a one-time game. Only in an ongoing relationship is there an ability to punish, and thus a stick to motivate cooperation. A collapse of cooperation carries an automatic cost in the form of a loss of future profits. If this cost is large enough, cheating will be deterred and cooperation sustained.

There are some caveats to this general principle. The first arises when the relationship has some natural end, such as the end of a term in an elected office. In these situations, the game is repeated only a fixed number of times. Using the principle of looking ahead and reasoning back, we see that cooperation must end when there is no longer any time left to punish. Yet neither wants to be left cooperating while the other cheats. If ever someone cooperates, then someone must get stuck in the end. Since neither is willing to play the fool, cooperation never gets started. This is true no matter how long the game is, provided the end is known.

Let us look at this argument a little more carefully. Right from the start, both players should look ahead to predict the last play. On this last play, there will be no future to consider, and the dominant strategy is to cheat. The outcome of the last play is a foregone conclusion. Since there is no way to affect the last play of the game, the penultimate play effectively becomes the last one to consider.

Once again, cheating is a dominant strategy. The reason is that the play in the next-to-last period has no effect on the strategies chosen in the final period. Thus the penultimate period can be considered in isolation. For any period in isolation, cheating is a dominant strategy.

Now the play of the final two periods can be taken as given. Cooperating early on won't help, as both players are resigned to cheat in the final two periods. Hence, the third-to-last period is effectively the last one to consider. The same argument applies and cheating is a dominant strategy. This argument unwinds all the way back, so that there is no cooperation even in the first play.

The logic of this argument is impeccable, and yet in the real world we find episodes of successful cooperation. There are various ways to explain this. One is that all actual games of this kind are repeated only a finite number of times, but that number is unknown. Since there is no fixed last time, there is always the possibility that the relationship will go on. Then the players have some incentive to sustain the cooperation for the sake of such future contingencies; if this incentive is large enough, the cooperation will persist.

Another explanation is that the world contains some "nice" people who will cooperate no matter what the material advantages of cheating may be. Now suppose you are not so nice. If you behaved true to your type in a finitely repeated game of prisoners' dilemma, you would start cheating right away. That would reveal your nature to the other player. To hide the truth (at least for a while) you have to behave nicely. Why would you want to do that? Suppose you started by acting nicely. Then the other player would think it possible that you are one of the few nice people around. There are real gains to be had by cooperating for a while, and the other player would plan to reciprocate your niceness to achieve these gains. That helps you, too. Of course you are planning to sneak in a defection near the end of the game, just as the other player is.

But you two can still have an initial phase of mutually ben-
eficial cooperation. Thus while each side is waiting to take
advantage of the other, both are benefiting from this mutual
deception.

A third qualification to the emergence of trust in a repeated
prisoners' dilemma is that the gains from cheating take place
before the costs of the breakdown of cooperation occur. Therefore the relative importance of the two depends on the relative
importance of the present versus the future. In business contexts, current and future profits are compared using an appropriate interest rate to discount the future. In politics, the judgment of present versus future is more subjective, but it seems
that time beyond the next election counts for very little. This
makes cooperation hard to achieve. Even in business, when
times are bad, the whole industry is on the verge of collapse,
and the management feels that there is no tomorrow, competition may become more fierce than in normal times. Similarly,
the needs of war made current profits more important to Iran
and Iraq, and contributed to the difficulties of OPEC.

4. The Punishment Is Guaranteed

The neatest trick is enforcing price collusion through a punishment guarantee, all in the name of competition. Here we
turn to New York City and its stereo wars. Crazy Eddie has
made his trademark "We cannot be undersold. We will not
be undersold. Our prices are the lowest — guaranteed. Our
prices are insane." His main competitor, Newmark & Lewis,
is no less ambitious. With any purchase, you get the store's
"Lifetime low-price guarantee." It promises to rebate double
the difference if you can find a lower price elsewhere.

"If, after your purchase, you find the same model advertised or
available for sale for less (confirmed printed proof required) by any
other local stocking merchant, in this marketing area, during the life-

time of your purchase, we, Newmark & Lewis, will gladly refund (by check) 100% of the difference, plus an additional 25% of the difference, or if you prefer, Newmark & Lewis will give you a 200% gift certificate refund (100% of the difference plus an additional 100% of the difference, in gift certificates)."

— from Newmark & Lewis's Lifetime Low-Price Guarantee

Yet, although they sound competitive, these promises to beat the rival's price can enforce discipline in a price-setting cartel. How can this happen?

Suppose each VCR costs $150 wholesale, and for the moment both Crazy Eddie and Newmark & Lewis are selling it for $300. Crazy Eddie is contemplating a sneaky cut to $275. Without the beat-the-rival promise, Crazy Eddie would hope that his lower price would attract some of the customers who would otherwise have gone to his rival — say, because they lived nearer to a Newmark & Lewis outlet, or had bought from them before. Unfortunately for Crazy Eddie, his price cut has the reverse effect. With the Newmark & Lewis price guarantee, these people are now tempted just to walk over to Newmark & Lewis and buy the VCR for $300 and then claim a $50 rebate. This is just as if Newmark & Lewis had reduced its price to $250, automatically undercutting Crazy Eddie. But of course Newmark & Lewis would prefer not to give away the fifty dollars. Its response will be to lower the price to $275. In any event, Crazy Eddie is worse off than where he started. So why bother? The price stays at $300.

Although cartels are illegal in the United States, Crazy Eddie and Newmark & Lewis have the makings of one. You can see how their implicit cartel works in terms of the requirements of enforcement we mentioned before: detection of cheating, and punishment of cheaters. Newmark & Lewis can more easily detect Crazy Eddie's cheating. The customers who bring them the news of Crazy Eddie's lower price, and ask them to beat that, are acting as unwitting enforcement agents for the cartel. The punishment comes in the form of the collapse of the pricing agreement and consequently lower profits. The "beat-the-competition" ads also set the punishment in motion, automatically and quickly.

A celebrated antitrust case before the Federal Trade Commission concerned the use of a similar device that appears to make competition more fierce, but can in fact serve as a cartel enforcement mechanism. E. I. Du Pont, Ethyl, and other manufacturers of antiknock gasoline additives were charged with using a "most-favored-customer" clause. This clause says that the seller will offer to these favored customers the best price they offer to anyone. Taken at face value, it seems that the manufacturers are looking out for their favored customers. But let's look deeper. The clause means that the manufacturer cannot compete by offering selective discounts to attract new customers away from his rival, while charging the old higher price to his established clientele. They must make general price cuts, which are more costly, because they reduce the profit margin on all sales. You can see the advantage of this clause to a cartel: the gain from cheating is less, and the cartel is more likely to hold.

In evaluating most-favored-customer clauses, the Federal Trade Commission ruled that there was an anticompetitive effect, and forbade the companies from using such clauses in their contracts with customers.* How would you rule if such a case were brought against Crazy Eddie and Newmark & Lewis? One yardstick by which to judge the fierceness of competition is the level of markups. Many "discount" stereo stores charge almost a hundred-percent markup over the wholesale cost of their components. It is hard to say what part of the markup is due to the costs of carrying inventory and adver-

---

* This ruling was not without some controversy. The Commission's chairman, James Miller, dissented. He wrote that the clauses "arguably reduce buyers' search costs and facilitate their ability to find the best price-value among buyers." For more information, see "In the matter of Ethyl Corporation et al." FTC Docket 9128, *FTC Decisions*, pp. 425–686.

tising, but there is at least a prima facie case that there is
method to Crazy Eddie's madness.

5. A CHOICE OF PUNISHMENT

When several alternative punishments could deter cheating
and sustain cooperation, how should one choose among them?
Several criteria have a role.

Perhaps most important are simplicity and clarity, so that
a player thinking of cheating can easily and accurately calculate its consequences. A criterion that infers someone has
cheated if your discounted mean of profits from the last sev-
enteen months is 10 percent less than the average real rate of
return to industrial capital over the same period, for example,
is too complicated for most firms to figure out, and therefore
not a good deterrent.

Next comes certainty. Players should have confidence that
defection will be punished and cooperation rewarded. This is
a major problem for the European countries looking to enforce
the General Agreement on Tariffs and Trade. When one country complains that another has cheated on the trade agreement, GATT initiates an administrative process that drags on
for months or years. The facts of the case have little bearing
on the judgment, which usually depends more on dictates of
international politics and diplomacy. Such enforcement procedures are unlikely to be effective.

Next we ask how severe a punishment should be. Most
people's instinctive feeling is that it should "fit the crime." But
that may not be big enough to deter cheating. The surest
way to deter cheating is to make the punishment as big as
possible. Since the punishment threat succeeds in sustaining
cooperation, it should not matter how dire it is. The fear keeps
everyone from defecting, hence the breakdown never actually
occurs and its cost is irrelevant.

The problem with this approach is that it ignores the risk of mistakes. The detection process may go wrong, indicating cheating by a member of the cartel when the real cause of low prices is an innocent one such as low demand. If punishments are as big as possible, then mistakes will be very costly. To reduce the cost of mistakes, the punishment should be the smallest size that suffices to deter cheating. Minimal deterrence accomplishes its purpose without imposing any extra costs when the inevitable mistakes occur.

6. TIT-FOR-TAT

This list of the desirable properties of a punishment mechanism looks quite demanding. But University of Michigan political scientist Robert Axelrod claims that the rule of *tit-for-tat* does very well in meeting these demands.[2] Tit-for-tat is a variation of the "eye for an eye" rule of behavior: do unto others as they have done onto you.* More precisely, the strategy cooperates in the first period and from then on mimics the rival's action from the previous period.

Axelrod argues that tit-for-tat embodies four principles that should be evident in any effective strategy: clarity, niceness,

---

* In Exodus (21:22), we are told, "If men who are fighting hit a pregnant woman and she gives birth prematurely but there is no serious injury, the offender must be fined whatever the woman's husband demands. But if there is a serious injury, you are to take life for a life, eye for eye, tooth for tooth, hand for hand, burn for burn, wound for wound, bruise for bruise." The New Testament suggests more cooperative behavior. In Matthew (5:38) we have, "You have heard that it was said, 'Eye for Eye, and Tooth for Tooth.' But I tell you, do not resist an evil person. If someone strikes you on the right cheek, turn to him the other also." We move from "Do unto others as they have done onto you" to the golden rule, "Do unto others as you would have them do unto you" (Luke 6:31). If people were to follow the golden rule, there would be no prisoners' dilemma. And if we think in the larger perspective, although cooperation might lower your payoffs in any particular game, the potential reward in an afterlife makes this a rational strategy even for a selfish individual.

provocability, and forgivingness. Tit-for-tat is as *clear* and simple as you can get. It is *nice* in that it never initiates cheating. It is *provocable*, that is, it never lets cheating go unpunished. And it is *forgiving*, because it does not hold a grudge for too long and is willing to restore cooperation.

Axelrod confirmed the power of tit-for-tat through experiment, not just theory. He staged a tournament of two-person prisoners'-dilemma games. Game theorists from around the world submitted their strategies in the form of computer programs. The programs were matched against each other in pairs to play a prisoners'-dilemma game repeated 150 times. Contestants were then ranked by the sum of their scores.

The winner was Anatol Rapoport, a mathematics professor at the University of Toronto. His winning strategy was tit-for-tat. Axelrod was surprised by this. He repeated the tournament with an enlarged set of contestants. Once again Anatol Rapoport submitted tit-for-tat and beat the competition.

One of the impressive features about tit-for-tat is that it did so well overall even though it did not (nor could it) beat any one of its rivals in a head-on competition. At best, tit-for-tat ties its rival. Hence if Axelrod had scored the competition as a winner-take-all contest, tit-for-tat would have scored below .500 and so could not have won.

But Axelrod did not score the pairwise plays as winner-take-all: close counted. The big advantage of tit-for-tat is that it always comes close. At worst, tit-for-tat ends up getting beaten by one defection; i.e., it gets taken advantage of once and then ties from then on. The reason tit-for-tat won the tournament is that it usually managed to encourage cooperation whenever possible while avoiding exploitation. The other entries were either too trusting and open to exploitation or too aggressive and knocked one another out.

In spite of all this, we believe that tit-for-tat is a flawed strategy. The slightest possibility of misperceptions results in a complete breakdown in the success of tit-for-tat. This flaw was not apparent in the artificial setting of a computer tournament, because misperceptions did not arise. But when tit-for-tat is applied to real-world problems, misperceptions cannot be avoided and the result can be disastrous.

For instance, in 1987 the United States responded to the Soviet spying and wiretapping of the U.S. embassy in Moscow by reducing the number of Soviet diplomats permitted to work in the United States. The Soviets responded by withdrawing the native support staff employed at the U.S. Moscow embassy and placed tighter limits on the size of the American delegation. As a result, both sides found it more difficult to carry out their diplomatic functions. Another series of tit-for-tat retaliations occurred in 1988, when the Canadians discovered spying on the part of the visiting Soviet diplomats. They reduced the size of the Soviet delegation and the Soviets reduced the Canadian representation in the Soviet Union. In the end, both countries were bitter, and future diplomatic cooperation was more difficult.

The problem with tit-for-tat is that any mistake "echoes" back and forth. One side punishes the other for a defection, and this sets off a chain reaction. The rival responds to the punishment by hitting back. This response calls for a second punishment. At no point does the strategy accept a punishment without hitting back. The Israelis punish the Palestinians for an attack. The Palestinians refuse to accept the punishment and retaliate. The circle is complete and the punishments and reprisals become self-perpetuating.

The long-standing feuds between the Hatfields and the McCoys or Mark Twain's Grangerfords and Shepherdsons offer more examples of how tit-for-tat behavior leads to mutual loss. Feudists on either side are not willing to end the feud until they consider themselves even. But in a continuing attempt to get even, they end up knocking each other further and further down. Eventually they'll end up dead even. Rarely is there any hope of going back and solving the dispute at its origin, for once begun, it takes on a life of its own. When Huck Finn tries to understand the origins of the Grangerfords-Shepherdsons feud, he runs into the chicken-or-egg problem:

"What was the trouble about, Buck? — Land?"

"I reckon maybe — I don't know."

"Well, who done the shooting? Was it a Grangerford or a Shepherdson?"

"Laws, how do *I* know? It was so long ago."

"Don't anyone know?"

"Oh yes, pa knows, I reckon, and some of the other old people, but they don't know now what the row was about in the first place."

What tit-for-tat lacks is a way of saying "Enough is enough." It is dangerous to apply this simple rule in situations in which misperceptions are endemic. Tit-for-tat is *too easily provoked.* You should be more forgiving when a defection seems to be a mistake rather than the rule. Even if the defection was intentional, after a long-enough cycle of punishments it may still be time to call it quits and try reestablishing cooperation. At the same time, you don't want to be too forgiving and risk exploitation. How do you make this trade-off?

A useful way to evaluate a strategy is to measure how well it performs against itself. If one thinks in terms of evolution, the "fittest strategies" will become dominant in the population. As a result, they will encounter each other often. Unless a strategy performs well against itself, any initial success will eventually become self-defeating.

At first glance, tit-for-tat does very well against itself. Two tit-for-tatters will start off cooperating, and since each is responding in kind, this cooperation seems destined to go on forever. The pair of strategies appears to completely avoid the problem of the prisoners' dilemma.

But what happens if there is a chance that one side misperceives the other's move? To find out, we follow two families, the Hatfields and the McCoys, as they use tit-for-tat in their neighborly relations. They begin peacefully (*P*).

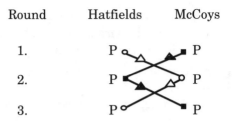

Suppose that in round 4 a Hatfield misinterprets a McCoy. Although the McCoys were truly peaceful, the Hatfields mistakenly saw an act of aggression (*A*).

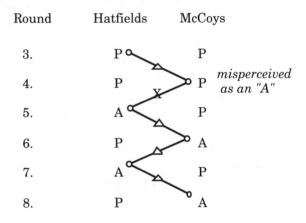

The single misunderstanding "echoes" back and forth. In round 5, the imagined McCoy aggression becomes real in the Hatfield response. Now the two tit-for-tat clans are trapped in a situation in which they alternate retaliating against the other for the previous retaliation. In round 6, the McCoys punish the Hatfields for their aggression in round 5, which leads the Hatfields to retaliate once more in round 7. And so it goes. Trying to get even for being down one just doesn't work.

The situation continues like this until a second misinterpretation arises. Two developments are possible. The Hatfields could misinterpret peace for aggression or they could misinterpret aggression as peace.* If aggression is misinterpreted as peace, the feud is ended (at least until the next misperception).

If the second misperception is peace as aggression, both sides will resort to continual retaliation. This is illustrated below in round 9. Here the single helixlike twisting strand of peace is misinterpreted as aggression. Consequently, the Hatfields respond by retaliating in round 11. Until another misperception occurs, both sides continue to punish the other for the other's previous punishments. Although tit-for-tatters can give it, they can't take it.

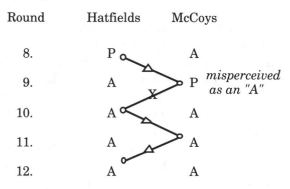

Round	Hatfields	McCoys
8.	P	A
9.	A	P *misperceived as an "A"*
10.	A	A
11.	A	A
12.	A	A

What can we conclude about the performance of tit-for-tat? When misperceptions are possible, *in the long run tit-for-tat will spend half the time cooperating and half of it defecting.* The reason is that once misperceptions arise, they are just as likely to get compounded as they are to get cleared up. Hence, tit-for-tat will do no better than a strategy based on a coin toss that cooperates and defects with equal probability.

In this discussion, we seem to have left out an important ingredient: the probability that a misperception occurs. In fact, our conclusion does not depend on this probability! No

---

* Alternatively, these misunderstandings could also arise on the part of the McCoys, and the effect would be the same.

matter how unlikely a misperception is (even if it is one in a trillion), in the long run tit-for-tat will spend half of its time cooperating and half defecting, just as a random strategy does. When the probability of a misperception is small, it will take a lot longer for the trouble to arise. But then once a mistake happens, it will also take a lot longer to clear it up.

The possibility of misperceptions means that you have to be more forgiving, but not forgetting, than simple tit-for-tat. This is true when there is a presumption that the chance of a misperception is small, say five percent. But what strategy would you adopt in a prisoners' dilemma in which there is a fifty percent chance that the other side will misinterpret (reverse) your actions? How forgiving should you be?

Once the probability of misunderstanding reaches fifty percent there is *no* hope for achieving any cooperation in the prisoners' dilemma. You should always defect. Why? Consider two extremes. Imagine that you always cooperate. Your opponent will misinterpret your moves half the time. As a result, he will believe that you have defected half the time and cooperated half the time. What if you always defect? Again, you will be misinterpreted half the time. Now this is to your benefit, as the opponent believes that you spend half your time cooperating.

No matter what strategy you choose, you cannot have any effect on what your partner sees. It is as if your partner flips a coin to determine what he thinks you did. There is simply no connection with reality once the probability of a mistake reaches fifty percent. Since you have no hope of influencing your partner's subsequent choices, you might as well defect. Each period you will gather a higher payoff and it won't hurt you in the future.

The moral is that it pays to be more forgiving up to a point. Once the probability of mistakes gets too high, the possibility of maintaining cooperation in a prisoners' dilemma breaks down. It is just too easy to be taken advantage of. The large chance of misunderstandings makes it impossible to send clear messages through your actions. Without an ability to communicate through deeds, any hope for cooperation disappears.

A 50 percent chance of a misperception is the worst possible case. If misperceptions were certain to occur, you would interpret every message as its opposite, and there would be no misunderstandings. A stock forecaster whose advice is always dead wrong is as good a predictor as one who is always right. You just have to know how to decode the forecasts.

With this in mind, we look for a way out of the dilemma when there is a chance of misperception, but not too big of a chance.

7. AN ALTERNATIVE TO TIT-FOR-TAT

The basic properties of clarity, niceness, provocability, and forgivingness seem likely to be true of any good rule of behavior for extricating oneself from a prisoners' dilemma. But tit-for-tat is too quick to punish someone who has a history of cooperating. We need to find a strategy that is more discriminating: it should be more forgiving when a defection appears to be an exception, and it should punish when defection appears to be the rule.

You can consider the following guidelines as a step in that direction. (1) Begin cooperating. (2) Continue cooperating. (3) Keep count of how many times the other side appears to have defected while you have cooperated. (4) If this percentage becomes unacceptable, revert to tit-for-tat. Note that unlike before, tit-for-tat is not used as a reward for good behavior; instead, tit-for-tat is the *punishment* if it appears that the other side is trying to take advantage of you.

To determine what is an unacceptable percentage of defections, you need to know both a short-, medium-, and long-term history of the other side's actions. The long run is not enough.

Just because someone has been cooperating for a long time does not mean that he now won't take advantage of you while he runs down his reputation. You also need to know "What have you done for me lately?"

Here is an example of one such strategy. It is nicer, more forgiving, not quite as provocable, and a little more complicated than tit-for-tat. Start cooperating and continue to do so until one of the four tests below fails.

- First impression: A defection on the first move is unacceptable. Revert to tit-for-tat.
- Short term: Two defections in any three turns is unacceptable. Revert to tit-for-tat.
- Medium term: Three defections out of the last twenty periods is unacceptable. Revert to tit-for-tat.
- Long term: Five defections out of the last one hundred periods is unacceptable. Revert to tit-for-tat.

The punishment of tit-for-tat need not last forever. Keep track of how often the other side has violated any of these four tests. On the first violation, return to cooperation after twenty periods of the tit-for-tat "echo" of alternating defections. But put the other side on probation. Reduce the number of defections allowed in the medium- and long-term tests by one. If the other side does not violate the probation for fifty periods, then strike the record clean and return to the original standards. If the other side violates the probation, resort to tit-for-tat forever.

The exact rules for first, short-term, medium-term, and long-term impressions will depend on the probabilities of error or misperception, the importance you place on future gains and current losses, and so on. But this type of strategy is likely to outperform tit-for-tat in the imperfect real world.

The important principle to remember is that when misperceptions are possible, you shouldn't punish every defection you see. You have to make a guess as to whether a misperception has occurred, either by you or by your partner. This extra forgiveness allows others to cheat a little on you. But if they cheat, they use up their goodwill. When the eventual misperceptions arise you will no longer be inclined to let the incident pass. Opportunism on the part of your opponent will be self-defeating.

8. CASE STUDY #4: *CONGRESS* V. *FEDERAL RESERVE*

The United States Congress and the Federal Reserve often clash over economic policy. To explain why the conflict arises and where it leads, we present Princeton economist Alan Blinder's game-theoretical analysis of the conflict.[3] The two institutions have separate and largely independent powers in making economic policy. Fiscal policy (taxation and expenditures) is the responsibility of the Congress, and monetary policy (money supply and interest rates) that of the Federal Reserve. Each can deploy its policies in an expansionary mode or a contractionary mode. Expansionary fiscal policy means high expenditures and low taxes; this reduces unemployment but carries a risk of inflation. Expansionary monetary policy means low interest rates and therefore easier borrowing conditions, but again at the risk of inflation.

The two branches have also developed separate preferences about economic outcomes. Voters like the benefits they get from government spending, as in cheaper mortgages, and dislike paying taxes. Congress responds to this by favoring expansionary policies, unless inflation is imminent and serious. In contrast, the Fed takes a longer viewpoint and thinks inflation the greater problem; therefore it favors contractionary policies.

In 1981–82, Congress no longer regarded inflation as a sufficiently great risk. It felt that the economy could afford an expansionary fiscal policy and wanted the Fed to accommodate by pursuing an expansionary monetary policy. But the Fed under Paul Volcker was afraid that this would just rekindle the fires of inflation. The Fed's first preference was for both fiscal and monetary policies to be contractionary. What seemed best for the Congress was worst for the Fed and vice versa.

The interests of the Congress and the Fed were not entirely opposed. In search of a compromise, the two sides debated the relative merits of combining one expansionary and one contractionary policy. Either way the policies were mixed would have similar effects on general employment and inflation, but differed in other important respects. Fiscal expansion and monetary contraction would lead to a large budget deficit and high interest rates as the need to finance this deficit ran up against the tight money. The high interest rates would hurt such important sectors as autos and construction especially hard. Foreign capital would flow in, attracted by the high U.S. interest rates. The dollar would rise and our international competitiveness would suffer.

Fiscal contraction and monetary expansion would have just the opposite effects — low interest rates and a low dollar — favoring our auto and construction industries, and making our traded goods more competitive. Both Congress and the Fed preferred this second combination of policies to the first.

What would you predict in this situation? How would you judge the outcome? What reforms in the policy-making process would you prescribe?

Case Discussion

This is a prisoners' dilemma. (Otherwise the case wouldn't be in this chapter, would it?) Let the Congress and the Fed rank the four possible policy combinations, 1 being the best and 4 the worst in each case. Then we have this table.

Rankings of Outcomes for (Fed, Congress)

Congress's Choice

		High Expen-ditures	Low Expen-ditures
Fed's Choice	Easy Money	1 · · · 4	2 · · · 2
	Tight Money	3 · · · 3	4 · · · 1

High expenditures is a dominant strategy for the Congress; tight money, for the Fed. When the two think in this way and each selects its preferred strategy, the result is a budget deficit and tight money. This is exactly what happened in the early 1980s. But there is a better outcome for both, namely a budget surplus and looser money.

What prevents them from reaching an outcome both prefer? The answer lies, once again, in the interdependence of decisions. The jointly preferred outcome arises when each chooses its *individually worse* strategy. Congress must restrict spending to achieve a balanced budget. Having done so, how can it be sure that the Fed will not respond with a tight money supply? It knows that the Fed has a temptation to sneak a switch to a tight money supply to achieve its ideal outcome, which would result in the worst possible outcome for the Congress. Congress does not trust the Fed to refrain from this temptation. It is their inability to make credible promises to each other that locks the adversaries into an outcome they could jointly improve upon.

Can we suggest a way out of this dilemma? The two have an ongoing relationship, and cooperation might emerge in the repeated game. However, that only happens if the players put sufficient weight on future benefits; Congressmen who must run for reelection every two years find it hard to act with such forethought.

Let us try a different avenue. The Federal Reserve is itself a creation of Congress. In most other countries, the government (the Treasury Department) exercises much more control over the central bank. If the same were true in the United States, the Congress could impose an expansionary monetary policy on the Fed and achieve its most preferred outcome. Of course those who share the Fed's concern for inflation would find this regrettable.

This seems a no-win situation: coordination of fiscal and monetary policies is tantamount to a triumph of the short-sighted political objectives of the Congress, but the checks and balances supplied by an independent Federal Reserve lead to a prisoners' dilemma. Perhaps a solution is to let the Fed choose expenditures and taxes, and let the Congress set the money supply?

5

Strategic Moves

"We must organize a merciless fight. The enemy must not lay hands on a single loaf of bread, on a single liter of fuel. Collective farmers must drive their livestock away and remove their grain. What cannot be removed must be destroyed. Bridges and roads must be dynamited. Forests and depots must be burned down. Intolerable conditions must be created for the enemy." — Joseph Stalin, proclaiming the Soviets' "scorched earth" defense against the Nazis, July 3, 1941.

Today Stalin's campaign lives on in the battlefields of corporate control. When Western Pacific attempted to "annex" the publishing company Houghton Mifflin, the publishing house responded by threatening to empty its stable of authors. John Kenneth Galbraith, Archibald MacLeish, Arthur Schlesinger Jr., and many profitable textbook authors threatened to find new publishers if Houghton Mifflin were acquired. "When Western Pacific Chairman Howard (Mickey) Newman got the first few letters from authors, he thought it was a big laugh, and called it a 'put-up job.' When he began getting more letters, he began to realize, 'I'm going to buy this company and I ain't going to have nothing.'"[1] Western Pacific withdrew its bid, and Houghton Mifflin remained independent.

This strategy doesn't always work. When Rupert Murdoch was interested in acquiring *New York* magazine, the incumbent management attempted to fight him off. Many of the magazine's best-known writers threatened to quit if Murdoch attained control. Murdoch was not deterred. He acquired *New*

York magazine. The writers quit. But the advertisers stayed on. And Murdoch got what he was looking for. The writers burned the wrong fields. For the scorched earth strategy to be effective, you must destroy what the invader wants, which may not coincide with what the present occupants value.

We do not mean to imply any moral approval of such tactics or their outcomes — successful or not. We can easily imagine circumstances where society would wish to prevent the wasteful destruction. Our purpose is to explain the nature of these strategies so that you may better use them or prevent them.

The scorched earth defense is but one example of devices game theorists call *strategic moves.*[2] A strategic move is designed to alter the beliefs and actions of others in a direction favorable to yourself. The distinguishing feature is that the move purposefully limits your freedom of action. This can be done in an unconditional way; a presidential candidate pledges he will not raise taxes, period. Or, freedom can be limited because the strategic move specifies a rule for how to respond under different circumstances. For example, many states have mandatory sentencing laws for crimes with handguns; these statutes purposefully limit judicial discretion.

You might have thought that leaving options open is always preferable. But in the realm of game theory that is no longer true. Your lack of freedom has strategic value. It changes other players' expectations about your future responses, and you can turn this to your advantage. Others know that when you have the freedom to act, you also have the freedom to capitulate. To quote Oscar Wilde, "I can resist anything except temptation."[3]

1. Unconditional Moves

Picture a rivalry between the United States and Japan to develop high-definition TV. Although the United States has a technological edge, it also has more limited resources owing to accumulated budget deficits. The Japanese play off of this handicap and once again beat the United States. But a strategic move that at first glance appears to handicap the United States further can change all that.

In the absence of any unconditional moves, Washington and Tokyo simultaneously choose their strategies. Each country decides between a low or high level of research and development effort; a high-effort level shortens development time, incurring much greater costs. We depict this as a game, and set up the payoff table. Each side has two strategies, so there are four possible outcomes.

We suppose both sides regard a high-effort race as the worst scenario — the Japanese because the United States is more likely to win an all-out race, and the United States because of the greater cost. Call this payoff 1 for each side. Each side's second worst outcome (payoff 2) is pursuing low effort while the other goes all out: this is spending money with little chance of success.

Payoffs for High-Definition TV Race (U.S., Japan)

Japanese Effort

	Low	High
U.S. Effort Low	3 4	4 2
High	2 3	1 1

The Japanese like best (labeled as payoff 4) the situation in which they pursue high effort and the United States follows low effort; their chances of winning are high, and resource costs matter less for them. For the United States, the best

situation is when both sides make low effort; they are likely
to win at low cost.

Low effort is the dominant strategy for the United States.
The problem for the United States is that the Japanese can
anticipate this. The Japanese best response is to follow high
effort. The equilibrium of the game is the top right cell, where
the United States gets its second worst payoff. To improve its
position calls for a strategic move.

Suppose the United States preempts. It announces its unconditional effort level before the Japanese reach their decision. This turns the simultaneous-move game into a sequential-
move game, one in which the United States goes first. The
table turns into a tree.*

Tree and Payoffs in Sequential-Move Game

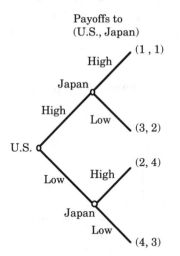

This game is solved by looking forward and reasoning back.
If the United States pursues low effort, the Japanese respond
with high, and the U.S. payoff is 2. If the United States

---

* It takes a clever carpenter to turn a tree into a table; a clever strategist
knows how to turn a table into a tree.

pursues high effort, the Japanese respond with low, and the U.S. payoff is 3. Therefore the United States should announce high, and expect the Japanese to respond low. This is the equilibrium of the sequential-move game. It gives the United States a payoff of 3, more than the 2 it got in the simultaneous-move game.

The strategic move that brings the United States this advantage is a unilateral and unconditional declaration of its choice. The choice is *not* what the United States would have made in simultaneous play. This is where the strategic thinking enters. The United States has nothing to gain by declaring the choice of low effort; the Japanese expect that anyway in the absence of any declaration.

To behave strategically, you must commit *not* to follow your equilibrium strategy of the simultaneous-move game. The strategic move changes Japanese expectations, and therefore their response. Once they believe that the United States is committed to high effort, the Japanese will choose low effort. Of course, after the Japanese choose their path, the United States would do better to change its mind and switch to low effort, too.

This raises several questions: Why should the Japanese believe the U.S. declaration? Would they not anticipate a change of mind? And if they anticipate such a reversal, would they not choose high effort?

In other words, the *credibility* of the U.S. unconditional first move is suspect. Without credibility, the move has no effect. Most strategic moves must confront this problem of credibility. Recall the examples at the opening of the chapter. Although the politician's pledge not to raise taxes is unconditional, it is not irreversible. Once elected, excuses are often found to raise taxes. Conditional rules are also subject to exceptions when the time comes; the mandatory sentence is waived when a neurologist uses an illegal handgun in self-defense against a deranged patient.

To give a strategic move credibility, you have to take some other supporting action that makes reversing the move too costly or even impossible. Credibility requires a *commitment* to the strategic move. In the case of Stalin's threat to starve the enemy, burning the fields made his threat credible. In other situations, credibility is a matter of degree. Precedent in the legal system gives credibility to the mandatory sentencing rule (in most cases); for politicians' promises, exceptions are more the rule. In the race for high-definition TV, the United States might commit funds to which interested companies can lay claim in order to make a high R&D effort credible.

Strategic moves thus contain two elements: the planned course of action and the commitment that makes this course credible. In this chapter we focus attention on the actions. We classify and explain different types of strategic behavior, leaving aside for the moment the problem of how to make them credible. To make an analogy with cooking, the next chapter offers recipes for commitment. We continue here with a menu of moves.

2. THREATS AND PROMISES

An unconditional move gives a strategic advantage to a player able to seize the initiative and move first. Even when you don't actually move first, you can achieve a similar strategic advantage through a commitment to a *response rule*. The response rule prescribes your action as a response to the others' moves. Although you act as a follower, the commitment to the response rule must be in place *before* others make their moves. A parent telling a child "No dessert unless you eat your spinach" is establishing such a response rule. Of course this rule must be in place and clearly communicated before the child feeds its spinach to the dog.

Response rules fall under two broad categories: threats and

promises. A *threat* is a response rule that punishes others who fail to cooperate with you. There are compellent threats, as when a terrorist hijacks a plane and establishes a response rule that the passengers will be killed if his demands are rejected, and there are deterrent threats, as when the United States threatens that it will respond with nuclear weapons if the Soviet Union attacks any NATO country. A compellent threat is designed to induce someone to action, while a deterrent threat is designed to prevent someone from taking an action. The two threats share a common feature: *both* sides will suffer if the threat has to be carried out.

The second category of response rules is *promises*. This is an offer to reward someone who cooperates with you. In search of a witness, a prosecutor promises one defendant a more lenient sentence if he turns state's evidence against his codefendants. Again there can be compellent and deterrent promises. A compellent promise is designed to induce someone to take a favorable action, such as turning state's evidence. A deterrent promise is designed to prevent someone from taking an unfavorable action, such as when the mobsters promise the witness they will take care of him if he keeps his mouth shut. The two promises also share a common feature: once the action is taken (or not taken), there is an incentive to go back on one's word.

Sometimes the distinctions between threats and promises are blurred. A friend was mugged in New York City with the following promise: If you "lend" me twenty dollars, I promise I won't hurt you. More relevant was the mugger's implicit threat that if our friend *didn't* lend him the money, he would be hurt.

As this story suggests, the distinction between a threat and a promise depends only on what you call the status quo. The traditional mugger threatens to hurt you if you don't give him some money. If you don't, he starts hurting you, making that the new status quo, and promises to stop once you give him money. A compellent threat is just like a deterrent promise with a change of status quo; likewise, a deterrent threat and a compellent promise differ only in their status quo.

3. WARNINGS AND ASSURANCES

The common feature to all threats and promises is this: the response rule commits you to actions that you would not take in its absence. If the rule merely says you will do what is best at the time, this is as if there is no rule. There is no *change* in others' expectations about your future actions and hence no influence of the rule. Still, there is an informational role for stating what will happen without a rule; these statements are called *warnings* and *assurances*.

When it is in your interest to carry out a "threat," we call this a *warning*. For example, if the president warns he will veto a bill not to his liking, this is simply an indication of his intentions. It would be a threat if he were willing to sign the bill, but strategically committed to veto it in order to induce Congress to offer something even better.

A warning is used to inform others of the effect of their actions. A parent who warns a child that a stove-top is hot, makes a statement of fact, not strategy.

When it is in your interest to carry out a "promise," we call this an *assurance*. A child who ignores the warning that the stove-top is hot and gets burned assures the parent that he won't do this again.

We emphasize this distinction for a reason. Threats and promises are truly strategic moves, whereas warnings and assurances play more of an informational role. Warnings or assurances do not change your response rule in order to influence another party. Instead, you are simply informing them of how you will want to respond based on their actions. In stark contrast, the sole purpose of a threat or promise is to change your response rule away from what will be best when the time comes. This is done not to inform but to manipulate. Because threats and promises indicate that you will act against your own interest, there is an issue of credibility. After others have moved, you have an incentive to break your threat or promise. A commitment is needed to ensure credibility.

We summarize the options for strategic moves in a chart below. An *unconditional* move is a response rule in which you move first and your action is fixed. Threats and promises arise when you move second. They are *conditional* moves because the response dictated by the rule depends on what the other side does.

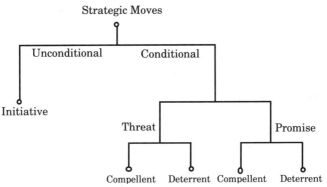

A strategic move is always a preemptive action. The response rule must be in place before the other side moves. That means that whatever strategic move is made, the game should be analyzed as one with sequential moves. When you are intransigent, others respond to your unconditional action. With threats and promises, you first lay down a response rule, then others move and you respond according to your response rule.

As a result, commitment to an action or response rule transforms an otherwise simultaneous-move game into a sequential-move game. Although the payoffs remain unchanged, a game played with simultaneous moves in one case and sequential moves in another can have dramatically different outcomes.

The different outcomes are due to the different rules of play. We illustrated this effect with an unconditional move in the story of U.S.-Japanese rivalry; let us now look at threats and promises arising in a confrontation between the United States and the Soviets and then the Democrats and the Republicans.

4. NUCLEAR DETERRENCE

For over forty years, the North Atlantic Treaty Organization (NATO) sought a credible deterrence to any Soviet attempt to invade Western Europe. A conventional defense by NATO forces was not likely to succeed. A primary component of the NATO deterrence was based on the U.S. nuclear forces. Yet, a nuclear response would be devastating for the whole world. How could this work?

Let us show the game in a tree. The Soviets have the first move. If they do not attack, we have the status quo; score this 0 for each side. If they attack and NATO attempts a conventional defense, suppose the Soviets have the payoff 1 and the United States has -1. A nuclear response gives -100 to each side.

Tree and Payoffs in Sequential-Move Game

Payoffs to (USSR , USA)

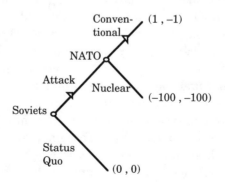

In this game, the Soviets look ahead and forecast that their aggression will not bring forth a nuclear response. It is not in the U.S. interests after the fact. Thus attacking will give them the payoff 1; not attacking, 0. Therefore they will attack.

If you think this an unlikely scenario, the European members of NATO thought it all too likely that the United States would desert them in their time of need in just this way. They wanted the United States to commit credibly to a nuclear response.

Let us leave aside the issue of credibility for now, and examine the mechanics of how such a threat could work. Now the United States has the first move, namely the response rule it puts in place. The pertinent rule is the threat: "If the Soviets attack Western Europe, our response will be nuclear." If the United States does not make the threat, the rest of the game unfolds as before. With the threat in place, the choice of a conventional defense no longer exists. The full game tree is as follows.

Payoffs in Sequential-Move
Game with Threat in Place

Payoffs to (USSR , USA)

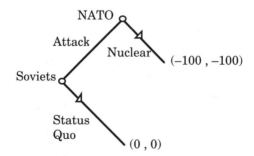

Once the U.S. threat is in place, the Soviets look ahead and recognize that aggression will meet a nuclear response and result in a Soviet payoff of −100. They prefer the status quo, and so do not invade. Now the United States in its first move looks ahead to all this and sees that its payoff is 0 with the threat and   1 without. Therefore U.S. interests dictate making the threat.

Once again, observe that the U.S. response rule requires doing something that is not the best response after the fact. Therein lies the strategic purpose: by credibly altering the Soviets' perception of the U.S. response after the fact, the United States can change "the fact" — namely, the Soviet decision whether or not to invade Western Europe.

The rule must be in place before the other party has already taken the action you want to influence. After the fact, neither an unconditional move nor threats and promises have any relevance.

This first move must be either observed or inferred by the rival, or else you cannot use it for strategic effect. In the film *Dr. Strangelove*, the Soviets install their sure deterrent, the doomsday device, on a Friday, but delay telling the Americans until Monday. Over the weekend, U.S. Air Force General Jack D. Ripper orders his squadron of planes to launch a nuclear attack. The deterrent fails by being unobservable.

Observability is not as straightforward as it seems. One need not actually observe the other person's actions if the action can be inferred from the consequence. If I am allergic to shellfish, I can tell that you cooked with shrimp even if I did not actually observe you in the kitchen.*

Just as your unconditional move must be observable if it is to influence your rival, his actions must be observable if you

---

* Secrecy of the ballot is supposed to make the voters immune from pressure in this way. But once again, inference will do the job without actual observation. It is not sufficient that I can observe that you have moved; I must actually be able to infer what your move was. Although my ballot may be secret when it goes into the box, the final vote cannot be secret. If a candidate bribes 100 people and then receives only 47 votes, he knows that *someone* (actually, 53 someones) has cheated him. If he punishes all 100 people whom he bribed, in the process he'll get the right person. Although blunt, this technique can circumvent the secrecy of the ballot box when the election has only a small number of voters (in each precinct).

are to influence them by threats or promises. Otherwise you cannot check his compliance, and he knows this.

Now that you have seen how credible unconditional moves and threats have their effects, you will be able to analyze most simple situations of this kind without drawing a game tree in all its detail. A verbal argument will usually suffice. If ever it does not, and you doubt if the prose has covered all the cases correctly, you can always check the reasoning by drawing the tree.

5. STRATEGIES OF THE TIMES

In 1981, Ronald Reagan was a newly elected president with tremendous popular appeal. But, could he carry his vision for tax reform through Congress? The battle lines were drawn in the fight over his first budget proposal. The Democrats wanted Reagan to compromise, sacrificing part of the tax cut for the sake of a smaller deficit. The Republicans wanted the full dose of supply-side economics. The outcome would depend on how the two parties played the game.

In the Senate, the Democrats went along with Reagan's budget, hoping to induce some Republican compromise in return for the bipartisan support. But the Republicans held firm to the original plan. Thus the scene turned to the House of Representatives. Was there some better strategy for the Democrats?

A pair of *New York Times* columns by Leonard Silk neatly laid out the strategic possibilities.[4] As he described the negotiations, each party had two choices and there were four possible outcomes. We reproduce Silk's table of the game.

Ranking of Outcomes for [Democrats, Republicans]

Republicans

	Support Reagan Completely	Compromise
Democrats	*1st*	*2nd*
	Republicans triumph, Democrats avoid blame.	Republicans win, but vex Reagan; Democrats share credit.
Mainly Support Reagan	*3rd*	*2nd*
	3rd	*4th*
	Republican program blocked in House; Democrats incur blame.	Republicans lose much of program; Democrats look fiscally responsible.
Attack Reagan	*4th*	*1st*

The Democrats regard as best the outcome where they attack Reagan and the Republicans compromise, because the Democrats can claim the credit for fiscal responsibility while implementing their favored budget. For the Republicans, the best outcome occurs in the top left, where Reagan's budget gets bipartisan support. When the Democrats attack while the Republicans hold firm, the result is a stalemate and both parties lose. The Democrats would be willing to moderate their attack if the Republicans would compromise; both parties would get their second-best outcome.

The Democrats' main problem is that the Republicans have a dominant strategy: support Reagan completely. If the Democrats mainly support Reagan, the Republicans should support Reagan completely to attain their top outcome. If the Democrats attack Reagan, the Republicans should support Reagan to avoid their worst outcome. Whatever the Democrats do, it is always better for the Republicans to support Reagan completely.*

Thus the Republican strategy seems easy to predict. The Democrats should expect the Republicans to support Reagan completely, and then the Democrats do best by following suit and mainly supporting Reagan. This is exactly what happened in the Senate.

So far, the outcome greatly favors the Republicans. To improve their position, the Democrats need to make some type of strategic move. They must turn the situation into a sequential-move game, moving first and then letting the Republicans respond to their strategy.† Thus we consider what type of threats, promises, or other moves shift the outcome in favor of the Democrats.

None of the basic strategies seem to work for the Democrats. Unconditional moves, promises, even threats all fail. Only the combined use of a threat and promise can induce Republican compromise.

The problem with unconditionality is that it doesn't influence the Republican position. The Democrats are currently expected to support Reagan. Committing themselves to this action does not alter the Republicans' perception and thus

---

* Additionally, Silk noted that supporting Reagan completely leaves the Republicans in a better position than the Democrats, no matter what strategy the Democrats choose. In the top left compartment, the Republicans' 1st place is better than the Democrats' 3rd, and in the bottom left compartment, the Republicans' 3rd is better than the Democrats' 4th. Thus the Republicans always come out on top. But as we explained in Chapter 2, each player should attempt to maximize his own position, without concern for who ends up on top. The correct sense of dominance is that a strategy does better for you than other strategies, not that it leaves you better off than an opponent. To the extent that players are concerned about their relative position, these concerns should already be included as part of the rankings or payoffs listed in the table.

† Since the Republicans are already at their most preferred outcome, there is nothing they can do to improve their position. Their goal is simply to maintain the status quo. It is in their interest to prevent the Democrats from making any strategic move that changes the outcome of the game.

leads to the same outcome. The only strategic possibility is for
the Democrats to attack Reagan unconditionally. In this case,
they can look forward and reason that the Republicans will
still respond by supporting Reagan completely. (The Republicans always prefer to support Reagan completely — it is their
dominant strategy.) But the combination of Democrats attacking with the Republicans giving complete support is worse for
the Democrats than the alternative of both parties supporting
Reagan.

The Democrats want to induce the Republicans to move
from completely supporting Reagan to compromise. Therefore, they might promise to support Reagan *if* the Republicans agree to compromise.* But this promise will not help
them. The Republicans know that if they ignore the promise
and choose to support Reagan completely, the Democrats' best
response is to support Reagan. The effect of the Democrats'
promise is that they end up unconditionally supporting Reagan. The Republicans appreciate this gesture and proceed to
support Reagan completely, maintaining their best outcome.
The promise is pointless. The Republicans can safely ignore
it.

The Democrats have only one threat that they can use to
stop the Republican support of Reagan. They can threaten to
attack Reagan if the Republicans support him completely. But
the threat is not enough. The effect of the threat is that the
Democrats have unconditionally committed to attack Reagan.
If the Republicans support Reagan, the Democrats carry out
their threat and attack Reagan; if the Republicans compromise, it is in the Democrats' best interest to attack Reagan.
Since the Democrats attack Reagan whatever the Republicans
do, the Republicans support Reagan completely, making the
best of the two possibilities.

---

* If the Republicans agree, the Democrats will have an incentive to renege
on the deal. This promise must be irreversible in order to have an effect.

A promise ends up being equivalent to unconditional Democrat support for Reagan, while a threat is equivalent to an unconditional Democrat attack on Reagan. Neither is effective in changing the Republicans' actions.

If the Democrats combine a promise with a threat, they can achieve a better result for themselves. They should promise to support Reagan if the Republicans compromise and threaten to attack Reagan if the Republicans support Reagan completely. This strategy achieves the Democrats' goals. With this threat and promise in place, the Republicans must choose between compromising and getting the Democrats to mainly support Reagan, or supporting Reagan completely and thereby provoking the Democrats to attack Reagan. Between these two alternatives, they prefer the compromise.

What actually happened was that Republicans supported Reagan completely in both the Senate and in the House. The Senate Democrats went along with the Republicans. In the House, the Democrats's initial resistance quickly gave way to a third strategy: they out-Reaganed Reagan in the tax-cutting game. The result was a bipartisan "Christmas-tree" tax cut. The economic bills for that are just coming due, and the negotiations to get out of the difficulty are developing into new strategic games.

6. MORE STRATEGIC MOVES

In addition to the three basic strategic moves, there are more complicated options. Instead of establishing a response rule directly, you can purposefully allow someone else to take advantage of one of these strategies. Three options are

- You may allow someone to make an unconditional move before you respond.
- You may wait for a threat before taking any action.
- You may wait for a promise before taking any action.

We have already seen examples in which someone who could move first does even better by relinquishing this option, allowing the other side to make an unconditional move. This is true whenever it is better to follow than to lead, as in the tales of the America's Cup race and gambling at the Cambridge May Ball. While it can be advantageous to give up the initiative, this is not a general rule. Sometimes your goal will be to prevent your opponent from making an unconditional commitment. Chinese military strategist Sun Tzu wrote: "When you surround an enemy, leave an outlet free."[5] One leaves an outlet free so that the enemy may believe there is a road to safety. If the enemy does not see an escape outlet, he will fight with the courage of desperation. Sun Tzu aimed to deny the enemy an opportunity to make his own very credible commitment of fighting to the death.

It is never advantageous to allow others to threaten you. You could always do what they wanted you to do without the threat. The fact that they can make you worse off if you do not cooperate cannot help, because it limits your available options. But this maxim applies only to allowing threats alone. If the other side can make both promises and threats, then you can both be better off.

7. A SLEDGEHAMMER TO CRACK A NUT?

It is clear that when making a promise, you should not promise more than you have to. If the promise is successful in influencing the other party's behavior, you expect to carry out your word. This should be done as cheaply as possible, and that means promising the minimum amount necessary.

It is less apparent that moderation applies equally well to threats. You shouldn't threaten someone any more than necessary. The reason is more subtle.

Why doesn't the United States threaten a military attack

against the Japanese if they don't agree to import more American rice, beef, and oranges?* The idea may have some appeal to some American farmers and politicians. But there are several good reasons against it.

1. Nobody would believe the threat, and thus it wouldn't work.
2. Even if the threat did work, the Japanese might wisely want to reconsider whether the Americans are really their allies.
3. If the Japanese didn't import more oranges and the U.S. actually carried out its threat, the rest of the world and especially the Japanese would sanction the U.S. for selecting an inappropriate method of punishment. But if the U.S. didn't carry out its threat, that hurts its reputation in the future. Either way the United States loses.
4. The threat dilutes the clarity of the original problem by introducing the otherwise extraneous issue of military force.

The essence of all these points is that the threat is excessively large — too big to be credible, too big to carry out, and too serious to stake a reputation over.

The first concern of a player making a threat would be just the opposite — a threat must be large enough to achieve the desired deterrence or compellence. The next thing that matters is credibility — the other side's belief that if it defies the threat, it *will* suffer the stated consequences. Under ideal circumstances, nothing else should matter. If the threatened player knows and fears the consequences of defiance, he will comply. The threatened action will never have to be carried out. Then why does it matter how terrible it would have been if it were carried out?

The point is that circumstances are never ideal in this sense. If we examine the reasons for our not threatening to use

---

* In fact, just such a threat was used 1853. The black warships of Admiral Matthew C. Perry persuaded the shogunate to open the Japanese market to American commerce. Today, the Japanese describe excessive U.S. pressure to open up Japanese markets as "the second coming of the black ships."

military power in this case, we see more clearly how reality differs from the ideal.

First, the very act of making a threat may be costly. Nations, businesses, and even people are engaged in many games, and what they did in one game has an impact on all the other games. In our dealings with Japan in the future, and with other countries now and in the future, our use of an excessive threat will be remembered. They will be reluctant to deal with us at all, and we will forgo the benefits of many other trades and alliances.

Second, an excessive threat may be counterproductive even in the game in which it is used. The Japanese will throw up their hands in horror, appeal to world opinion and the decency of the American people, and more generally delay the negotiation to the point where our timetable for compelling them to open their markets is slowed rather than speeded.

Third, the theory that a successful threat need never be carried out is fine so long as we are absolutely sure no unforeseen errors will occur. Suppose we have misjudged the Japanese farmers' power, and they are willing to let their nation go to war rather than see their protected market disappear. Or suppose that the Japanese agree to our terms, but some U.S. military commander down the line who remembers his experience as a P.O.W. and is itching for revenge takes the opportunity to launch an attack all the same. The possibility of such errors should give us pause before we commit ourselves to a very large threat.

Finally, in view of this, a threat starts to lose credibility just for being too large. If the Japanese do not believe we are truly committed to carrying out the threat, it will not deter them either.

The conclusion is that one should strive for the smallest and the most appropriate threat that will do the job — make the punishment fit the crime. When the United States wants to stimulate the Japanese to import more oranges, it uses a more reciprocal threat, one that more closely fits the crime. The United States might retaliate in kind by limiting the quotas on imports of Japanese cars or electronic goods.

Sometimes fitting threats are readily available. At other times, there are only excessive threats, which must somehow be scaled down before they can be used. Brinkmanship is perhaps the best scaling device of this kind, and we shall explain it in Chapter 9.

8. CASE STUDY #5: BOEING, BOEING, GONE?

Developing a new commercial airplane is a gigantic gamble. The cost of designing a new engine alone can reach two billion dollars. It is no exaggeration to say that building a new and better plane requires "betting the company".[6] No wonder governments get involved, each trying to make a larger market for its domestic firm.

Here we look at the market for 150-passenger medium-range jets: the Boeing 727 and the Airbus 320. Boeing developed the 727 first. Did it make sense for Airbus to enter the market?

The primary market for these aircraft was in the United States and in the European Economic Community (E.E.C.) countries. We assume each of these markets is worth $900 million to a monopoly firm. Were the two firms to compete head-on, total profits fall from $900 to $600 million, divided evenly between the two firms. Although profits fall, competition results in cheaper planes and lower airfares, so consumers benefit. These benefits to consumers are worth $700 million in each market.

Airbus Industries estimates that it will cost $1 billion to develop the Airbus 320. If they go ahead without any government assistance, they can expect to make a profit of $300 million in each of the markets, American and E.E.C. The total of $600 million is not enough to cover the development costs.

The E.E.C. governments cannot offer direct assistance in the form of subsidies because their budget is already committed to subsidizing farmers. In the traditional trade-off between guns and butter, the E.E.C. has gone for butter and has little left for either guns or Airbuses.

You are called to Brussels and asked for advice on whether the E.E.C. should assist Airbus by giving it a protected market, that is, requiring European airlines to buy the Airbus 320 over the Boeing 727. What do you suggest? How do you expect the United States government to respond?

Case Discussion

If the E.E.C. protects its home market and the American market stays open, Airbus will earn $900 million as a monopolist in Europe and $300 million as a duopolist in the United States. This is enough to cover the development costs of $1 billion.

Is this policy in the interests of the E.E.C. as a whole? We have to consider the gain to Airbus versus the loss to European consumers. Without a protected market, Airbus would not enter. Boeing would have a monopoly in Europe. Consumers would be no better off. Therefore there is no loss to consumers. The economic gains to the E.E.C. as a whole coincide with the profits of Airbus. It seems that the E.E.C. should support the venture by promising a protected market.

It is important that the E.E.C. *commit* itself to protectionist policy. Suppose it keeps its options open, and Airbus enters the market. At this point it does not have an incentive to protect Airbus. Keeping the markets open will reduce Airbus's expected profit by $600 million (from $200 million to negative $400 million), but the competition from Boeing will raise the E.E.C. consumers' benefits by $700 million. Knowing this, Airbus will not enter, because it does not have a credible commitment that the E.E.C. governments will maintain a protected market.

What about the American response? If the Americans act quickly, they too can commit to protecting their domestic market before Airbus begins production. Let us look ahead and reason backward. If the American market is kept open, the picture unfolds as before. Boeing is shut out of Europe and makes $300 million in competition with Airbus in the American market. The American consumer gets an extra $700 million of benefits from the competition. The total gain to the U.S. economy if it maintains an open market is $1,000 million.

Say the United States reciprocates and requires American airlines to purchase the Boeing 727 over the Airbus 320. Then even the monopoly profit of $900 million in Europe falls short of the Airbus development costs. So the Airbus 320 will never be built. Boeing will enjoy a monopoly in both markets, making profits of $1,800 million. This total economic gain to the United States is considerably higher than when its market is open.[7]

The United States can defeat the E.E.C. support for Airbus by reciprocating protectionism. It is in its interest to do so.

6

Credible Commitments

In most situations, mere verbal promises should not be trusted. As Sam Goldwyn put it, "A verbal contract isn't worth the paper it's written on."[1] An incident in *The Maltese Falcon* by Dashiell Hammett (filmed by Goldwyn's competitor Warner Brothers, with Humphrey Bogart as Sam Spade and Sydney Greenstreet as Gutman) illustrates this point. Gutman gives Sam Spade an envelope containing ten thousand dollars.

> Spade looked up smiling. He said mildly: "We were talking about more money than this." "Yes sir, we were," Gutman agreed, "but, we were *talking* then. This is *actual* money, genuine coin of the realm. With a dollar of this, you can buy more than with ten dollars of talk."[2]

This lesson can be traced all the way back to Thomas Hobbes: "The bonds of words are too weak to bridle men's avarice."[3] Women's too, as King Lear discovered.

Credibility is a problem with all strategic moves. If your unconditional move, or threat or promise, is purely oral, why should you carry it out if it turns out not to be in your interest to do so? But then others will look forward and reason backward to predict that you have no incentive to follow through, and your strategic move will not have the desired effect.

The whole point behind the strategies of Chapter 5 is to change an opponent's expectations about your responses to his actions. This will fail if he believes that you will not carry out the threats or promises you make. Without any effect on his expectations, there will be no effect on his actions.

An action that can be changed loses strategic effect against a rival who thinks strategically. He knows that your utterances may not match your actions and so is on the lookout for tactical bluffing.

A famous example of the reversal was made by the Rothschilds following the Battle of Waterloo. The Rothschilds supposedly used carrier pigeons and hence were the first to know the battle's outcome. When they discovered that the English had won, they sold British bonds publicly and thus led others to believe that England had lost. The price of British government bonds plummeted. Before the truth was discovered, the Rothschilds secretly bought an even greater number of bonds at the rock-bottom price.*

Had the others in the London stock exchange recognized that the Rothschilds might reverse their move in this way, they would have anticipated the tactical bluffing and it would not have worked. A strategically aware opponent will expect you to mislead him and therefore will not be influenced by actions that he perceives as being put on display for his benefit.

Establishing credibility in the strategic sense means that you are expected to carry out your unconditional moves, keep your promises, and make good on your threats. Unlike the Rothschilds, you cannot count on an ability to fool people. Commitments are unlikely to be taken at face value. Your commitment may be tested. Credibility must be earned.

Credibility requires finding a way to prevent going back. If there is no tomorrow, today's commitment cannot be reversed.

---

* There is some question as to whether carrier pigeons is a modern-day embellishment of the story. Frederic Morton in his book *The Rothschilds*, claims "On June 19, 1815, late in the afternoon a Rothschild agent named Rothworth jumped into a boat at Oostend. In his hand he held a Dutch gazette still damp from the printer. By the dawn light of June 20 Nathan Rothschild stood at Folkstone harbor and let his eye fly over the lead paragraphs. A moment later he was on his way to London (beating Wellington's envoy by several hours) to tell the government that Napoleon had been crushed. Then he proceeded to the stock market."

The fact that deathbed testimony can never be altered leads the courts to give it tremendous weight. More commonly, there is a tomorrow (and a day after) so that we must explore the problem of how to maintain commitment over the long haul. "Feast today, for tomorrow we fast" is the excuse for putting on today what can be taken off tomorrow.

1. THE EIGHTFOLD PATH TO CREDIBILITY

Making your strategic moves credible is not easy. But it is not impossible, either. When we first raised this issue in Chapter 5, we said that to make a strategic move credible, you must take a supporting or collateral action. We called such an action *commitment*.

We now offer eight devices for achieving credible commitments. Like the Buddhist prescription for Nirvana, we call this the "eightfold path" to credibility. Depending on the circumstances, one or more of these tactics may prove effective for you. Behind this system are three underlying principles.

The first principle is to change the payoffs of the game. The idea is to make it in your interest to follow through on your commitment: turn a threat into a warning, a promise into an assurance. This can be done through a variety of ways.

1. Establish and use a reputation.

2. Write contracts.

Both these tactics make it more costly to break the commitment than to keep it.

A second avenue is to change the game to limit your ability to back out of a commitment. In this category, we consider three possibilities. The most radical is simply to deny yourself any opportunity to back down, either by cutting yourself off from the situation or by destroying any avenues of retreat. There is even the possibility of removing yourself from the decision-making position and leaving the outcome to chance.

3. Cut off communication.

4. Burn bridges behind you.

5. Leave the outcome to chance.

These two principles can be combined: both the possible actions and their outcomes can be changed. If a large commitment is broken down into many smaller ones, then the gain from breaking a little one may be more than offset by the loss of the remaining contract. Thus we have

6. Move in small steps.

A third route is to use others to help you maintain commitment. A team may achieve credibility more easily than an individual. Or you may simply hire others to act in your behalf.

7. Develop credibility through teamwork.

8. Employ mandated negotiating agents.

Reputation

If you try a strategic move in a game and then back off, you may lose your reputation for credibility. In a once-in-a-lifetime situation, reputation may be unimportant and therefore of little commitment value. But, you typically play several games with different rivals at the same time, or the same rivals at different times. Then you have an incentive to establish a reputation, and this serves as a commitment that makes your strategic moves credible.

During the Berlin crisis in 1961, John F. Kennedy explained the importance of the U.S. reputation:

> If we do not meet our commitments to Berlin, where will we later stand? If we are not true to our word there, all that we have achieved in collective security, which relies on these words, will mean nothing.[4]

Another example is Israel's standing policy not to negotiate with terrorists. This is a threat intended to deter terrorists from taking hostages to barter for ransom or release of prisoners. If the no-negotiation threat is credible, terrorists will come to recognize the futility of their actions. In the meantime, Israel's resolve will be tested. Each time the threat must be carried out, Israel suffers; a refusal to compromise may sacrifice Israeli hostages' lives. Each confrontation with terrorists puts Israel's reputation and credibilty on the line. Giving in means more than just meeting the current demands; it makes future terrorism more attractive.*

Reputation effect is a two-edged sword for commitment. Sometimes destroying your reputation can create the possibility for a commitment. Destroying your reputation commits you *not* to take actions in the future that you can predict will not be in your best interests.

The question of whether to negotiate with hijackers helps illustrate the point. Before any particular hijacking has occurred, the government might decide to deter hijackings by threatening never to negotiate. However, the hijackers predict that after they commandeer the jet, the government will find it impossible to enforce a no-negotiation posture. How can a government deny itself the ability to negotiate with hijackers?

One answer is to destroy the credibility of its promises. Imagine that after reaching a negotiated settlement, the government breaks its commitment and attacks the hijackers. This destroys any reputation the government has for trustworthy treatment of hijackers. It loses the ability to make a credible promise, and irreversibly denies itself the temptation to respond to a hijacker's threat. This destruction of the credibility of a promise makes credible the threat never to negotiate.

---

* Even the Israelis have lost some of their reputation for toughness. Their willingness to swap 3,000 Arab prisoners for 3 of their air force pilots suggests that exceptions will sometimes be made.

Congress has a similar problem of maintaining consistency over time when it comes to tax amnesty programs. Such programs allow those who owe back taxes to pay up without penalty. This appears to be a costless way of raising more revenue. All those who have second thoughts about having cheated on their taxes give the government money owed. In fact, if it could be credibly established that there would never be another amnesty, then Congress could raise additional tax revenues at no cost. But if amnesty was such a good idea once, why not try it again in a few years? Nothing prevents Congress from offering an amnesty on a regular basis. Then a problem arises. Cheating becomes more attractive, since there is the possibility of getting amnesty in the future.

Congress must find a way to prevent itself from ever repeating the amnesty program. In a *Wall Street Journal* article, Robert Barro and Alan Stockman propose that the government offer a tax amnesty, then renege on its promise and prosecute those who turn themselves in.[5] This would raise even more revenue than a simple amnesty. And once the government cheats on its amnesty, who would believe the government were it to try again? By destroying its credibility, the government can make a credible commitment not to offer an amnesty again.

You will probably think this is an absurd idea, and with good reason. First, it will not work against strategically aware taxpayers. They will expect the government to renege on its promise, so they will not participate in the amnesty at all. Secondly, and more importantly, catching tax cheaters is not the only game in town. Any benefits from double-crossing tax cheaters will be more than offset by the harm to the government's reputation in other areas.

One of the most impressive examples of how to build a reputation belongs to the Mayflower Furniture Company. On a large billboard located along the Massachusetts Turnpike, they proudly advertise that they have gone 127 years with-

out a sale. (Are they still waiting for their first customer?)
This unconditional commitment to everyday low prices brings
in a steady stream of customers. A sale might temporarily
raise profits, but it would be another 127 years before they
could repeat such a clever advertisement. Next year, we expect the sign will read 128 years. The reputation becomes
self-perpetuating as it becomes more valuable.*

In all these instances, the player cultivates a reputation
with the direct and conscious aim of creating credibility for
his future unconditional commitments, threats, and promises.
However, reputation can also arise for nonstrategic reasons,
and yet be just as powerful in achieving credibility. The feeling of *pride* in not breaking one's word is an example. Thomas
Hobbes wrote that the weak bonds of words can be strength-
ened in two ways: a fear of the consequence of breaking one's
word; or a glory, or pride, in not breaking it. Such pride is often
instilled in people's value system through education or general
social conditioning. It may even have the implicit social aim of
improving the credibility of our manifold daily relationships.
Yet we are not told to take pride in being honorable *because* it
will bring us strategic advantage by making our threats and
promises credible; we are told that honor is a good thing in
itself.

Someone who has a reputation for being crazy can make
successful threats that would be incredible coming from a saner
and cooler person. In this way, apparent *irrationality* can become good strategic rationality. One can even cultivate such
a reputation. A seeming madman, therefore, may be a superior strategist, because his threats are more readily believed.
Could Colonel Ghadafi and Ayatollah Khomeini have understood this principle better than the cool, rational leaders of
Western nations trying to deal with them? We do not know,

---

* Sadly, we must report that the Mayflower Furniture Company recently
had its first sale, a going out of business sale.

but we are willing to bet that your child who is too irrational to be deterred by your threats of punishment is a better instinctive game-player than you are.

Contracts

A straightforward way to make your commitment credible is to agree to a punishment if you fail to follow through. If your kitchen remodeler gets a large payment up front, he is tempted to slow down the work. But a contract that specifies payment linked to the progress of the work and penalty clauses for delay can make it in his interest to stick to the schedule. The contract is the commitment device.

Actually, it's not quite that simple. Imagine that a dieting man offers to pay $500 to anyone who catches him eating fattening food. Every time the man thinks of a dessert he knows that it just isn't worth $500. Don't dismiss this example as incredible; just such a contract was offered by a Mr. Nick Russo — except the amount was $25,000. According to the *Wall Street Journal*:

> So, fed up with various weight-loss programs, Mr. Russo decided to take his problem to the public. In addition to going on a 1,000-calorie-a-day diet, he is offering a bounty —$25,000 to the charity of one's choosing — to anyone who spots him eating in a restaurant. He has peppered local eateries ... with "wanted" pictures of himself.[6]

But this contract has a fatal flaw: there is no mechanism to prevent renegotiation. With visions of eclairs dancing in his head, Mr. Russo should argue that under the present contractual agreement, no one will ever get the $25,000 penalty since he will never violate the contract. Hence, the contract is worthless. Renegotiation would be in their mutual interest. For example, Mr. Russo might offer to buy a round of drinks in exchange for being released from the contract. The restaurant diners prefer a drink to nothing and let him out of the contract.[7]

For the contracting approach to be successful, the party that

enforces the action or collects the penalty must have some inde-
pendent incentive to do so. In the dieting problem, Mr. Russo's
family might also want him to be skinnier and thus not be
tempted by a mere free drink.

The contracting approach is better suited to business dealings. A broken contract typically produces damages, so that
the injured party is not willing to give up on the contract for
naught. For example, a producer might demand a penalty
from a supplier who fails to deliver. The producer is not indifferent about whether the supplier delivers or not. He would
rather get his supply than receive the penalty sum. Renegoti-
ating the contract is no longer a mutually attractive option.

What happens if the supplier tries the dieter's argument?
Suppose he attempts to renegotiate on the grounds that the
penalty is so large that the contract will always be honored
and the producer will never receive the penalty. This is just
what the producer wants, and hence he is not interested in
renegotiation. The contract works because the producer is not
solely interested in the penalty; he cares about the actions
promised in the contract.

It is possible to write contracts with neutral parties as en-
forcers. A neutral party is someone who does not have any
personal interest in whether the contract is upheld. To make
enforcement credible, the neutral party must be made to care
about whether or not the commitment is kept by creating a
reputation effect. In some instances, the contract holder might
lose his job if he allows the contract to be rewritten. Thomas
Schelling provides a remarkable example of how these ideas
have been implemented.[8] In Denver, one rehabilitation center
treats wealthy cocaine addicts by having them write a self-
incriminating letter which will be made public if they fail random urine analysis. After placing themselves voluntarily in
this position, many people will try to buy their way back out
of the contract. But the person who holds the contract will
lose his job if the contract is rewritten; the center will lose its

reputation if it fails to fire employees who allow contracts to be rewritten.

The moral is that contracts alone cannot overcome the credibility problem. Success requires some additional credibility tool, such as employing parties with independent interests in enforcement or a reputation at stake. In fact, if the reputation effect is strong enough, it may be unnecessary to formalize a contract. This is the sense of a person's word being his bond.*

Cutting Off Communication

Cutting off communication succeeds as a credible commitment device because it can make an action truly irreversible. An extreme form of this tactic arises in the terms of a last will and testament. Once the party has died, renegotiation is virtually impossible. (For example, it took an act of the British parliament to change Cecil Rhodes's will in order to allow female Rhodes Scholars.) In general, where there is a will, there is a way to make your strategy credible.

For example, most universities set a price for endowing a chair. The going rate is about $1.5 million. These prices are not carved in stone (nor covered with ivy). Universities have been known to bend their rules in order to accept the terms and the money of deceased donors who fail to meet the current prices.

One need not die trying to make commitments credible. Irreversibility stands watch at every mailbox. Who has not mailed a letter and then wished to retrieve it? And it works the other way. Who has not received a letter he wishes he hadn't? But you can't send it back and pretend you've never read it once you've opened the letter.

Before the practice became widespread, a successful commitment device was to mail one's bill payments in unstamped

---

* On the other hand, among college professors, there is a saying, "A handshake is good enough between businessmen. But when your university's dean promises you something, get it in writing."

letters with no return address. Mailing a letter with no re-turn address is an irreversible commitment. The post office used to deliver such letters, and the receiver could accept de-livery by paying the postage due. A utility or phone company knew that such a letter was likely to contain a check. It would rather pay the postage due than wait another billing cycle be-fore receiving payment (or another unstamped letter with no return address).

The solution to the companies' problem came when the post office changed its policy. Letters without postage are no longer delivered to the addressee; they are returned to the sender if there is a return address and not delivered if there is no return address. Now the company can commit itself not to receive a letter with postage due.

But what if you put the company's address as both the mailing address and the return address? Now the post office has someone to return the letter to. Remember, you didn't hear this idea here first. And if it begins to spread, rest assured that the post office rules will be changed so that letters without a stamp are not even returned to the sender.

There is a serious difficulty with the use of cutting off com-munication as a device to maintain commitment. If you are incommunicado, it may be difficult if not impossible to make sure that the rival has accorded with your wishes. You must hire others to ensure that the contract is being honored. For example, wills are carried out by trustees, not the deceased. A parental rule against smoking may be exempt from debate while the parents are away, but unenforceable too.

Burning Bridges behind You

Armies often achieve commitment by denying themselves an opportunity to retreat. This strategy goes back at least to 1066, when William the Conqueror's invading army burned its own ships, thus making an unconditional commitment to fight rather than retreat. Cortés followed the same strategy in his conquest of Mexico. Upon his arrival in Cempoalla, Mexico, he gave orders that led to all but one of his ships being burnt or disabled. Although his soldiers were vastly outnumbered, they had no other choice but to fight and win. "Had [Cortés] failed, it might well seem an act of madness.... Yet it was the fruit of deliberate calculation.... There was no alternative in his mind but to succeed or perish."[9]

Destroying the ships gave Cortés two advantages. First, his own soldiers were united, each knowing that they would *all* fight until the end since desertion (or even retreat) was an impossibility. Second, and more important, is the effect this commitment had on the opposition. They knew that Cortés must either succeed or perish, while they had the option to retreat into the hinterland. They chose to retreat rather than fight such a determined opponent. For this type of commitment to have the proposed effects, it must be understood by the soldiers (yours and the enemy's), not just by the armchair strategists. Thus it is especially interesting that "the destruction of the fleet [was] accomplished not only with the knowledge, but the approbation of the army, though at the suggestion of Cortés."[10]

This idea of burning one's own ships demonstrates the evolution of strategic thinking over time. The Trojans seemed to get it all backward when the Greeks sailed to Troy to rescue Helen.* The Greeks tried to conquer the city, while the Trojans tried to burn the Greek ships. But if the Trojans had succeeded in burning the Greek fleet, they would simply have made the Greeks all the more determined opponents. In fact, the Trojans failed to burn the Greek fleet and saw the Greeks

* Although the Trojans may have gotten it backward, the Greeks were ahead of the game. Schelling cites the Greek general Xenophon as an early example of this type of strategic thinking. Although Xenophon did not literally burn his bridges behind him, he did write about the advantages of fighting with one's back against a gully. See Schelling's "Strategic Analysis and Social Problems," published in his collected essays, *Choice and Consequence* (Cambridge, Mass.: Harvard University Press, 1984).

sail home in retreat. Of course the Greeks left behind a gift horse, which in retrospect the Trojans were a bit too quick to accept.[11]

In modern times, this strategy applies to attacks on land as well as by sea. For many years, Edwin Land's Polaroid corporation purposefully refused to diversify out of the instant photography business. With all its chips in instant photography, it was committed to fight against any intruder in the market.

On April 20, 1976, after twenty-eight years of a Polaroid monopoly on the instant photography market, Eastman Kodak entered the fray: it announced a new instant film and camera. Polaroid responded aggressively, suing Kodak for patent infringement. Edwin Land, founder and chairman, was prepared to defend his turf:

> This is our very soul we are involved with. This is our whole life. For them it's just another field. ::: We will stay in our lot and protect that lot.[12]

Mark Twain explained this philosophy in *Pudd'nhead Wilson*:

> Behold, the fool saith, "Put not all thine eggs in one basket" ::: but the wise man saith, "Put all your eggs in one basket and WATCH THAT BASKET."[13]

The battle ended on October 12, 1990. The courts awarded Polaroid a $909.4 million judgment against Kodak.* Kodak was forced to withdraw its instant film and camera from the market. Although Polaroid restored its dominance over the instant photography market, it lost ground to competition from portable videocassette recorders and minilabs that developed and printed conventional film in one hour. Lacking bridges, Polaroid began to feel trapped on a sinking island. With a

---

* Polaroid's stock actually fell in response to this award, as the market was expecting a judgment closer to $1.5 billion.

change in philosophy, the company has begun to branch out into video film and even conventional film.

One need not literally burn bridges, nor ships that bridge oceans. One can burn bridges figuratively by taking a political position that will antagonize certain voters. When Walter Mondale said in accepting the 1984 Democratic presidential nomination that he *would* raise taxes if elected, he was making such a commitment. Voters who believed in supply-side economics were irretrievably lost, and this made Mondale's position more credible to those who favored a tax increase in order to reduce the deficit. Unfortunately (for Mondale) the group of voters antagonized by this move turned out to be far too large.

Finally, building rather than burning bridges can also serve as a credible source of commitment. In the December 1989 reforms in Eastern Europe, building bridges meant knocking down walls. Responding to massive protests and emigration, East Germany's Prime Minister Egon Krenz wanted to promise reform but didn't have a specific package. The population was skeptical. Why should they believe that the vague promise of reform would be genuine and far-reaching? Even if Krenz was truly in favor of reform, he might fall out of power. Dismantling parts of the Berlin Wall helped the East German government make a credible commitment to reform without having to detail all the specifics. By (re)opening a bridge to the West, the government forced itself to reform or risk an exodus. Since it would be possible to leave in the future, the promise of reform was both credible and worth waiting for. Reunification was to be less than a year away.

Leaving the Outcome beyond Your Control

The doomsday device in the movie *Dr. Strangelove* consisted of large buried nuclear bombs whose explosion would emit enough radioactivity to exterminate all life on earth. The device would be detonated automatically in the event of an attack on the Soviet Union. When President Milton Muffley of the United States asked if such an automatic trigger was possible, Dr. Strangelove answered: "It is not merely possible; it is *essential*."

The device is such a good deterrent because it makes aggression tantamount to suicide.* Faced with an American attack, Soviet premier Dimitri Kissov might refrain from retaliating and risking mutually assured destruction. As long as the Soviet premier has the freedom not to respond, the Americans might risk an attack. But with the doomsday device in place, the Soviet response is automatic and the deterrent threat is credible.

However, this strategic advantage does not come without a cost. There might be a small accident or unauthorized attack, after which the Soviets would not want to carry out their dire threat, but have no choice as execution is out of their control. This is exactly what happened in *Dr. Strangelove*.

To reduce the consequences of errors, you want a threat that is no stronger than is necessary to deter the rival. What do you do if the action is indivisible, as a nuclear explosion surely is? You can make the threat milder by creating a risk, but not a certainty, that the dreadful event will occur. This is Thomas Schelling's idea of *brinkmanship*. He explained it in his book *The Strategy of Conflict*:

> Brinkmanship is ... the deliberate creation of a recognizable risk, a risk that one does not completely control. It is the tactic of deliberately letting the situation get somewhat out of hand, just because its being out of hand may be intolerable to the other party and force his accommodation. It means harassing and intimidating an adversary by exposing him to a shared risk, or deterring him by showing that if he makes a contrary move he may disturb us so that we slip over the brink whether we want to or not, carrying him with us.[14]

* Apparently, Khrushchev attempted to use this strategy, threatening that Soviet rockets would fly *automatically* in the event of armed conflict in Berlin; see Tom Schelling's *Arms and Influence* p. 39.

The use of brinkmanship formed the basis of the U.S. nuclear deterrent policy. During the cold war, the United States did not need to guarantee a nuclear retaliation if the Soviets invaded Europe. Even a small chance of nuclear war, say 10 percent, was enough to deter the Soviets. A 10 percent chance is one-tenth the threat and consequently required much less commitment in order to establish credibility. While the Soviets might not have believed that the United States would surely retaliate, they couldn't be *sure* that Americans wouldn't either. There was always the possibility that a Soviet attack would start an escalatory cycle that got out of control.

This brief description does not do brinkmanship justice. To better understand the probabilistic threats behind brinkmanship, Chapter 7 develops the role of mixed strategies. Then in Chapter 8 we give brinkmanship the full attention it deserves.

Moving in Steps

Although two parties may not trust each other when the stakes are large, if the problem of commitment can be reduced to a small-enough scale, then the issue of credibility will resolve itself. The threat or promise is broken up into many pieces, and each one is solved separately.

Honor among thieves is restored if they have to trust each other only a little bit at a time. Consider the difference between making a single $1 million payment to another person for a kilogram of cocaine and engaging in 1,000 sequential transactions with this other party, with each transaction limited to $1,000 worth of cocaine. While it might be worthwhile to double-cross your "partner" for $1 million, the gain of $1,000 is too small, since it brings a premature end to a profitable ongoing relationship.

Whenever a large degree of commitment is infeasible, one should make do with a small amount and reuse it frequently. Homeowners and contractors are mutually suspicious. The homeowner is afraid of paying up front and finding incomplete

or shoddy work. The contractors are afraid that after they
have completed the job, the homeowner may refuse to pay. So
at the end of each day (or each week), contractors are paid on
the basis of their progress. At most each side risks losing one
day's (or one week's) work.

As with brinkmanship, moving in small steps reduces the
size of the threat or promise and correspondingly the scale of
commitment. There is just one feature to watch out for. Those
who understand strategic thinking will reason forward and
look backward, and they will worry about the last step. If you
expect to be cheated on the last round, you should break off
the relationship one round earlier. But then the penultimate
round will become the final round, and so you will not have
escaped the problem. To avoid the unraveling of trust, there
should be no clear final step. As long as there remains a chance
of continued business, it will never be worthwhile to cheat. So
when a shady character tells you this will be his last deal
before retiring, be especially cautious.

Teamwork

Often others can help us achieve credible commitment. Although people may be weak on their own, they can build resolve by forming a group. The successful use of peer pressure
to achieve commitment has been made famous by Alcoholics
Anonymous (and diet centers too). The AA approach changes
the payoffs from breaking your word. It sets up a social insti-
tution in which pride and self-respect are lost when commitments are broken.

Sometimes teamwork goes far beyond social pressure and
employs strong-arm tactics to force us to keep true to our
promises. Consider the problem for the front line of an advancing army. If everyone else charges forward, one soldier who
hangs back ever so slightly will increase his chance of survival
without significantly lowering the probability that the attack

will be successful. If every soldier thought the same way, however, the attack would become a retreat.

Of course it doesn't happen that way. A soldier is conditioned through honor to his country, loyalty to fellow soldiers, and belief in the million-dollar wound — an injury that is serious enough to send him home, out of action, but not so serious that he won't fully recover.[15] Those soldiers who lack the will and the courage to follow orders can be motivated by penalties for desertion. If the punishment for desertion is certain and ignominious death, the alternative of advancing forward becomes much more attractive. But soldiers are not interested in killing their fellow countrymen, even deserters. How can soldiers who have difficulty committing to attack the enemy make a credible commitment to killing their countrymen for desertion?

The ancient Roman army made falling behind in an attack a capital offense. As the army advanced in a line, any soldier who saw the one next to him falling behind was ordered to kill the deserter immediately. To make this order credible, failing to kill a deserter was also a capital offense. Thus even though a soldier would rather get on with the battle than go back after a deserter, failing to do so could cost him his own life.*

The tactics of the Roman army live on today in the honor code required of students at West Point. Exams are not monitored, and cheating is an offense that leads to expulsion. But, because students are not inclined to "rat" on their classmates, failure to report observed cheating is also a violation of the honor code. This violation also leads to expulsion. When the honor code is violated, students report crimes because they do not want to become guilty accomplices by their silence. Sim-

---

* The motive for punishing deserters is made even stronger if the deserter is given clemency for killing those in line next to him who fail to punish him. Thus if a soldier fails to kill a deserter, there are now two people who can punish: his neighbor and the deserter, who could save his own life by punishing those who failed to punish him.

ilarly, criminal law provides penalties for those who fail to report a crime as an accessory after the fact.

Mandated Negotiating Agents

If a worker says he cannot accept any wage increase less than 5 percent, why should the employer believe that he will not subsequently back down and accept 4 percent? Money on the table induces people to try negotiating one more time.

The worker's situation can be improved if he has someone else negotiate for him. When the union leader is the negotiator, his position may be less flexible. He may be forced to keep his promise or lose support from his electorate. The union leader may secure a restrictive mandate from his members, or put his prestige on the line by declaring his inflexible position in public. In effect, the labor leader becomes a mandated negotiating agent. His authority to act as a negotiator is based on his position. In some cases he simply does not have the authority to compromise; the workers, not the leader, must ratify the contract. In other cases, compromise by the leader would result in his removal.

In practice we are concerned with the means as well as the ends of achieving commitment. If the labor leader *voluntarily* commits his prestige to a certain position, should you (do you) treat his loss of face as you would if it were externally imposed? Someone who tries to stop a train by tying himself to the railroad tracks may get less sympathy than someone else who has been tied there against his will.

A second type of mandated negotiating agent is a machine. Very few people haggle with vending machines over the price; even fewer do so successfully.*

---

* According to the U.S. Defense Department, over a five-year period seven servicemen or dependents were killed and 39 injured by soft-drink machines that toppled over while being rocked in an attempt to dislodge beverages or change — *The International Herald Tribune*, June 15, 1988.

This completes our account of the eightfold way to successful commitment. In practice, any particular situation may require more than one. Here are two examples.

2. BUT ONE LIFE TO LAY DOWN FOR YOUR COUNTRY

How can an army get the enemy to believe that its soldiers will in fact lay down their lives for their country when called upon to do so? Most armies would be finished if each soldier on the battlefield started to make a rational calculation of the costs and the benefits of risking his life. Other devices have to be found, and they include many of the ones above. We have already mentioned the tactic of burning bridges, and the role of punishments and teamwork in deterring desertion. Now we concentrate on the devices to motivate individual soldiers.

The process begins in the boot camp. Basic training in the armed forces everywhere is a traumatic experience. The new recruit is maltreated, humiliated, and put under such immense physical and mental strain that the few weeks quite alter his personality. An important habit acquired in this process is an automatic, unquestioning obedience. There is no reason why socks should be folded, or beds made, in a particular way, except that the officer has so ordered. The idea is that the same obedience will occur when the order is of greater importance. Trained not to question orders, the army becomes a fighting machine; commitment is automatic.

The seeming irrationality of each soldier thus turns into strategic rationality. Shakespeare knew this perfectly well; in the night before the battle of Agincourt, King Henry V prays:

> O God of battles! steel my soldiers' hearts;
> Possess them not with fear; *take from them now*
> *The sense of reckoning*, if th'opposed numbers
> Pluck their hearts from them ... (italics added)

Next comes the pride that is instilled in each soldier: pride in one's country, pride in being a soldier, and, perhaps above all, pride in the tradition of the fighting unit. The U.S. Marine Corps, famous regiments of the British Army, and the French Foreign Legion exemplify this approach. Great deeds from past battles fought by the unit are constantly remembered, heroic deaths are glorified. Constant repetition of this history is meant to give new recruits a pride in this tradition, and a resolve not to flinch from similar deeds when the time comes.

Commanders of troops also appeal to a far more personal sense of pride of their men. According to Shakespeare, King Henry V inspired his troops at Harfleur thus: "Dishonour not your mothers; now attest that those you call'd fathers did beget you." Pride is often an elitist emotion; it consists in doing or having something that most others lack. Thus, again, we have Henry V speaking to his troops before the battle of Agincourt:

> We few, we happy few, we band of brothers;
> For he to-day that sheds his blood with me
> Shall be my brother; ...
> And gentlemen in England now a-bed
> Shall think themselves accurs'd they were not here
> And hold their manhoods cheap whiles any speaks
> That fought with us upon Saint Crispin's day.

There is also the use of commitment through a combination of teamwork, contracting, and burning one's bridges. Once again we turn to Shakespeare's Henry V speaking to his troops before the battle of Agincourt.

> That he which hath no stomach to this fight,
> Let him depart; his passport shall be made,
> And crowns for convoy put into his purse:
> We would not die in that man's company
> That fears his fellowship to die with us.

Of course everyone is too ashamed to take this offer up publicly. But even so, by their act of rejecting the offer, the soldiers have psychologically burned their ships home. They have established an implicit contract with each other not to flinch from death if the time comes. Henry V's brilliant understanding of how to motivate and commit his army to battle is reflected in success on the battlefield, even when vastly outnumbered.

3. AN OFFER YOU CAN'T REFUSE

It's not only in the film *The Godfather* that one hears an "offer you can't refuse." With minor variations, this situation arises surprisingly often.

At the end of what appeared to be a successful job interview, our friend Larry was asked where the firm ranked in his list of potential employers. Before answering, he was told that the firm hired only those applicants who ranked it first. If the firm was in fact his first choice, then they wanted him to accept in advance a job offer should one be made.* With this prospect of an "offer you can't refuse" (because otherwise you don't get it), what should Larry have done?

With the X-ray vision of game theory, we can see through this ploy. The firm claims that it wants to hire only people who rank it first. However, the effect these pressure tactics have is the opposite of what they claim. If the firm truly wanted to have employees who ranked it first, then it should not make job offers conditional on the applicant's ranking of the firm. If, after completing the interview process, the firm was in fact Larry's first choice, then the firm can expect him to accept its offer. No firm need worry about having its offer turned down by someone who most wants to work there. On the other hand, if the firm was in fact Larry's second choice, but Larry's first-

---

* For the starting position, there was a standard starting salary which was pretty much identical across competitors. Hence, he could predict what he would be accepting even before it was offered.

choice firm had yet to make an offer, then he might be willing to accept his second-choice job to avoid the risk of getting none. The firm's pressure tactic of saying that it will offer jobs only to those who accept first has the effect of hiring candidates who do not in fact rank the firm first.

More truthful and what they really mean is, "We want you to work for us. If you rank us first, then we know we'll get you. However, if you rank us second, we might lose you. To get you even if we are not your first choice, we want you to agree in advance to accept our offer or you will get none at all." Seen in this light, this does not seem to be a credible threat. The firm wants to hire Larry so much that it is willing to take him even if it is not his first choice. At the same time, it claims that if Larry refuses to accept in advance, but instead comes back later to accept, it will no longer offer him a job. It is possible but unlikely.

Our friend Larry explained that he was only beginning his interviews and thus had too little information to make a ranking. The firm reminded him that unless he accepted in advance, he would not be offered a job. He left the Wednesday interview without an offer. That Friday, he received an offer on his answering machine. Monday there was another message reiterating the offer. On Wednesday, a telegram arrived offering a sign-on bonus. It is hard to make a credible commitment not to offer a job to someone you want to hire.

What could the firm have done to make its threat credible? Here, teamwork can help, but not in the usual sense. Once there are several people with hiring power, it is possible that should you not accept immediately, the coalition that supported your candidacy may break down in favor of some later applicant. As we will see in Chapter 10 on voting, the order in which candidates are considered may determine the ultimate decision. In this way a decision made by a committee is sufficiently dependent on chance that it cannot promise that given the same inputs it will reach the same verdict. A committee's inability to commit itself to "rational" decision-making makes the take-it-or-leave-it threat credible.

An offer valid now but not necessarily later prevents people from comparison shopping. Stereo stores and car dealers use this tactic to great effect. But how do these salesmen make credible their threat to turn down tomorrow an offer that they would accept today? The answer is that business may turn up, cash-flow problems may be lessened. As they are fond of saying, this is a once-in-a-lifetime opportunity.

4. CASE STUDY #6: WOULD YOU RATHER RENT A COMPUTER FROM IBM?

After a battle that lasted longer than twelve years, *United States* v. *IBM* stands as a monumental eyesore of antitrust litigation. One of the many issues revolved around IBM's policy of leasing rather than selling its mainframe computers.

The government argued that IBM's emphasis on short-term leases constituted an entry barrier resulting in monopoly profits. IBM defended the practice as being in consumers' interest. It argued that a short-term lease insulates customers from the risk of obsolescence, provides flexibility when needs change, commits IBM to maintain its leased equipment (since it is responsible for the operation of the leased computers), and provides financing from the company with the deepest pockets.[16]

Many find these arguments a convincing defense. Yet there is a strategic advantage to leasing that seems to have been overlooked by both sides. How would you expect prices to differ if IBM primarily sold its large mainframe machines rather than leased them?

Case Discussion

Even a company without an outside competitor must worry about competing with its future self. When a new computer is introduced, IBM can sell the first models at very high prices to customers impatiently awaiting the technological advance. Once the computers are available in large numbers, there is the temptation to lower the price and attract more customers. The main cost of producing the computer has already been incurred in the development stage. Each additional sale is gravy.

Herein lies the problem. If customers expect that IBM is about to lower its price, they will wait to make their purchase. When the majority of customers are waiting, IBM has an incentive to speed up its price reductions and capture the customers sooner. This idea, first expressed by University of Chicago law professor Ronald Coase, is that for *durable* goods, in effect, a monopolist competes with its future self in a way that makes the market competitive.[17]

Leasing serves as a commitment device that enables IBM to keep prices high. The leasing contracts make it much more costly for IBM to lower its price. When its machines are on short-term leases, any price reduction must be passed along to *all* customers, not just the ones who haven't yet bought. The loss in revenue from the existing customer base may outweigh the increase in new leases. In contrast, when the existing customer base owns its computers, this trade-off does not arise; the customers who already bought the computer at a high price are not eligible for refunds.

Thus leasing is an example of moving in small steps. The steps are the length of the lease. The shorter the lease, the smaller the step. Customers don't expect IBM to keep its price high when the steps are too big; they will wait for a price reduction and get the same machine a little later at a lower price. But if IBM leases its computers only on short, renewable contracts, then it can credibly maintain high prices, customers have no reason to wait, and IBM earns higher profits.

As college professors and authors, we encounter the same problem closer to home in the market for academic textbooks.

If commitment were possible, publishers could raise profits by bringing out new editions of a textbook on a five-year cycle, rather than the more common three-year cycle. Greater longevity would increase the text's value on the used-book market and consequently the student's initial willingness to pay when a new edition appears. The problem is that once the used books are out there, the publisher has a strong incentive to undercut this competition by bringing out a new edition. Because everyone expects this to happen, students get a lower price for their used books and thus are less willing to pay for the new editions. The solution for the publisher is the same as for IBM: rent books rather than sell them.

7

Unpredictability

In the 1986 baseball National League championship series, the New York Mets won a crucial game against the Houston Astros when Len Dykstra hit Dave Smith's second pitch for a two-run home run in the ninth inning. The two players later talked about what happened.[1] Dykstra said, "He threw me a fastball on the first pitch and I fouled it off. I had a gut feeling then that he'd throw me a forkball next, and he did. I got a pitch I saw real well, and hit it real well." According to Smith, "What it boils down to, is that it was bad pitch selection." By that he meant Dykstra was guessing that, because the first pitch was a fastball, Smith would alter the velocity. "If I had it to do over again? It would be [another] fastball."

Should Smith adopt the strategy of throwing another fastball the next time such a situation arises? Of course not. The batter can see through this level of Smith's thinking, and expect a fastball. But then Smith should move gears to the next level of thinking, and throw a forkball, after all. And so on. There is no definite stopping point to this process. The batter can see through and exploit any *systematic* thinking and action by the pitcher, and vice versa. The only sensible course of action for both is to be unpredictable.*

---

* To be unpredictable, the pitcher should make a random selection from accurate pitches. He should not throw inaccurate pitches. An inaccurate pitcher is unpredictable because he himself does not know where the ball will go. Without accuracy, there is no control over the placement and relative frequencies of the different types of pitches. The best example of an accurate

In these situations, a classic mistake in strategic thinking is to believe that you can predict your rival's moves simply by wearing his shoes. We see this mistake in David Halberstam's book *The Summer of '49* as he describes the strategic awakening of the seventeen-year-old Ted Williams.[2]

Like so many other young players, Williams had trouble with breaking pitches. He was never ready for them. Once a pitcher got him out on a curve. Williams, furious with himself, trotted back to his position in the outfield. One of the San Diego pitchers, a former major-leaguer, yelled over to him, "Hey kid, what'd he get you out on?" "A goddamn slow curve," Williams answered. "Can you hit his fastball?" the pitcher continued. "You bet," Williams answered. "What do you think he'll be looking to put past you next time?" the pitcher asked. There was a brief pause. Ted Williams had never thought about pitching to Ted Williams — that was something pitchers did. "A curve," he answered. "Hey kid," the pitcher said, "why don't you go up there and wait on it the next time." Williams did, and hit the ball out for a home run. Thus began a twenty-five-year study of the mind of the pitcher.

Apparently the pitcher hadn't learned the need to be unpredictable, but then neither had Williams, for if Williams were thinking about how to pitch to Williams, he wouldn't throw a curve when he recognized that Williams was expecting it! This chapter shows what to expect when both sides are trying to outsmart the other. Even though you can't guess right all the time, you can at least recognize the odds.

Correctly anticipating and responding to unpredictability is useful well beyond the baseball diamond. Unpredictability is a critical element of strategy whenever one side likes a co-incidence of actions, while the other wishes to avoid it. The IRS wants to audit those who have evaded taxes, while those

---

but unpredictable pitch is the knuckleball. Because the ball hardly spins, the seams lead to sudden movements through the air and no one can quite predict its outcome — but few pitchers can throw good knuckleballs.

who have cheated hope to avoid an audit. Among children, the older sibling usually wants to avoid having the younger one tag along; the younger often looks to follow the older's footsteps, literally. An invading army wants to achieve tactical surprise in its choice of the place to attack; the defending army wants to concentrate its force on the spot where the attack comes.

The setters of fashion in nightclubs, restaurants, clothing, and art want exclusivity; the general public wants to mingle with the trendsetters. Eventually, the "in" places are discovered. But by then the beautiful people have moved on to somewhere else. This helps explain the short life span of nightclubs. Once a nightclub gets to be successful, too many people want to go there. This drives the trendsetters away and they start a new fad somewhere else. As Yogi Berra said, "The place is so crowded, no one goes there anymore."

While the baseball player's choice of pitch or the IRS's decision of whom to audit on any one occasion may be unpredictable, there are rules that govern the selection. *The right amount of unpredictability should not be left to chance.* In fact, the odds of choosing one pitch over another or of whom to audit can be precisely determined from the particulars of the game. "Though this be madness, yet there is method in't." Here we explain the method.

1. How to Even the Odds

Many of you will remember a game from elementary school called "one-two-three shoot" or "matching fingers." In this contest, one of the players chooses "evens" and the other player gets "odds." On the count of three, each of the two players simultaneously casts out either one or two fingers. If the total number of fingers is even, the "evens" player wins, while if the sum is odd, the "odds" player wins. Suppose the loser pays the winner a dollar. We can compute the usual table of wins and losses in relation to the choices of strategies.

Payoffs to ["Evens," "Odds"]

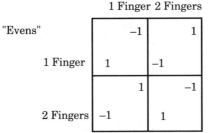

"Odds"

		1 Finger	2 Fingers
"Evens"		−1	1
1 Finger		1	−1
		1	−1
2 Fingers		−1	1

There is *no* equilibrium to this game if the two players do not act randomly. Imagine that "Odds" were to play 1 finger with certainty. "Evens" would always choose to play 1 finger as well. Now the logic turns on itself. Since "Odds" is certain that his opponent will display 1 finger, he will choose to show 2 fingers. This leads "Evens" to respond with 2 fingers. In which case, "Odds" will play 1 finger. We are back where we started, and there is no end in sight to this circular reasoning.

An easy way to check if randomness is needed is to consider whether there is any harm in letting the other player see your move *before* he responds. When unpredictability is needed, it would be disadvantageous to move first. Think what would happen in "one-two-three shoot" if you moved first: you would always lose.

Not just any randomness will do. Suppose Odds chooses 1 finger 75 percent of the time and 2 fingers 25 percent of the time. Then Evens, by choosing 1, can win 75 percent of the time, and on average get $.75 \times 1 + .25 \times (-1) = .5$ dollars per play. Similarly, the choice of 2 would lose Evens fifty cents per play on average. So Evens would choose 1. But then Odds should be choosing 2, not the 75:25 mixture. The mixture would not survive the successive rounds of thinking about each other's strategy.

In other words, there is an *equilibrium pattern* of randomness, and it has to be calculated. In this example, the whole situation is so symmetric that the equilibrium mix has to be 50:50 for each player. Let us try that out. If Odds chooses 1 and 2 equally often, then Evens wins $.5 \times 1 + .5 \times (-1) = 0$ per play on average, whether he plays 1 or 2. Therefore he also wins 0 on average when he plays his 50:50 mix. The argument also works the other way around. So the two 50:50 mixes are best responses to each other, that is, an equilibrium. The name for this solution is a "mixed-strategy" equilibrium, reflecting the necessity for the individuals to randomly mix their moves.

The equilibrium mix in more general situations is not so evident from symmetry, but there are some simple rules for calculating it. We develop the rules using the game of tennis.

2. ANYONE FOR TENNIS?

One of the first strategic lessons in tennis is not to commit to a direction until the last possible fraction of a second. Otherwise, the opponent can exploit your guess and hit the ball the other way. But even when one can't observe the opponent's move, there is a great advantage to predicting it. If the server always aims to the receiver's backhand, the receiver will prepare his grip and start to move toward that side in anticipation, and consequently will be more effective in the return of serve. The server, therefore, attempts to be unpredictable in order to prevent the receiver from successfully second-guessing his aim. Conversely, the receiver must not exclusively favor one side or the other in making his initial move. Unlike matching fingers, players should not equate unpredictability with even odds. Players can improve their performance by systematically favoring one side, although in an unpredictable way.

For concreteness, let us think of a pair of players with particular skills. The receiver's forehand is somewhat stronger. If he anticipates correctly, his forehand return will be successful 90 percent of the time, while an anticipated backhand return will be successful only 60 percent of the time. Of course, the returner fares worse if he starts to move to one side and the service goes to the other. If he goes to the backhand side while the service is to his forehand, he can shift and return successfully only 30 percent of the time. The other way around, his chances are 20 percent. We can show all this using the table below.

**Probability That Receiver
Successfully Returns Serve**

Server's Aim

Forehand Backhand

		Forehand	Backhand
Receiver's Move	Forehand	90%	20%
	Backhand	30%	60%

The server wants to keep the successful return percentage as low as possible; the returner has exactly the opposite interest. Before the match, the two players choose their game plans. What is the best strategy for each side?

If the server always aims his serves toward the forehand, the receiver will anticipate the move to his forehand and successfully return the serves 90 percent of the time. If the server always aims his serves to the backhand, the receiver will anticipate the move toward his backhand and will return 60 percent of the serves successfully.

Only by mixing his aim can the server reduce the receiver's effectiveness. He keeps the receiver guessing and therefore unable to take full advantage of anticipating the correct position.

Suppose the server tosses an imaginary coin just before each serve, and aims to the forehand or backhand according to whether the coin shows heads or tails. Now look what happens when the receiver moves to the forehand position. This guess will be correct only half the time. When correct, the forehand return is successful 90 percent of the time, and when the move to the forehand is an incorrect guess, the receiver's successful return rate falls to 20 percent. His overall success rate is $(1/2)90\% + (1/2)20\% = 55\%$. By a similar argument, a move toward the backhand leads to successful returns $(1/2)60\% + (1/2)30\% = 45\%$ of the time.

Given the 50:50 mixing rule of the server, the receiver chooses the options best from his perspective. He should move toward his forehand, and the percentage of successful returns will be 55%. For the server, this is already an improvement over the outcome when he aims his serve the same way all the time. For comparison, the receiver's success rate is 90 percent or 60 percent if the server aims exclusively toward forehand or backhand serves, respectively.

The next obvious question is, what is the server's *best* mix? To answer this, we show the consequences of the various mixes in a chart. The percentage of times the server aims toward forehand goes horizontally from 0 percent to 100 percent. For each of these mixtures, one of the two lines in the chart shows the receiver's success rate when he anticipates a move toward the forehand; the other, his success rate when he expects a move toward the backhand. For example, if the receiver anticipates a move to the forehand, the zero-percent-forehand (i.e., backhand) serve policy holds the receiver to a 20 percent success rate, while the hundred-percent-forehand serve policy allows a 90 percent success rate. The receiver's success percentage rises along the straight line from one end to the other.

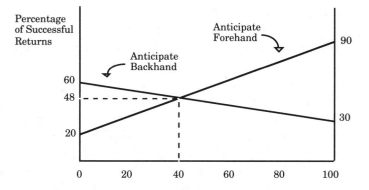

Percentage of Times Server Aims Serve to Forehand

The two lines meet at the point where the server aims at the forehand 40 percent of the time. To the left of this, the receiver does better by anticipating a service to the backhand; to the right, he does better by anticipating a service to the forehand.*

The 40:60 mixture of forehands to backhands is the only one that cannot be exploited by the receiver to his own advantage in this way. Only at this mixture is it the case that the receiver does equally well with either of his choices. Both ensure the receiver a 48 percent success rate. Any other mix by the server, when properly exploited, will give the receiver a success percentage along the *upper* of the two lines in the chart, and therefore more than 48 percent. Thus the mix of aiming to his forehand 40 percent of the time is the server's best choice.

The exact proportions of the mix are governed by the four outcomes of the combinations of the basic pairs of actions. For players of different absolute and relative strengths, the num-

---

* Note that the receiver does better betting on his forehand as soon as the odds of a serve to the forehand are above 40 percent — not 50 percent. Even though the odds may be against a service to the forehand, *his skills are not equal*. Anticipating a forehand is the right bet whenever the odds are better than 40 percent.

bers that here are 90, 60, 30, and 20 will be different, and then so will the best mixes to use. We will soon find some surprising results of making such changes. Here the point is simply that you will have to work out your own best mix by estimating the four basic outcomes for the actual game you are playing.

There is a shortcut; one can calculate the equilibrium strategies without drawing a chart like the one above. The simple arithmetic method is due to J. D. Williams.[3] Go back to the table of the basic outcomes. For the server, take his aim to the forehand strategy and find the difference of its yields against the two choices of the receiver; we have 90 − 30 = 60. Do the same for his aim to the backhand strategy: 60 − 20 = 40. The numbers *in reverse order* are the odds of using the two strategies in the best mix.* So the server should aim to the forehand or the backhand in proportions of 40:60.

Now let us look at the same game from the receiver's point of view. The next figure shows the chart of the consequences of his choices. If the serve is aimed at his backhand, then a move toward the backhand means 60 percent successful returns, whereas a move to the forehand means 20 percent suc-

---

* We can confirm this result using a little algebra. If the table of payoffs for the Column player is as drawn below, then the equilibrium ratio of Left to Right is $(D − B) : (A − C)$. Column chooses a probability p of playing Left so that Row is indifferent between Up and Down; $pA + (1 − p)B = pC + (1 − p)D$ implies $p/(1 − p) = (D − B)/(A − C)$ as claimed. Since the Row player's payoffs are the negative of the Column player's, his equilibrium mixture of Up to Down is $(D − C) : (A − B)$.

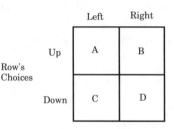

Column's Choices

cessful returns. Changing the proportion of moves to the forehand from 0 percent to 100 percent traces out a line joining these two points. Similarly we have a line rising from 30 to 90 when the server aims at his forehand side. The two lines meet where the receiver moves toward his forehand 30 percent of the time, and his percentage of successful returns is 48 percent no matter where the server aims. Any other mix would be exploited by the server, choosing the better of his strategies and reducing the receiver to a success rate below 48 percent.

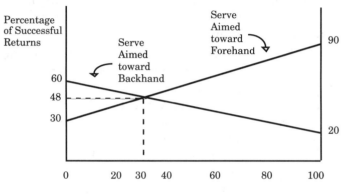

Percentage of Times Receiver Moves toward Forehand

Alternatively, we can use Williams's method. The table gives us the differences of outcomes for the two choices of the receiver. For a move to the forehand we have 90 − 20 = 70; for a move to the backhand, 60 − 30 = 30. The best mix has these proportions in reverse order: 30 percent of the time, anticipate a forehand; the other 70 percent, anticipate a backhand.

You may have noticed an interesting common feature of the best mixes calculated from the two players' separate points of view. The two give the same successful return percentage, namely 48 percent. Using his best mix, the receiver is able to hold the server down to exactly the same success percentage as the server is able to achieve using his own best mix. This is not a coincidence but a general property of all games with two players whose interests are strictly opposed to each other.

This result, called the min-max theorem, is due to the former Princeton mathematicians John von Neumann and Oscar Morgenstern. The theorem states that in zero-sum games in which the players' interests are strictly opposed (one's gain is the other's loss), one player should attempt to minimize his opponent's maximum payoff while his opponent attempts to maximize his own minimum payoff. When they do so, the surprising conclusion is that the minimum of the maximum (mini-max) payoffs equals the maximum of the minimum (maxi-min) payoffs. Neither player can improve his position, and so these strategies form an equilibrium of the game.

We illustrate the argument when each player has only two strategies using the tennis example. If the server tries to minimize the receiver's maximal success rate, he should act as if the receiver has correctly anticipated his mixing strategy and has responded optimally. That is, the receiver's success rate would be the maximum of the two lines as drawn below. The minimum of the maximum occurs where the lines cross, which is at a 48 percent success rate.

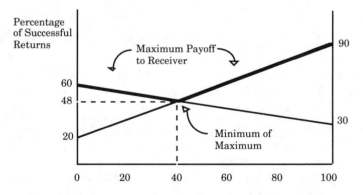

Percentage of Times Server Aims Serve to Forehand

Next we look at the problem from the receiver's perspective; he is trying to maximize his minimal payoff. If the receiver moves to the forehand and backhand equally often, his new payoff curve will be the average of the original two lines, shown as a dotted line. Because this line is sloped upward, its minimum occurs all the way at the left, at a 40 percent success rate. No matter what mixture the receiver uses, the line must go through the 48 percent success rate because the server has the option of using a 40:60 mixture. If the line has any slope at all, one end must fall below 48 percent. Only when the receiver mixes in the ratio of 30:70 is the line perfectly flat, and the minimum is then 48 percent. Thus the minimum of the maximum equals the maximum of the minimum — 48 percent.

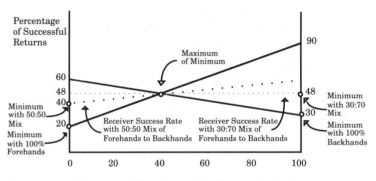

Percentage of Times Server Aims Serve to Forehand

The general proof of the min-max theorem is quite complicated, but the result is useful and worth remembering. If all you want to know is the gain of one player or the loss of the other when both play their best mixes, you need only compute the best mix for one of them and determine its result.

Our other tools, Williams's method and these charts, work well for any zero-sum game with two players each with two strategies. Unfortunately, they do not apply when games are not zero-sum, or have more than two players, or allow more than two strategies for any player. Economists and mathematicians have developed more general techniques, such as linear programming, to solve for equilibrium strategies in even the most complicated zero-sum games. Although these techniques are beyond the scope of this book, we can still make use of the results.

A general feature of all mixed-strategy equilibria is that each person is indifferent between any strategy he uses in the equilibrium. When mixing is necessary, the way to find your own equilibrium mixture is to act so as to make others indifferent about their actions. Although this may sound backward, it fits exactly with the motivation for randomization in zero-sum games: you want to prevent others from exploiting any systematic behavior of yours. If they had a preference for a particular action, that would mean only that they had chosen the worst course from your perspective.

At this point we have explained the advantages, even the strategic necessity, of using mixed or random strategies. The basic idea is that one resorts to chance as the means of keeping the other player from exploiting any systematic behavior on your part. Turning this idea into practice is more subtle. The next five sections act as a mini user's guide to mixed strategies.

3. WHY YOU SHOULD CHOOSE THE RIGHT MIX

If it is ever discovered that one player is pursuing a course of action other than the equilibrium random mix, the other player can exploit this to his own advantage. In the tennis example, the receiver could achieve a 48 percent success rate when the server followed his equilibrium strategy of mixing 40 percent forehands to 60 percent backhands. The receiver can do better *if* the server uses any other mix of strategy. For example, if the server foolishly aimed all his serves at the receiver's weak backhand, the receiver could anticipate his move and improve his success rate to 60 percent. In general, if the receiver knows the server and is sure of his foibles, he can react accordingly. But then there is always the danger that, like the pool shark, the server is a superior strategist who used poor strategies in unimportant matches to deceive the receiver into reacting thus, and will exploit him on a really important occasion. Once the receiver deviates from his equilibrium mixture in order to take advantage of the server's "perceived" deviation, the receiver becomes subject to exploitation by the server. The server's apparently poor mixing could be a setup. Only by playing one's equilibrium mixture is this danger avoided.

Just as important as the proper proportions of the mixture is the nature of the randomness. If a server adopts the system of serving four times to the forehand, then six times to the backhand, then four times to the forehand again, and so on, this will achieve the right proportions. But it is systematic behavior that will be noticed by the receiver. He will respond by moving appropriately, and achieve $(4/10)90\% + (6/10)60\% = 72\%$ success. In order to be maximally effective, the server needs genuine unpredictability of *each* serve. Messrs. Smith and Dykstra in our baseball story seemed not to realize this principle.

4. WHY NOT RELY ON THE OTHER PLAYER'S RANDOMIZATION?

If one player is using his best mix, then his success percentage is the same no matter what the other does. Suppose you are the receiver in the tennis example, and the server is using his best mix of 40:60. Then you will return successfully 48 percent of the time whether you move to the forehand, or the backhand, or any mixture of the two. Observing this, you might be tempted to spare yourself the calculation of your own best mix, just stick to any one action, and rely on the other player using his best mix. The problem is that unless you use your best mix, the other does not have the incentive to go on using his. If you pick a forehand move, for example, he will switch to serving to your backhand. The reason why you *should* use your best mix is to *keep* the other player using his.

5. HOW YOUR BEST MIX CHANGES AS YOUR SKILLS CHANGE

Suppose the receiver practices to improve his backhand return, until his percentage of successful returns on that side goes up from 60 to 65. We can modify the chart from which we computed his best mix. This is done in the next figure. We see that the proportion of the receiver's moves to the forehand side goes up from 30 percent to 33.3 percent, and the overall percentage of successful returns goes up from 48 to 50.

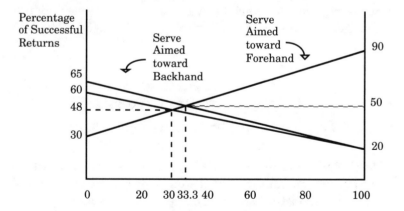

Percentage of Times Receiver Moves Toward Forehand

It is natural that the receiver's success rate should increase as his skill improves. But it is rather surprising that the success is achieved by using the improved backhand *less* often. In the hot hand story of Chapter 1, we said this could happen; now we explain how.

The reason lies in the interaction of the two players' strategies. When the receiver is better at returning backhands, the server goes to the forehand more often (43 percent instead of 40 percent). In response, the receiver moves to his forehand more often, too. A better backhand unlocks the power of your forehand. Similarly for Larry Bird, an improvement in his left-handed shooting changes the way he is defended and allows him to shoot right-handed more often.

As another example of the same phenomenon, suppose the receiver trains to become more agile, so that he can shift from an initial forehand move to return a backhand service more accurately. His success figure of 20 percent for this shot rises to 25 percent. Once again, his proportion of forehand moves will increase from 30 percent to 31.6 percent (using Williams's method, the ratio of forehand to backhand moves increases from 30:70 to 30:65). The receiver moves to the forehand side more often since this is the source of his improved skill. In response, the server diminishes the receiver's gain by going to the forehand less often.

6. How to Act Randomly

What should you do if you are told to mix forkballs and fastballs randomly in equal proportions? One way is to pick a number at random between 1 and 10. If the number is 5 or less then you throw a fastball; if the number is 6 or above then go for the forkball. Of course, this only reduces the problem one layer. How do you go about picking a random number between 1 and 10?

Let us start with the simpler problem of trying to write

down what a random sequence of coin tosses will look like. If the sequence is truly random, then anyone who tries to guess what you write down will be correct no more than 50 percent on average. But writing down such a "random" sequence is more difficult than you might imagine.

Psychologists have found that people tend to forget that a head is just as likely to be followed by a head as by a tail; therefore they have too many reversals, and too few strings of heads, in their successive guesses. If a fair coin toss comes up heads thirty times in a row, the next toss is still equally likely to be heads or tails. There is no such thing as "being due" for a tails. Similarly, in the lottery, last week's number is just as likely to win again as any other number. To avoid getting caught putting order into the randomness, you need a more objective or independent mechanism.

One such trick is to choose some fixed rule, but one that is both secret and sufficiently complicated that it is difficult to discover. Look, for example, at the length of our sentences. If the sentence has an odd number of words, call it a heads; if the sentence length is even, call it a tails. That should be a good random number generator. Working backward over the previous ten sentences yields T, H, H, T, H, T, H, H, H, T. If our book isn't handy, don't worry; we carry random number sequences with us all the time. Take a succession of your friends' and relatives' birthdates. For even dates, guess heads; for odd, tails. Or look at the second hand on your watch. Provided your watch is not too accurate, no one else will know the current position of the second hand. Our advice to the pitcher who must mix in proportions of 50:50 is to glance at his wristwatch just before each pitch. If the second hand points toward an even number, then throw a fastball; an odd number, then throw a forkball. The second hand can be used to achieve any ratio. To throw fastballs 40 percent of the time and forkballs 60 percent, choose fastball if the second hand is between 1 and 24, and forkball if it is between 25 and 60.

7. UNIQUE SITUATIONS

All of this reasoning makes sense in games like football or baseball or tennis, in which the same situation arises many times in one game, and the same players confront each other from one game to the next. Then there is time and opportunity to observe any systematic behavior, and respond to it. Correspondingly, it is important to avoid patterns that can be exploited, and stick to the best mix. But what about games that are played just once?

Consider the choices of points of attack and defense in a battle. Here the situation is usually so unique that no system from your previous actions can be inferred by the other side. But a case for random choice arises from the possibility of espionage. If you choose a definite course of action, and the enemy discovers what you are going to do, he will adapt his course of action to your maximum disadvantage. *You want to surprise him; the surest way to do so is to surprise yourself.* You should keep the options open as long as possible, and at the last moment choose between them by an unpredictable and therefore espionage-proof device. The relative proportions of the device should also be such that if the enemy discovered them, he would not be able to turn the knowledge to his advantage. But that is just the best mix calculated in the description above.

Finally, a *warning*. Even when you are using your best mix, there will be occasions when you have a poor outcome. Even if Dave Smith is unpredictable, sometimes Lenny Dykstra will still guess right and knock the ball out of the park. In football, on third down and a yard to go, a run up the middle is the percentage play; but it is important to throw an occasional bomb to keep the defense honest. When such a pass succeeds, fans and sportscasters will marvel at the cunning choice of play, and say the coach is a genius. When it fails, the coach will come in for a lot of criticism: how could he gamble on a long pass instead of going for the percentage play?

The time to justify the coach's strategy is *before* using it on any particular occasion. The coach should publicize the fact that mixing is vital; the run up the middle remains such a good percentage play precisely because some defensive resources must be diverted to guard against the occasional costly bomb. However, we suspect that even if the coach shouts this message in all newspapers and television channels before the game, and then uses a bomb in such a situation and it fails, he will come in for just as much criticism as if he had not tried to educate the public in the elements of game theory.

8. BODYGUARD OF LIES

If you are using your best mix, then it does not matter if the other player discovers this fact, so long as he does not find out in advance the particular course of action that is indicated by your random device in a particular instance. He can do nothing to take advantage of your random strategy: the equilibrium strategy is chosen to defend against being exploited in just this way. However, if for whatever reason you are doing something other than using your best mix, then secrecy is vital. Leakage of this knowledge would rebound to your cost. By the same token, you can gain by getting your rival to believe the wrong thing about your plan.

In preparation for their landings on the Normandy beaches in June 1944, the Allies used many devices to make the Germans believe the invasion would be at Calais. One of the most ingenious was to turn a German spy into a double agent — but no ordinary double agent. The English made sure that the Germans knew that their agent had been turned, but did not let the Germans know that this was intentional. To build up his (lack of) credibility as a double agent, the spy transmitted home some of the worst information possible. The Germans found this information useful simply by reversing that which they were told. This was the setup for the big sting. When the double agent told the truth that the Allied landing would occur at Normandy, the Germans took this to be further evidence that Calais was the chosen spot.

This strategy had the further advantage that after the landing, the Germans were no longer sure that their spy was really a double agent. He had been one of their only sources of correct information. With his credibility restored, the English could now send false information and have it believed.[4]

The problem with this story is that the Germans should have predicted the English strategy and thus calculated that there was some probability that their agent had been turned. When playing mixed or random strategies, you can't fool the opposition every time or on any one particular time. The best you can hope for is to keep them guessing and fool them some of the time. In this regard, when you know that the person you are talking to has in his interest a desire to mislead you, it may be best to *ignore* any statements he makes rather than accept them at face value or to infer that exactly the opposite must be the truth.

There is the story of the two rival businessmen who meet in the Warsaw train station.

"Where are you going?" says the first man.

"To Minsk," replies the other.

"To Minsk, eh? What a nerve you have! I know that you are telling me that you are going to Minsk because you want me to believe that you are going to Pinsk. But it so happens that I know you really *are* going to Minsk. *So why are you lying to me?*"[5]

Actions do speak a little louder than words. By seeing what your rival does, you can judge the relative likelihood of matters that he wants to conceal from you. It is clear from our examples that you cannot simply take a rival's statements at face value. But that does not mean that you should ignore what he does when trying to discern where his true interests lie.

The right proportions to mix one's equilibrium play critically depend on one's payoffs. Thus observing a player's move gives some information about the mixing being used and is valuable evidence to help infer the rival's payoffs. Bidding strategies in poker provide a prime example.

Poker players are well acquainted with the need to mix their plays. John McDonald gives the following advice: "The poker hand must at all times be concealed behind the mask of inconsistency. The good poker player must avoid set practices and act at random, going so far, on occasion, as to violate the elementary principles of correct play."[6] A "tight" player who never bluffs seldom wins a large pot; nobody will ever raise him. He may win many small pots, but invariably ends up a loser. A "loose" player who bluffs too often will always be called, and thus he too goes down to defeat. The best strategy requires a mix of these two.

Suppose you know that a regular poker rival raises two-thirds of the time and calls one-third of the time when he has a good hand. If he has a poor hand, he folds two-thirds of the time and raises the other third of the time. (In general, it is a bad idea to call when you are bluffing, since you do not expect to have a winning hand.) Then you can construct the following table for the probabilities of his actions.

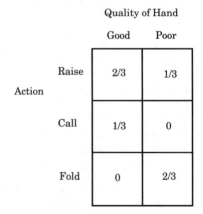

		Quality of Hand	
		Good	Poor
	Raise	2/3	1/3
Action	Call	1/3	0
	Fold	0	2/3

Before he bids, you believe that good and poor hands are equally likely. Because his mixing probabilities depend on his hand, you get additional information from the bid. If you see him fold, you can be sure he had a poor hand. If he calls, you know his hand is good. But in both these cases, the betting is over. If he raises, the odds are 2:1 that he has a good hand. His bid does not always perfectly reveal his hand, but you know more than when you started. After hearing a raise, you increase the chance that his hand is good from 1/2 to 2/3.*

9. SURPRISE

So far, our applications of randomized strategies have focused exclusively on games in which the players' interests are strictly opposed. Somewhat more surprising is the possibility of finding an equilibrium with random behavior even when the players have common interests. In this case, mixing one's plays leads to an inferior outcome for all parties. But just because the outcome is inferior does not mean the strategies are not an equilibrium: equilibrium is a description not a prescription.

The reason for mixing one's moves arises from a failure of coordination. This problem only arises when there is not

---

* The estimation of probabilities conditional on hearing the bid is made using a mathematical technique called Bayes rule. The probability the other player has a good hand conditional on hearing the bid "X" is the chance that this person would both have a good hand and bid "X" divided by the chance that he ever bids "X." Thus, hearing a "Fold" implies that his hand must be bad, since a person with a good hand never "Folds." Hearing a "Call" implies that his hand must be good, since the only time a player calls is when his hand is good. After hearing a "Raise," the calculations are only slightly more complicated. The odds that a player both has a good hand and raises is (1/2)(2/3) = 1/3, while the chance that the player both has a bad hand and raises, i.e., bluffs, is (1/2)(1/3) = 1/6. Hence the total chance of hearing a raise is 1/3 + 1/6 = 1/2. According to Bayes rule, the probability that the hand is good conditional on hearing a raise is the fraction of the total probability of hearing a raise that is due to the times when the player has a strong hand: in this case that fraction is (1/3)/(1/2) = 2/3.

a unique equilibrium. For example, two people disconnected during a phone call don't always know who should call whom back. Without the ability to communicate, the players don't know which equilibrium to expect. In a loose sense, the equilibrium with randomization is a way of playing a compromise between the coordinated equilibria. The nature of this compromise is illustrated in the story below.

Della and Jim are the sort of couple you read about in fiction, O. Henry's *The Gift of the Magi*, to be precise. "Nobody could ever count" their love for each other, and each was willing, even eager, to make any sacrifice to get a really worthy Christmas gift for the other. Della would sell her hair to get Jim a chain for his heirloom watch, and Jim would sell the watch to buy a comb for Della's beautiful hair.

If they know each other well enough, they should both recognize the possibility that each will sell his or her one treasure to buy the other a gift, and the result will be a tragic mistake. Della should pause and consider whether it would be better to keep her hair and await Jim's gift. Likewise, Jim should consider not selling his watch. Of course, if they both refrain, neither gives a gift, which would be a different mistake.

This story can be represented as a game.

Payoffs to [Della, Jim]

Jim's Choice

		Sell Watch	Keep Watch
Della's Choice	Keep Hair	1 ⟍ 2	0 ⟍ 0
	Sell Hair	0 ⟍ 0	2 ⟍ 1

The couple's strategies interact even though their interests largely coincide. For each, both kinds of mistake would be a bad outcome. For concreteness, we give this a point score of zero. As between the two outcomes in which one gives a gift and the other receives it, suppose each thinks it better to give (2 points) than to receive (1 point).

The situation in which Della keeps her hair and Jim sells his watch is a possible equilibrium; each spouse's strategy is the best response to the other's. But the situation in which Della sells her hair and Jim keeps his watch is also an equilibrium. Is there a mutually understood convention to select one equilibrium over the other? Surprise is an important aspect of a gift; therefore they cannot communicate in advance to establish a convention.

Mixing can help preserve the surprise, although at a cost. It is easy to check that the strategies in which each chooses to give with probability 2/3 and receive with probability 1/3 also constitute an equilibrium. Suppose Della uses such a mixture. If Jim sells his watch, there is a 1/3 chance that Della has kept her hair (2 points) and a 2/3 chance that she has sold it (0 point). The average outcome is 2/3 point. A similar calculation shows that if Jim keeps his watch, the average outcome is again 2/3 point. So Jim has no clear reason to choose one strategy rather than another, or indeed any mix. Once again, note that the function of Della's best mix is to keep Jim willing to mix, and vice versa.

The probabilities of mistakes are quite large: 4 times in 9 the couple finds that each has sold the item for which the other has bought the gift (as in the O. Henry story), and 1 time in 9 neither gets any gift. Because of these mistakes, the average score (2/3 point for each) is worse than that of either of the two equilibria in which one gives and the other receives (2 points for the giver and 1 for the receiver). This is unlike the tennis example, in which each could actually raise his success rate by mixing.

Why the difference? Tennis is a zero-sum game, in which the players' interests are strictly opposed. They do better when they choose the mixing probabilities independently. In our account of *The Gift of the Magi*, the couple's interests are largely aligned. They need, therefore, to coordinate their mixing. They should toss *one* coin, and depending on the outcome decide who gives and who receives. The couple has a slight conflict of interest; Jim prefers the top left outcome, and Della the bottom right. Coordinated mixing can offer them a compromise, splitting the difference. When a common coin toss decides who gives and who receives, the average outcome for each becomes 1.5 points. Of course the element of surprise is lost.

10. CATCH AS CATCH CAN

So far there have been very few examples of mixed strategy outside the sporting world. Why are there so few instances of businesses using randomized behavior out in the real world? First, it may be difficult to build in the idea of leaving the outcome to chance in a corporate culture that wants to maintain control over the outcome. This is especially true when things go wrong, as they must occasionally when moves are chosen randomly. While some people understand that a football coach has to fake a punt once in a while in order to keep the defense honest, a similarly risky strategy in business can get you fired if it fails. But the point isn't that the risky will always work, but rather that it avoids the danger of set patterns and predictability.

One application in which mixed strategies improve business performance is price couponing. Companies use price discount coupons to build market share. The idea is to attract new customers, and not just to give a discount to your present market. If competitors simultaneously offer coupons, then customers don't have any special incentive to switch brands. Instead, they stay with their current brand and take the discount. Only when one company offers coupons while the others don't are new customers attracted to try the product.

The price coupon strategic game for competitors such as Coke and Pepsi is then quite analogous to the coordination problem of Jim and Della. Both companies want to be the one to give coupons. But if they try to do this simultaneously, the effects cancel out and both are worse off. One solution would be to follow a predictable pattern of offering coupons every six months, and the competitors could learn to alternate. The problem with this approach is that when Coke predicts Pepsi is just about to offer coupons, Coke should step in first to preempt. The only way to avoid preemption is to keep the element of surprise that comes from using a randomized strategy.*

There are other cases in which businesses must avoid set patterns and predictability. Some airlines offer discount tickets to travelers who are willing to buy tickets at the last minute. But they won't tell you how many seats are left in order to help you estimate the chances of success. If last-minute ticket availability were more predictable, then there would be a much greater possibility of exploiting the system, and the airlines would lose more of their otherwise regular paying customers.

The most widespread use of randomized strategies in business is to motivate compliance at a lower monitoring cost. This applies to everything from tax audits to drug testing to parking meters. It also explains why the punishment should not necessarily fit the crime.

The typical fine for illegal parking at a meter is many times

---

* There is some strong statistical evidence that Coke and Pepsi reached a cooperative solution for their couponing. As reported on "60 Minutes," there was a span of 52 weeks in which Coke and Pepsi each offered 26 price promotions and there was no overlap. The chance that this would occur by luck if the two companies were acting independently and each offered 26 weeks of couponing is 1/495918532948104 — or less than 1 in 1,000 trillion.

the meter fee. If the meter rate is a dollar per hour, would a fine of $1.01 not suffice to keep people honest? It would, provided the traffic police were *sure* to catch you each time you parked without putting money in the meter. Such enforcement would be very costly. The salaries of the traffic wardens would be the largest item, but the cost of administering the collection mechanism needed to keep the policy credible would be quite substantial, too.

The authorities have an equally effective and less costly strategy, namely to have larger fines and relax the enforcement efforts. When the fine is $25, a 1 in 25 risk of being caught is enough to keep you honest. A much smaller police force will do the job, and the fines collected will come closer to covering the administrative costs.

This is another instance of the usefulness of mixed strategies. It is similar to the tennis example in some ways, and different in other respects. Once again, the authorities choose a random strategy because it is better than any systematic action: no enforcement at all would mean misuse of scarce parking places, and a 100 percent enforcement would be too costly. However, the other side, the parking public, does not necessarily have a random strategy. In fact the authorities want to make the detection probability and the fine large enough to induce the public to comply with the parking regulations.

Random drug testing has many of the same features as parking meter enforcement. It is too time-consuming and costly to test every employee every day for evidence of drug use. It is also unnecessary. Random testing will uncover those who are unable to work drug free and discourage others from recreational use. Again, the probability of detection is small, but the fine when caught is high. That is one of the problems with the IRS audit strategy. The penalties are small given the chances of getting caught. When enforcement is random, it must be that the punishment is worse than the crime. The rule should be that the *expected* punishment should fit the crime, where the expectation takes into account the chance of being caught.

Those hoping to defeat enforcement can also use random strategies to their benefit. They can hide the true crime in the midst of many false alarms or decoys, and the enforcer's resources become spread too thin to be effective. For example, an air defense must be able to destroy nearly 100 percent of all incoming missiles. A cost-effective way of defeating the air defense is for the attacker to surround the real missile with a bodyguard of decoys. It is much cheaper to build a decoy missile than the real thing. Unless the defender can perfectly distinguish among them, he will be required to stop all incoming missiles, real and fake.

The practice of shooting dud shells began in World War II, not by the intentional design of building decoy missiles, but as a response to the problem of quality control. As John McDonald explained in his book *Strategy in Poker, Business, and War*, "The elimination of defective shells in production is expensive. Someone got the idea then of manufacturing duds and shooting them on a random basis. A military commander cannot afford to have a delayed time bomb buried under his position, and he never knew which was which. The bluff made him work at every unexploded shell that came over."

When the cost of defense is proportional to the number of missiles that can be shot down, attackers can make this enforcement cost unbearably high. This problem is one of the major challenges facing those involved in the "Star Wars" defense; it may have no solution.

11. CASE STUDY #7: OPERATION OVERLORD

In 1944, the Allies were planning an operation for the liberation of Europe, and the Nazis were planning their defense against it. There were two possibilities for the initial landing

— the Normandy beaches and Pas de Calais. A landing would surely succeed against a weak defense, so the Germans would have to concentrate their attention on one of these two places. Calais was more difficult to invade, but more valuable to win, being closer to the Allies' ultimate targets in France, Belgium, and Germany itself.

Suppose the probabilities of success are as follows:

Probabilities of Allied Success

German Defense

		Normandy	Calais
Allied Landing	Normandy	75%	100%
	Calais	100%	20%

The payoffs are given on a scale of 0 to 100. The Allies count a successful landing at Calais as 100, a successful landing at Normandy as 80, and a failure at either place as 0 (and the Germans get the negative of these payoffs).

Put yourself simultaneously in the boots of General Eisenhower, the Allied Supreme Commander, and Field Marshal Rommel, the German commander of their coastal defenses in France. What strategies would you choose?

Case Discussion

First combine the information on the probabilities of success and the point score value of success to construct a table of the average point scores. The scores listed are from the Allied perspective; the German scores can be taken as the negative of these numbers, as the sides' interests are strictly opposed.

Allied Point Scores

German Defense

Normandy   Calais

	Normandy	Calais
Normandy	60	80
Calais	100	20

Allied Landing (row labels)

There is no equilibrium in the basic strategies, and we must look for mixtures. Using Williams's method, the Allies should choose to land at Normandy or Calais with the odds of $(100-20):(80-60)$, or 4:1, while the Germans should deploy their defenses at Normandy or Calais with the odds $(80-20):(100-60)$, or 3:2. The average point score for the Allies when both use their best mixtures is 68.

The probabilities and point scores we chose are plausible, but it is hard to be precise or dogmatic about such matters. Therefore let us compare our results with what actually happened. In retrospect, we know that the Allies' mixing proportions were overwhelmingly weighted toward Normandy, and that is what they in fact chose. For the Germans, it was a closer call. It is less surprising, therefore, that the German decision-making was swayed by the Allies' double-agent trick, differences of opinion in their commanding ranks, and some plain bad luck, such as Rommel being away from the front at the crucial time. They failed to commit their reserves on the afternoon of D-Day when the Allied landings at Normandy seemed to be succeeding, believing that a bigger landing at Calais would come. Even then, the fate of Omaha Beach was in the balance for a while. But the Allies gained and consolidated their foothold on Normandy. The rest you know.

Epilogue to Part II

1. HISTORICAL NOTE

Game theory was pioneered by the Princeton polymath, John von Neumann. In the early years, the emphasis was on games of pure conflict (zero-sum games). Other games were considered in a cooperative form, that is, the participants were supposed to choose and implement their actions jointly. These approaches could not encompass most of the games played in reality, in which people choose actions separately but their links to others are not ones of pure conflict. For general games combining conflict and cooperation, our concept of an equilibrium is due to John Nash. Thomas Schelling broadened the analysis of sequential-move games, developing the ideas of strategic moves.

2. FURTHER READING

Pioneering books are often enjoyable to read. In this spirit, we recommend von Neumann and Morgenstern's *Theory of Games and Economic Behavior* (Princeton University Press, 1947) even though the mathematics may be hard to follow in places. Schelling's *The Strategy of Conflict* (Harvard University Press, 1960) is more than a pioneering book; it continues to provide instruction and insight.

For an entertaining exposition of zero-sum games, J. D. Williams's *The Compleat Strategyst* (revised edition, McGraw-Hill, 1966) still cannot be beat. The most thorough and highly mathematical treatment of pre-Schelling game theory is in Duncan Luce and Howard Raiffa, *Games and Decisions* (Wiley, 1957).

Among general expositions of game theory, Morton Davis, *Game Theory: A Nontechnical Introduction* (second edition, Basic Books, 1983) is probably the easiest to read. A far more detailed and mathematically harder treatment is Martin Shubik's *Game Theory in the Social Sciences* (MIT Press, 1982).

There are also several valuable books applying game theory to particular contexts. In the field of politics, the noteworthy books include Steven Brams, *Game Theory and Politics* (Free Press, 1979), William Riker, *The Art of Political Manipulation* (Yale University Press, 1986), and the more technical approach of Peter Ordeshook's *Game Theory and Political Theory* (Cambridge University Press, 1986). For applications to business, Michael Porter's *Competitive Strategy* (Free Press, 1982) and Howard Raiffa's *The Art and Science of Negotiation* (Harvard University Press, 1982) are two excellent resources.

3. OUR SINS OF OMISSION

We have blurred the distinction between zero-sum and non-zero-sum games. Equilibria of zero-sum games have some special properties that do not carry over to non-zero-sum games; therefore rigorous treatments of the subject are divided along this dimension.

We have simplified many situations to the point where each player had only two strategies. This was done when the most basic ideas could be conveyed without serious loss of content. In most cases the complications introduced by more strategies are purely computational. For example, randomization over three or more basic strategies can be done using a simple computer program. There is a new aspect: only a subset of the strategies might be active (be played with positive probability) in equilibrium. On this point, see Luce and Raiffa.

We have ignored the so-called "cooperative games" in which players choose and implement their actions jointly, and produce equilibria like the Core or the Shapley Value. This was done because we think any cooperation should emerge as the equilibrium outcome of a noncooperative game in which actions are chosen separately. That is, individuals' incentive to cheat on any agreement should be recognized and made a part of their strategy choice. However, interested readers can find treatments of cooperative games in the books by Davis, Luce and Raiffa, and Shubik.

4. FROM HERE ON

Part III takes the concepts and techniques developed thus far to several types of strategic interactions. These include bargaining, voting, brinkmanship, and the design of incentives. Once again we illustrate the strategic principles through examples and case studies and suggest further readings in footnotes for readers who wish to pursue some topics in more detail.

Part III

8

Brinkmanship

In October 1962, the Cuban missile crisis brought the world to the brink of nuclear war. The Soviet Union, under its mercurial leader Nikita Khrushchev, had begun to install nuclear missiles on Cuba, 90 miles from the American mainland. On October 14, our reconnaissance airplanes brought back photographs of missile sites under construction. After a week of tense discussions within his administration, on October 22 President John F. Kennedy announced a naval quarantine of Cuba. Had the Soviet Union taken up the challenge, the crisis could have escalated to the point of all-out nuclear war between the superpowers. Kennedy himself estimated the probability of this as "between one out of three and even." But after a few anxious days of public posturing and secret negotiation, Khrushchev shied away from the confrontation. In return for a face-saving compromise involving eventual withdrawal of U.S. missiles in Turkey, he ordered the Soviet missiles in Cuba dismantled and shipped back.[1]

Khrushchev looked over the nuclear brink, did not like what he saw, and pulled back. The name "brinkmanship" seems apt for the strategy of taking your opponent to the brink of disaster, and compelling him to pull back.* Kennedy's ac-

---

* Thomas Schelling more or less invented this concept, and certainly pioneered its analysis. This whole chapter owes more than we can say to his books, *The Strategy of Conflict* (Chapters 7, 8) and *Arms and Influence* (Chapter 3). Many people erroneously say "brinksmanship" — which sounds more like the art of robbing an armored truck.

tion in the Cuban missile crisis is generally accepted as an instance of successful exercise of brinkmanship.

The rest of us also practice brinkmanship, but with less than global stakes. A management team and a trade union facing a devastating strike, stubborn spouses whose failure to compromise is leading toward divorce, and a divided Congress risking a government shutdown if it fails to ratify a budget are all engaged in brinkmanship. They are deliberately creating and manipulating the risk of a mutually bad outcome in order to induce the other party to compromise.

Brinkmanship is a subtle strategy fraught with dangers, and if you want to practice it successfully, you must first understand it thoroughly. We aim to help you grasp the subtleties, using the Cuban missile crisis as a case study.

Upon discovering that the Soviets had secretly placed missiles in Cuba, the Kennedy administration contemplated a range of options: do nothing; take a complaint to the United Nations (in practice, almost the same thing as doing nothing); impose a quarantine or blockade (the course actually adopted); launch an air strike on the missile sites in Cuba; or — at the extreme end — make an immediate preemptive total nuclear strike on the Soviet Union.

After the United States imposed a naval quarantine, the Soviets had many possible responses. They could back down and remove the missiles; stop their ships carrying missiles in mid-Atlantic (the course actually adopted); try to run the blockade either without or with naval support; or take the extreme step of launching a preemptive strike on the United States.

In this spectrum of moves and countermoves, some of the possible actions were clearly safe (such as the United States doing nothing or the Soviets removing the missiles) while others were clearly dangerous (such as launching an air strike on

Cuba). But in the large middle range, where does safety end and danger begin? In other words, just where was the brink in the Cuban missile crisis? Was there a borderline such that the world was safe to the one side of it, and doomed as soon as the line was crossed?

The answer, of course, is that there was no such precise point, only a gradually increasing risk of uncontrollable future escalation. Had the Soviets tried to defy the blockade, for example, the United States was unlikely to launch its strategic missiles at once. But events and tempers would have heated up another notch, and the risk of Armageddon would have increased perceptibly. The key to understanding brinkmanship is to realize that the brink is not a sharp precipice, but a slippery slope, getting gradually steeper.

Kennedy took the world some way down this slope; Khrushchev did not risk going farther, and then the two arranged a pullback to the safe ground above. If this was the effect of Kennedy's actions, it is at least plausible that it was also his intention.* Let us examine the strategy of brinkmanship in this light.

The essence of brinkmanship is the deliberate creation of risk. This risk should be sufficiently intolerable to your opponent to induce him to eliminate the risk by following your wishes. This makes brinkmanship a strategic move, of the kind we introduced in Chapter 5. Like any strategic move, it aims to influence the other's actions by altering his expectations. In fact brinkmanship is a threat, but of a special kind. To use it successfully, you must understand its special features.

---

* In fact, it would be a mistake to think of the Cuban missile crisis as a game with two players, Kennedy and Khrushchev. On each side, there was another game of internal "politics," with the civilian and military authorities disagreeing among themselves and with one another. Graham Allison's *Essence of Decision* (see note 2) makes a compelling case for regarding the crisis as just such a complex many-person game. Later we will see how the presence of these other players (and institutions) can play an essential part in brinkmanship.

We approach these features through three questions. First, why not threaten your opponent with the *certainty* of a dire outcome, instead of a mere *risk* that it would happen? Second, what is the mechanism that ultimately determines whether the risk comes to pass? Third, just what is the right degree of this risk? We try to answer each of these questions in turn.

1. WHY UNCERTAINTY?

Given that the United States wanted the Soviets to pull their missiles out of Cuba, why could Kennedy not have threatened that he would annihilate Moscow unless Khrushchev removed the missiles? In the terminology we introduced before (Chapter 5), this would be a compellent threat; it must specify the precise conditions of compliance (missiles back to Russia, or in crates on a ship in Havana harbor?) and a deadline for compliance.

The problem is that in practice such a threat would not be believed, either by Khrushchev or by anyone else. The threatened action, surely leading to a global thermonuclear war, is simply too drastic to be credible. If the missiles were not out by the deadline, rather than annihilate the world, Kennedy would surely be tempted to extend the deadline by a day, and then another day.

In Chapter 6 we saw several ways of lending credibility to threats. The use of an automatic device seems the most promising in this context.* This approach is the basis for the movies *Failsafe* and *Dr. Strangelove*. In *Dr. Strangelove* the Soviets have installed a "doomsday machine" that monitors American transgressions and automatically launches So-

---

* Reputation won't work, because after the threat is carried out there is no tomorrow. Contracts won't work, because everyone will face the overwhelming temptation to renegotiate. And so on.

viet retaliation under circumstances specified in a tamperproof computer program. In *Failsafe* it is the Americans who have the doomsday machine. Those who have seen these movies (which we recommend highly) know why Kennedy should not use a similar device to make his threat credible.

In theory, under ideal circumstances, everything works just as planned. The very knowledge that an automatic device is in place makes the threat credible. Khrushchev backs down, the threat does not have to be carried out, and all is well. If a threat is sure to succeed, it need never be carried out, and it does not matter how big or dire it is, or how much it would hurt you too to carry it out. But in practice, you cannot be *absolutely* sure that it will work as planned.

There are in fact two kinds of errors that can occur. First, the threat may not succeed. Suppose Kennedy has totally misjudged Khrushchev's mindset. Then Khrushchev does not back down, and the doomsday device annihilates the world just as Kennedy is regretting having installed it. Second, the threat may be carried out even when it should not. Suppose the Soviets back down, but the news reaches the doomsday computer just too late.

Because such errors are always possible, Kennedy does not want to rely on threats that are too costly to carry out. Knowing this, Khrushchev will not believe the threats, and they will not deter or compel him. Kennedy may claim that an automatic launcher has the sole authority to fire at Moscow if the Soviet missiles are not out of Cuba by Monday, but Khrushchev can be sure that Kennedy controls an override button.

Although the threat of *certainty* of war is not credible, one of a *risk* or *probability* of war can be credible. If Khrushchev fails to comply, there is a risk, but not a certainty, that the missiles will fly. The uncertainty scales down the threat. The scaling down makes the threat more tolerable to the United States, and therefore more credible to the Soviets.

This is a lot like another device for credibility we mentioned in Chapter 6, namely moving in small steps. There we considered breaking up a large promise into a succession of small ones. If I am trying to sell you a valuable piece of information for a thousand dollars, I may not be willing to disclose it in return for your promise to pay, but may be willing to reveal installments one by one in return for corresponding payments. A similar principle applies to threats. And here the steps consist of degrees of risk. Each stage of escalation by the United States or the Soviet Union increases the risk of global war; each small concession reduces the risk. The calculation for each side is how far to proceed or retreat along this route. If Kennedy is willing to go farther than Khrushchev, then Kennedy's brinkmanship will succeed.

Kennedy cannot credibly threaten an immediate all-out nuclear strike, but he can credibly raise the risks to some degree by taking some confrontational actions. For example, he may be willing to risk one chance in six of nuclear war to ensure the removal of the missiles. Then Khrushchev can no longer conclude that Kennedy's threat is vacuous; it is in Kennedy's interest to expose himself to this risk if it will motivate the Soviets to remove the missiles. If Khrushchev finds this degree of risk intolerable, then the brinkmanship has accomplished its objective: to allow Kennedy to choose a more appropriately sized threat, one big enough to work and yet small enough to be believed.

We still have to ask how Kennedy can go about threatening a *risk* of war, short of a *certainty*. This is where the slippery slope comes in.

2. THE MECHANISM OF RISK

Just how does one go about generating a threat that involves a risk? In Chapter 7 we studied the idea of mixing one's moves, and suggested several random mechanisms that could be used when selecting one from the range of actions being mixed. We might try the same idea here. For example, suppose that during the Cuban missile crisis, one in six is the right risk of war for Kennedy to threaten. Then he might tell Khrushchev that unless the missiles were out of Cuba by Monday, he would roll a die, and if six came up he would order the U.S. missiles to be launched.

Quite apart from the horror this picture conjures up, it just won't work. If Khrushchev refuses to comply, and Kennedy rolls the die and six comes up, the actual decision is still in Kennedy's hands. He still has the powerful urge to give Khrushchev just one more roll of the die ("let's make it two out of three") before Armageddon. Khrushchev knows this, and knows that Kennedy knows that, too. The credibility of the threat collapses just as surely as if the elaborate mechanism of rolling the die had never been mentioned.

An essential insight is that when a sharp precipice is replaced by a slippery slope, even Kennedy does not know where safety lies. It is as if he is playing nuclear Russian roulette instead of rolling a die. One number leads to disaster but he does not know which one that is. If the number comes up, he cannot change his mind and roll again.

With rational opponents, no one would ever cross the nuclear brink. But it is possible to fall down a slippery slope by mistake. Brinkmanship deliberately hides the precipice by creating a situation that is slightly out of control.

The risk in brinkmanship is therefore fundamentally different from the element of chance in mixing your moves. If the best proportions of your tennis serve are 50:50 between forehand and backhand, and you toss a coin before a particular serve and it comes up heads, you have no reason to feel happy or sorry about the fact. You are *indifferent* as to your action on each occasion; it is only the unpredictability of individual occasions, and the right proportions of chance, that matter. With brinkmanship, you are willing to create the risk before the fact, but remain unwilling to carry out the threatened act if the occasion arises. To convince your rival that the threatened consequence will occur, you still need other devices.

The most common is to take the actual action out of your control. It is not a matter of "If you defy me, then there is a risk that I will choose to do such and such." Instead, it is "If you defy me, there is a risk that such and such will happen, however much both of us may regret it then." Thus the credibility of brinkmanship still needs a device of commitment; only that device contains within it a coin toss or a die that governs what happens.

This conjures up the image of an automaton or computer that will act in response to the roll of a die — an unlikely scenario. But in many circumstances, a generalized fear that "things may get out of hand" serves the same purpose. Kennedy does not have to spell out exactly how a chance of Armageddon will be created.

Soldiers and military experts speak of the "fog of war" — a situation in which both sides act with disrupted lines of communication, individual acts of fear or courage, and a great deal of general uncertainty. There is too much going on to keep everything under control. This serves some of the purpose of creating risk. The Cuban missile crisis itself provided instances of this. For example, even the president found it very difficult to control the operations of the naval blockade of Cuba once put into play. Kennedy tried to bring the blockade from 500 miles out to 800 miles off the shore of Cuba in order to give Khrushchev more time. Yet evidence based on the first ship boarded, the *Marcula* (a Lebanese freighter under charter to the Soviets), indicates that the blockade was never moved.[2]

Nor did Defense Secretary McNamara succeed in persuading Chief of Naval Operations Anderson to modify the Navy's standard operating procedure for a blockade. As recorded in

Graham Allison's book, *Essence of Decision*, McNamara explained to Anderson:

> By the conventional rules, blockade was an act of war and the first Soviet ship that refused to submit to boarding and search risked being sent to the bottom. But this was a military action with a political objective. Khrushchev must somehow be persuaded to pull back, rather than goaded into retaliation.[3]

Allison continues with his portrait of the meeting: "Sensing that Anderson was not moved by this logic, McNamara returned to the line of detailed questioning. Who would make the first interception? Were Russian-speaking officers on board? How would submarines be dealt with? ... What would he do if a Soviet captain refused to answer questions about his cargo? At that point the Navy man picked up the *Manual of Naval Regulations* and, waving it in McNamara's face, shouted, 'It's all in there.' To which McNamara replied, 'I don't give a damn what John Paul Jones would have done. I want to know what you are going to do, now.' The encounter ended on Anderson's remark: 'Now, Mr. Secretary, if you and your Deputy will go back to your offices, the Navy will run the blockade.'"

The standard operating procedures for a naval blockade may have imposed a much greater risk than Kennedy desired. This is where it is important to realize that the crisis was not a two-person game; neither the United States nor the Soviet Union was one individual player. The fact that Kennedy's decisions had to be carried out by parties with their own procedures (and sometimes their own agenda) provided a method for Kennedy to credibly commit to taking some of the control out of his hands. The ways in which a bureaucracy takes on a life of its own, the difficulty of stopping momentum, and the conflicting goals within an organization were some of the underlying ways in which Kennedy could threaten to start a process that he could not guarantee to stop.

3. THE CONTROL OF RISK

If you are trying to extract some exclusive information from
someone, your threat to kill him unless he reveals the secret
will not be credible. He knows that when the time comes,
you will realize that the secret dies with him, and will have
no incentive to carry out the threat. Hollywood films provide
two excellent illustrations of this problem, and of how to deal
with it. Schelling uses a scene from the film *High Wind in
Jamaica*.[4] "The pirate captain Chavez wants his captive to tell
where the money is hidden, and puts his knife to the man's
throat to make him talk. After a moment or two, during which
the man keeps his mouth shut, the mate laughs. 'If you cut his
throat he can't tell you. He knows it. And he knows you know
it.' Chavez puts his knife away and tries something else."

Chavez might have kept the knife out and tried brinkmanship, if only he had seen *The Maltese Falcon*. There Spade
(Humphrey Bogart) has hidden the valuable bird, and Gutman (Sydney Greenstreet) is trying to find out where it is.

Spade smiled at the Levantine and answered him evenly: "You
want the bird. I've got it. ... If you kill me how are you going to get
the bird? If I know that you can't afford to kill me till you have it,
how are you going to scare me into giving it to you?"

In response, Gutman explains how he intends to make his
threat credible.

"I see what you mean." Gutman chuckled. "That is an attitude, sir,
that calls for the most delicate judgement on both sides, because as
you know, sir, men are likely to forget in the heat of the action where
their best interest lies and let their emotions carry them away."[5]

Gutman concedes that he can't threaten Spade with certain
death. Instead, he can expose Spade to a risk, a probability
that things might get out of control in the heat of the moment.
The outcome is left to chance. It's not that Gutman would

actually want to kill Spade, but accidents do occur. And death is irreversible. Gutman cannot commit to killing Spade for sure if Spade refuses to talk. But he can threaten to put Spade in a position in which Gutman cannot guarantee that he will be able to prevent Spade from getting killed.* This ability to expose someone to a probability of punishment can be enough to make the threat effective if the punishment is bad enough.

The greater the risk of Spade getting killed in this way, the more effective the threat. But at the same time, the risk becomes less tolerable to Gutman, and therefore the threat becomes less credible. Gutman's brinkmanship will work if, and only if, there is an intermediate range of probabilities where the risk is large enough to compel Spade to reveal the bird's location, and yet small enough to be acceptable to Gutman. Such a range exists only if Spade values his own life more than Gutman values the bird, in the sense that the probability of death that will frighten Spade into talking is smaller than the risk of losing his information that gives Gutman pause. Brinkmanship is not just the creation of risk, but a careful control of the degree of that risk.

Now we have a problem. Many of the mechanisms that generate risk also prevent a sufficiently accurate control of the degree of that risk. We saw how Kennedy could use internal politics and standard operating procedures to ensure that the situation would get somewhat outside his control, and therefore not affected by Kennedy's temptation to back down. But those very things make it difficult for him to ensure that the risk does not climb to a degree that is intolerable to the United States. Kennedy's own estimate of the risk — between one out of three and even — is a wide range of risk, to the point where one worries if the risk is being controlled at all. We have no perfect or generally valid answer to this dilemma. Brinkman-

---

* This can be viewed as the strategic rationality of an irrational act, another device we discussed in Chapter 6. But here it is the probability, not the certainty, of an irrational act that is the crucial feature.

ship is often an effective device, but equally often it remains
something of an adventure.

4. Getting Off the Brink

There is a final aspect of control that is essential for effective brinkmanship. The threatened party must be able to reduce the risk sufficiently, often all the way to zero, by agreeing to the brinkman's terms. Spade must have the assurance
that Gutman's temper will cool down sufficiently quickly once
he knows the secret, and Khrushchev must be sure that the
United States forces will withdraw as soon as he complies.
Otherwise you are damned if you do and damned if you don't,
and there is no incentive to comply.

The conduct of America's trade policy illustrates brinkmanship without the control mechanism. The United States trade
administration tries to compel the Japanese and the Koreans
to open their markets to American exports (and also to export
less to the United States) by pointing out the risk of more serious protectionist actions by the Congress. "If we can't reach a
moderate agreement, the Congress will enact restrictions that
will be a lot worse for you." The so-called voluntary export restraints on automobiles agreed to by Japan in 1981 were the
result of just such a process. The problem with the regular
use of such tactics in trade negotiations is that they can create
risk, but cannot control it within the requisite range. When
other issues are occupying the legislators' attention, the risk
of protectionist action by Congress is too low to be an effective
threat. On the other hand, when the Congress is exercised
about trade deficits, the risk is either too high to be acceptable to our own administration, or simply unresponsive to a
modest foreign restraint and therefore an ineffective threat.
In other words, the American system of checks and balances
can create risk, but cannot control it effectively.

5. FALLING OFF THE BRINK

With any exercise of brinkmanship, there is always the danger of falling off the brink. While strategists look back at the Cuban missile crisis as a successful use of brinkmanship, our evaluation would be very different if the risk of a superpower war had turned into a reality.[6] The survivors would have cursed Kennedy for recklessly and unnecessarily flaming a crisis into a conflagration. Yet in an exercise of brinkmanship, the risk of falling off the brink will sometimes turn into a reality. The massacre of the Chinese students in June 1989 is a sad example. The students occupying Beijing's Tiananmen Square were on a collision course with the hard-liners in their government. One side would have to lose; either the hard-liners would cede power to more reform-minded leaders or the students would compromise on their demands. During the confrontation, there was a continual risk that the hard-liners would overreact and use force to squelch the democracy movement. When two sides are playing a game of brinkmanship and neither side is backing down, there is a chance that the situation will get out of control, with tragic consequences.

In the aftermath of Tiananmen Square, government leaders became more aware of the dangers in brinkmanship — for both sides. Faced with similar democracy protests in East Germany and Czechoslovakia, the communist leaders decided to give in to popular demands. In Romania, the government tried to hold firm against a reform movement, using violent repression to maintain power. The violence escalated almost to the level of a civil war, and in the end President Nicolae Ceausescu was executed for crimes against his people.

6. NUCLEAR BRINKMANSHIP

Let us put some of these ideas together and look at how the United States has used nuclear brinkmanship as an effective deterrent. Now that the cold war is over and the arms race is winding down, we can examine nuclear brinkmanship in a cool analytical way that was hard to achieve earlier. Many argue that there is a paradox in nuclear weapons because they pose too big a threat ever to use. If their use cannot be rational, then the threat cannot be rational either. This is just the Gutman-Spade exchange writ large. Without the threat value, nuclear weapons are impotent in deterring minor conflicts.

This is why the Europeans feared that NATO's nuclear umbrella might prove a poor shield against the rain of superior Soviet conventional forces. Even if the United States is resolved to defend Europe, the argument went, the threat of nuclear response is not credible against small Soviet transgressions. The Soviets can exploit this using "salami tactics," a slice at a time. Imagine that there are riots in West Berlin and some fires. East German fire brigades come to help. Does the U.S. president press the nuclear button? Of course not. East German police arrive in support. The button? No. They stay, and a few days later are replaced by East German troops. At each point, the incremental aggression is too small to merit a drastic response. NATO keeps on redrawing the line of its tolerance. Eventually, the Soviets could be at Trafalgar Square, and NATO headquarters in exile would be wondering just when it was that they missed their chance.[7]

This conclusion was mistaken. The threat of a U.S. nuclear response to conventional Soviet aggression in Europe was one of brinkmanship. There are two ways for getting around the problem of redrawing the line. Brinkmanship uses both. First, you arrange to take the control for punishment out of your hands so as to deny yourself the opportunity to redraw the line. Second, you transform the precipice into a slippery slope. With each step further down the slope there is the risk of losing control and falling into the abyss. In this way, an opponent who tries to avoid your threat through salami tactics finds himself constantly exposed to a small chance of disaster. Each slice he takes, no matter how small, *may* be the proverbial last straw. *The essential ingredient in making this type of threat credible is that neither you nor your rival knows just where the breaking point lies.*

A small risk of disaster can have the same threat value as the certainty of a smaller punishment. The United States has used the nuclear threat by creating a risk that the missiles will fly even though at that time the government will be trying as hard as it can to prevent the attack. The United States's threat would be carried out only in spite of itself. The threat of nuclear weaponry is that it will be used inadvertently. Nuclear deterrence becomes credible when there exists the possibility for any conventional conflict to escalate out of control. The threat is not a certainty but rather a probability of mutual destruction.

As a conflict escalates, the probability of a chain of events leading to a nuclear confrontation increases. Eventually the probability of war will be sufficiently high that one side will want to back down. But the wheels of war set in motion have a momentum all their own, and the concessions may come too late. Unanticipated, inadvertent, perhaps accidental or irrational actions beyond the leaders' control will provide the path of escalation to nuclear weapons. M.I.T. political science professor Barry Posen put this well:

> Escalation has generally been conceived of as either a rational policy choice, in which the leadership decides to preempt or to escalate in the face of a conventional defeat, or as an accident, the result of a mechanical failure, unauthorized use, or insanity. But escalation arising out of the normal conduct of intense conventional conflict falls between these two categories: it is neither a purposeful act of policy nor an accident. What might be called "inadvertent escalation" is rather the *unintended* consequence of a decision to fight a *conventional* war.[8]

Nuclear deterrence involves a fundamental trade-off. There

is a value in being able to make the threat of mutual destruction. The nuclear age has enjoyed forty years without a world war. But there is a cost in leaving our fate to chance. Nuclear deterrence requires accepting some risk of mutual destruction. Much of the debate about nuclear deterrence centers on this risk. What can we do to lower the probability of nuclear war without losing the value of deterrence?

The trick, as usual, is to keep such generalized risk within the bounds of effectiveness and acceptability. In this chapter we have given some pointers to how this can be done, but ultimately successful brinkmanship remains something of an art and an adventure.

7. CASE STUDY #8:
BRINKMANSHIP IN THE ATLANTIC

"At the outbreak of war, the Navy would move aggressively into the Norwegian Sea, first with submarines and then with several aircraft carriers. They would roll back the Soviet fleet, and attack its home base stations, striking ports and any bastions within reach of the carriers' attack planes." — John Lehman, U.S. Navy Secretary (1981–87)

"To threaten Soviet nuclear missile submarines is to wage nuclear war. It is very escalatory." — Barry Posen, Professor of Political Science, MIT [9]

Posen argues that the U.S. Navy is following a very dangerous and escalatory policy in the Atlantic. In the event of any conventional conflict with the U.S.S.R., the U.S. Navy will attempt to sink all Soviet subs in the Atlantic. The problem with this strategy is that, at present, the United States cannot distinguish nuclear from nonnuclear armed submarines. Hence there is the risk the United States will cross the nuclear threshold unknowingly by inadvertently sinking a Soviet submarine with nuclear weapons. At that point the Soviets will feel justified in attacking American nuclear weapons, and we will be one step too close to an all-out exchange.

Secretary of the Navy John Lehman defends the policy just as vigorously as Posen attacks it. He recognizes the increased chance that a conventional war would escalate into a nuclear conflict. But he reasons that the Soviets should recognize this too! The increased chance of escalation was justified because it would decrease the chance of a conventional conflict in the first place.

On which side of the fence does brinkmanship lie?

Case Discussion

Our understanding of brinkmanship is unlikely to please either side. When the goal is to prevent a nuclear war, the policy should not have any effect. The increased chance of a conventional conflict escalating should be *exactly* offset by a decrease in the probability of initiating a conventional conflict.

An analogy might prove helpful. Suppose we try to make dueling safer by reducing the accuracy of the pistols. The likely outcome is that the adversaries will come closer to one another before firing. Suppose that the adversaries are equally good shots, and that killing the other person earns the reward of 1, and that being killed incurs the penalty of -1. Then the optimal strategy is for the two to keep on approaching each other, and fire the moment the probability of hitting reaches 1/2. The probability of a fatal hit is the same (3/4) irrespective of the accuracy of the pistols. A change in the rules need not affect the outcome; all the players can adjust their strategies to offset it.

To deter the Soviets from initiating a conventional attack, the United States must expose them to some risk that the conflict will escalate to a nuclear exchange. If the risk along one route grows larger, then the Soviets will advance down

that route more slowly. And the Americans will be more likely
(as will the Soviets) to offer a concession, knowing that both
countries face this bigger risk.

Both the Americans and the Soviets should evaluate their
strategies by their consequences, not the actions per se. For
another helpful way to think about this, imagine that the two
parties are engaged in an auction. Instead of bidding dollars or
rubles, they are bidding probabilities of disaster. At some point
the bidding gets too rich. One side decides to back down rather
than escalate to a twenty-three percent chance of mutual loss.
But it may have waited too long, and the probability of a loss
could already have turned into the bad outcome.

In a conflict between the United States and the Soviet
Union, the bids are the probability that the conflict will escalate. How the two sides communicate their bids depends
critically on the rules of the game. But changing the rules
alone cannot make brinkmanship a safer game to play. If the
United States were to change its policy in the Atlantic, the
Soviets could simply adjust their bidding strategy to restore
the same pressure on the United States. In a safer world, the
countries can take more escalatory steps. When the threat is
a probability, the Soviets can always adjust their actions so as
to keep the probability the same.

This conclusion does not mean that you should give up and
be resigned to the risk of nuclear war. To reduce the risks, you
have to attack the problem at a more fundamental level — the
game must be changed. Were French and German aristocrats
to have used less accurate dueling pistols, that would not have
helped them to live longer. Rather, they would have to have
changed the honor code that initiated a duel at the drop of
a glove. As the United States and the Soviet Union begin to
share the same objectives, that changes the game, not just the
rules.

9

Cooperation and Coordination

"It is not from the benevolence of the butcher, the brewer or the baker that we expect our dinner, but from their regard to their own self interest.... [Every individual] intends only his own security, only his own gain. And he is in this led by an invisible hand to promote an end which was no part of his intention. By pursuing his own interest, he frequently promotes that of society more effectually than when he really intends to promote it."

Adam Smith wrote this in 1776 in *The Wealth of Nations*. Ever since, these words have been music to the ears of free-market advocates. The efficiency of the economic marketplace is then interpreted to suggest that a government should not interfere with individuals' selfish attempts to maximize their interests. Some free-marketers are inclined to take this idea beyond the economic realm and like Dr. Pangloss in *Candide* claim that "everything is for the best in this, the best of all possible worlds."

The sad reality is that Adam Smith's invisible hand has a relatively small span. There is no general presumption that when every person pursues his own interest, the outcome will be the best of all possible worlds. Even in the narrower sphere of economic affairs, there are important caveats and exceptions to the rule of the invisible hand.

Game theory provides a natural way to think about social interactions of individuals. Every person has his own aims and strategies; we bring them together and examine the equilibrium of the game in which these strategies interact. Remember that there is no presumption that an equilibrium must be good; we have to find out in each situation whether the outcome is a war of each against all, or the best of all possible worlds, or something between these extremes.

Why did Adam Smith think the invisible hand would produce good economic results for society? Very briefly, his argument went as follows. When I buy a loaf of bread, I am using up some socially valuable resources — the wheat, the fuel, the services of the oven, the labor, and so on — that go into making the loaf. What stops me from over-using these resources is the price of the loaf. I will buy the loaf only if its value to me exceeds the price I have to pay. In a well-functioning market the price equals the cost of all these resources — the baker will not sell me the loaf unless the price covers all his costs, and competition will preclude his charging me a higher price. Thus I will buy the loaf only if its value to me exceeds the cost of the resources to the rest of society. The market mechanism, therefore, controls my desire to buy more bread to just the right extent. It is as if the price were a "fine" I had to pay to compensate the rest of society for using up its resources. On the other side of the picture, the baker, representing the rest of society, is compensated for his costs in supplying the bread that I value, and therefore has just the right incentive to produce it.

The simplicity, the clarity, we daresay the beauty of this argument explain its appeal. In fact the clarity carries with it an equally clear message about its limitations. The invisible hand at best applies only to situations in which everything has a price. In many instances outside of economics, and even in many within, people are not charged a fine for doing harm to the rest of society, nor given a reward for doing good to someone else. For example, manufacturers are rarely charged an adequate price for using up clean air, nor compensated for training a worker who might then quit and find other employment. Here pollution is an unpriced good (actually a bad), and the problem is that there is no economic incentive to temper the firm's selfish interest in supplying a large amount of pollution. When a firm trains a worker, this good is not traded on a market, so there is no price to guide the firm's action; the firm must equate its own costs with benefits and cannot capture the willingness of others to pay for this service. In the prisoners' dilemma, when one prisoner confesses, he harms his colleague but is not fined. Because many unpriced or non-marketed activities matter, it is no wonder that individuals acting selfishly often do too much harm to others, and too little good.

Within this broad theme, the failures of the invisible hand can occur in many ways. Everyone might do the individually best thing, but this ends up worst from their collective viewpoint, as in the prisoners' dilemma. Too many people might do the wrong thing, or everyone might do too much of the wrong thing. Some of these problems are amenable to social policies; others, less so. The sections in this chapter discuss the different types of failures in turn. For each, we develop one central example, and then show how the same problem arises much more widely and suggest how it may be solved.

1. FOR WHOM THE BELL CURVE TOLLS

In the 1950s the Ivy League colleges were faced with a problem. Each school wanted to produce a winning football team. The colleges found themselves overemphasizing athletics and compromising their academic standards in order to build a championship team. Yet, no matter how often they practiced or how much money they spent, at the end of the season the standings were much as they had been before. The average win/loss record was still 50/50. The inescapable mathematical fact is that for every winner there had to be a loser. All the extra work canceled itself out.

The excitement of college sports depends as much on the closeness and intensity of the competition as on the level of skill. Many fans prefer college basketball and football to the professional versions; while the level of skill is lower, there is often more excitement and intensity to the competition. With this idea in mind, the colleges got smart. They joined together and agreed to limit spring training to one day. Although there were more fumbles, the games were no less exciting. Athletes had more time to concentrate on their studies. Everyone was better off, except some alumni who wanted their alma maters to excel at football and forget about academic work.

Many students would like to have a similar agreement with their fellow students before examinations. When grades are based on a traditional "bell curve," one's relative standing in the class matters more than the absolute level of one's knowledge. It matters not how much you know, only that others know less than you. The way to gain an advantage over the other students is to study more. If they all do so, they all have more knowledge, but the relative standings and therefore the bottom line — the grades — are largely unchanged. If only everyone in the class could agree to limit spring studying to one (preferably rainy) day, they would get the same grades with less effort.

The feature common to these situations is that success is determined by *relative* rather than *absolute* performance. When one participant improves his own ranking, he necessarily worsens everyone else's ranking. But the fact that one's victory requires someone else's defeat does not make the game zero-sum. In a zero-sum game it is not possible to make everyone better off. Here, it is. The scope for gain comes from reducing the inputs. While there might always be the same number of winners and losers, it can be less costly for everyone to play the game.

The source of the problem of why (some) students study too much is that they do not have to pay a price or compensation to the others. Each student's studying is akin to a factory's polluting: it makes it more difficult for all the other students to breathe. Because there is no market in buying and selling studying time, the result is a "rat race": each participant strives too hard, with too little to show for his efforts. But no one team or student is willing to be the only one, or the leader, in reducing the effort. This is just like a prisoners' dilemma with more than two prisoners. Escape from the horns of this dilemma requires an enforceable collective agreement.

As we saw with OPEC and the Ivy League, the trick is to form a cartel to limit competition. The problem for high-school students is that the cartel cannot easily detect cheating. For the collectivity of students, a cheater is one who studies more to sneak an advantage over the others. It is very hard to tell if some are secretly studying until after they have "aced" the test. By then it is too late. In some small towns, high-school students do have a way to enforce "no-studying" cartels. Everyone gets together and cruises Main Street at night. The absence of those home studying is noticed. Punishment can be social ostracism or worse.

To arrange a self-enforcing cartel is difficult. It is all the better if an outsider enforces the collective agreement limiting competition. This is just what happened for cigarette advertising, although not intentionally. In the old days, cigarette companies used to spend money to convince consumers to "walk a mile" for their product or to "fight rather than switch." The different campaigns made advertising agencies rich, but their main purpose was defensive — each company advertised because the others did, too. Then, in 1968, cigarette advertisements were banned from TV by law. The companies thought this restriction would hurt them and fought against it. But, when the smoke cleared, they saw that the ban helped them avoid mutually damaging and costly advertising campaigns and thus improved their profits.

2. THE ROUTE LESS TRAVELED

There are two main ways to commute from Berkeley to San Francisco. One is driving over the Bay Bridge, and the other is taking public transportation, the Bay Area Rapid Transit train called BART. Crossing the bridge is the shortest route, and with no traffic, a car can make the trip in 20 minutes. But that is rarely the case. The bridge has only four lanes and is easily congested.* We suppose that each additional 2,000 cars (per hour) causes a 10 minute delay for everyone on the road. For example, with 2,000 cars the travel time rises to 30 minutes; at 4,000 cars, to 40 minutes.

The BART train makes a number of stops, and one has to walk to the station and wait for the train. It is fair to say that the trip takes closer to 40 minutes along this route, but the train never fights traffic. When train usage rises, they put on more cars, and the commuting time stays roughly constant.

If, during the rush hour, 10,000 commuters want to go from Berkeley to San Francisco, how will the commuters be distributed over the two routes? Each commuter will act selfishly, choosing the route that minimizes his own transportation time. Left to their own devices, 40 percent will drive and 60 percent will take the train. The commuting time will be 40 minutes for everyone. This outcome is the equilibrium of a game.

We can see this result by asking what would happen if the split were different. Suppose only 2,000 drivers took the Bay Bridge. With less congestion, the trip would take less time (30 minutes) along this route. Then some of the 8,000 BART commuters would find out that they could save time by switching, and would do so. Conversely, if there were, say, 8,000 drivers using the Bay Bridge, each spending 60 minutes, some of them would switch to the train for the faster trip it

---

* Sometimes, after earthquakes, it is closed altogether.

provides. But when there are 4,000 drivers on the Bay Bridge and 6,000 on the train, no one can gain by switching: the commuters have reached an equilibrium.

We can show the equilibrium using a simple chart, which is quite similar in spirit to the one in Chapter 4 describing the classroom experiment of the prisoners' dilemma. The line *AB* represents the 10,000 commuters, with the number using the Bay Bridge measured from *A* and the number on the train from *B*. Vertical heights measure travel times. The rising line *DEF* shows how the trip time on the Bay Bridge increases as the number of drivers on it increases. The flat line shows the constant time of 40 minutes for the train. The lines intersect at E, showing that the trip times on the two routes are equal when the number of drivers on the Bay Bridge, namely the length *AC*, is 4,000. This graphic depiction of equilibrium is a very useful tool to describe the equilibrium; we will use it often in this chapter.

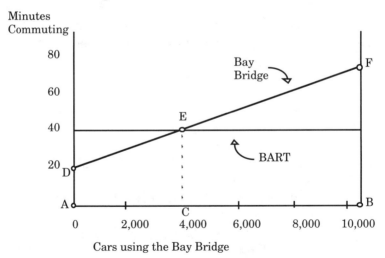

Cars using the Bay Bridge

Is this equilibrium good for the commuters as a whole? Not really. It is easy to find a better pattern. Suppose only 2,000 take the Bay Bridge. Each of them saves 10 minutes. The 2,000 who switch to the train are still spending the same time as they did before, namely 40 minutes. So are the 6,000 who continue to take the train. We have just saved 20,000 person-minutes (or almost two weeks) from the total travel time.

Why is this saving possible? Or in other words, why were the drivers left to themselves not guided by an invisible hand to the best mix of routes? The answer again lies in the cost that each user of the Bay Bridge inflicts on the others. When an extra driver takes this road, the travel time of all the other users goes up by a little bit. But the newcomer is not required to pay a price that reflects this cost. He takes into account only his own travel time.

What traffic pattern is best for the group of drivers as a whole? In fact, the one we constructed, with 2,000 cars on the Bay Bridge and a total time saving of 20,000 minutes, is best. To see this, try a couple of others. If there are 3,000 cars on the Bay Bridge, the travel time is 35 minutes, with a saving of 5 minutes each, or 15,000 minutes in all. With only 1,000 cars, the travel time is 25 minutes, and each saves 15 minutes, but the total saving is again only 15,000 minutes. The intermediate point with 2,000 drivers, each saving 10 minutes, is best.

How can the best pattern be achieved? Devotees of central planning will think of issuing 2,000 licenses to use the Bay Bridge. If they are worried about the inequity of allowing those with licenses to travel in 30 minutes while the other 8,000 must take the train and spend 40 minutes, they will devise an ingenious system of rotating the licenses among the population every month.

A market-based solution charges people for the harm they cause to others. Suppose each person values an hour of time at $12, that is, each would be willing to pay $12 to save an hour. Then charge a toll for driving on the Bay Bridge; set the toll $2 above the BART fare. By our supposition, people regard an extra $2 cost as equivalent to 10 minutes of time. Now the equilibrium commuting pattern will have 2,000 cars on the Bay Bridge and 8,000 riders on BART. Each user of the Bay Bridge spends 30 minutes plus an extra $2 in commuting costs; each BART rider spends 40 minutes. The total effective costs are the same, and no one wants to switch to the other route. In the process we have collected $4,000 of toll revenue (plus an additional 2,000 BART fares), which can then go into the county's budget, thus benefiting everyone because taxes can be lower than they would otherwise be.

A solution even closer to the spirit of free enterprise would be to allow private ownership of the Bay Bridge. The owner realizes that people are willing to pay for the advantage of a faster trip on a less congested road. He charges a price, therefore, for the privilege. How can he maximize his revenue? By maximizing the total value of the time saved, of course.

The invisible hand guides people to an optimal commuting pattern only when the good "commuting time" is priced. With the profit-maximizing toll on the bridge, time really is money. Those commuters who ride BART are selling time to those who use the bridge.

Finally, we recognize that the cost of collecting the toll sometimes exceeds the resulting benefit of saving people's time. Creating a marketplace is not a free lunch. The toll booths may be a primary cause of the congestion. If so, it may be best to tolerate the initial inefficient route choices.

3. CATCH-22?

Chapter 3 offered the first examples of games with many equilibria. Conventions for driving on one side of the road or who should return disconnected phone calls were the two cases. In those examples it was not important which of the conventions was chosen, so long as everyone agreed on the same convention. But sometimes one convention is much better than another. Even so, that doesn't mean it will always get adopted. If one convention has become established and then some change in circumstances makes another one more desirable, it is especially hard to bring about the change.

The keyboard design on most typewriters is a case in point. In the late 1800s, there was no standard pattern for the arrangement of letters on the typewriter keyboard. Then in 1873 Christopher Scholes helped design a "new improved" layout. The layout became known as QWERTY, after the letter arrangement of the six letters in the top left row. QWERTY was chosen to *maximize* the distance between the most frequently used letters. This was a good solution in its day; it deliberately slowed down the typist, and reduced the jamming of keys on manual typewriters. By 1904, the Remington Sewing Machine Company of New York was mass-producing typewriters with this layout, and it became the de facto industry standard. But with today's electric typewriters and word processors, this jamming problem is now completely irrelevant. Engineers have developed new keyboard layouts, such as DSK (Dvorak's Simplified Keyboard), which reduce the distance typists' fingers travel by over fifty percent. The same material can be typed in 5–10 percent less time using DSK than QWERTY.[1] But QWERTY is the established system. Almost all typewriters use it, so we all learn it and are reluctant to learn a second keyboard. Typewriter and keyboard manufacturers continue, therefore, with QWERTY. The vicious circle is complete.[2]

If history had worked differently, and if the DSK standard had been adopted from the outset, that would have been better for today's technology. However, given where we are, the question of whether or not we should switch standards involves a further consideration. There is a lot of inertia, in the form of machines, keyboards, and trained typists, behind QWERTY. Is it worthwhile to retool?

From the point of view of society as a whole, the answer would seem to be yes. During the Second World War, the U.S. Navy used DSK typewriters on a large scale, and retrained typists to use them. It found that the cost of retraining could be fully recouped in only ten days of use.

Would private employers do the retraining? They might if they knew it was cost-effective. Discovering the information about the efficacy of DSK is a costly endeavor. No wonder that few private employers are willing to perform this service, and it took someone as large as the U.S. Navy to try it first.

As mechanical typewriters are replaced by electronic ones and by computer keyboards, even the existing stock of QWERTY keyboards is a less significant barrier to change; the keys can be reassigned by changing just one chip or rewriting some software. However, it has proved impossible to get out of the vicious circle. No individual user would want to bear the cost of changing the social convention. Uncoordinated decisions of individuals keep us tied to QWERTY.

The problem is called a bandwagon effect and can be illustrated using the following chart. On the horizontal axis we show the fraction of typists using QWERTY. The vertical axis details the chance that a new typist will learn QWERTY as opposed to DSK. As drawn, if 85 percent of typists are using QWERTY, then the chances are 95 percent that a new typist will choose to learn QWERTY and only 5 percent that the new typist will learn DSK. The way the curve is drawn is meant to emphasize the superiority of the DSK layout. A majority of new typists will learn DSK rather than QWERTY provided that QWERTY has anything less than a 70 percent market share. In spite of this handicap, it is possible for QWERTY to dominate in equilibrium.

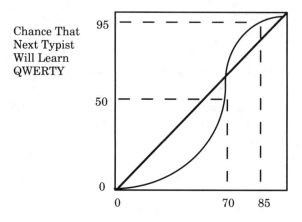

Percentage of Typists using QWERTY

The choice of which keyboard to use is a strategy. When the fraction using each technology is constant over time, we are at an equilibrium of the game. Showing that this game converges to an equilibrium is not easy. The random choice of each new typist is constantly disrupting the system. Recent high-powered mathematical tools, namely stochastic approximation theory, have allowed economists and statisticians to prove that this dynamic game does converge to an equilibrium.[3] We now describe the possible outcomes.

If the fraction of typists using QWERTY exceeds 72 percent, there is the expectation that an even greater fraction of people will learn QWERTY. The span of QWERTY expands until it reaches 98 percent. At that point, the fraction of new typists learning QWERTY just equals its predominance in the population, 98 percent, and so there is no more upward pressure.*

---

* If the number of typists using QWERTY is above 98 percent, the number is expected to fall back to 98 percent. There will always be a small number, somewhere up to 2 percent, of new typists who will choose to learn DSK because they are interested in the superior technology and are not concerned with the compatibility issue.

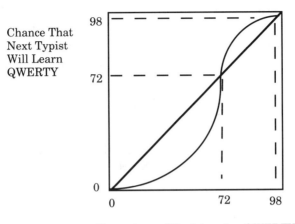

Percentage of Typists using QWERTY

Conversely, if the fraction of typists using QWERTY falls below 72 percent, then there is the expectation that DSK will take over. Fewer than 72 percent of the new typists learn QWERTY, and the subsequent fall in its usage gives new typists an even greater incentive to learn the superior layout of DSK. Once all typists are using DSK there is no reason for a new typist to learn QWERTY, and QWERTY will die out altogether.

The mathematics says only that we will end up at one of these two possible outcomes: everyone using DSK or 98 percent using QWERTY. It does not say which will occur. If we were starting from scratch, the odds are in favor of DSK being the predominant keyboard layout. But we are not. History matters. The historical accident that led to QWERTY capturing nearly 100 percent of typists ends up being self-perpetuating, even though the original motivation for QWERTY is long since obsolete.

Since bad luck or the convergence to an inferior equilibrium is self-perpetuating, there is the possibility of making everyone better off. But it requires coordinated action. If the major computer manufacturers coordinate on a new keyboard layout or a major employer such as the federal government trains its employees on a new keyboard, this can switch the equilibrium all the way from one extreme to the other. The essential point is that it is not necessary to convert everyone, just a critical mass. Given enough of a toehold, the better technology can take it from there.

The QWERTY problem is but one minor example of a more widespread problem. Our preference for gasoline engines over steam and light-water nuclear reactors over gas-cooled is better explained by historical accidents than by the superiority of the adopted technologies. Brian Arthur, an economist at Stanford and one of the developers of the mathematical tools used to study bandwagon effects, tells the story of how we ended up with gasoline-powered cars.[4]

In 1890 there were three ways to power automobiles — steam, gasoline, and electricity — and of these one was patently *inferior* to the other two: gasoline. ... [A turning point for gasoline was] an 1895 horseless carriage competition sponsored by the Chicago *Times-Herald*. This was won by a gasoline-powered Duryea — one of only two cars to finish out of six starters — and has been cited as the possible inspiration for R. E. Olds to patent in 1896 a gasoline power source, which he subsequently mass-produced in the "Curved-Dash Olds." Gasoline thus overcame its slow start. Steam continued viable as an automotive power source until 1914, when there was an outbreak of hoof-and-mouth disease in North America. This led to the withdrawal of horse troughs — which is where steam cars could fill with water. It took the Stanley brothers about three years to develop a condenser and boiler system that did not need to be filled every thirty or forty miles. But by then it was too late. The steam engine never recovered.

While there is little doubt that today's gasoline technology is better than steam, that's not the right comparison. How good would steam have been if it had had the benefit of seventy-five years of research and development? While we may never know, some engineers believe that steam was the better bet.[5]

In the United States, almost all nuclear power is generated by light-water reactors. Yet there are reasons to believe that the alternative technologies of heavy-water or gas-cooled reactors would have been superior, especially given the same amount of learning and experience. Canada's experience with heavy-water reactors allows them to generate power for 25 percent less cost than light-water reactors of equivalent size in the United States. Heavy-water reactors can operate without the need to reprocess fuel. Perhaps most important is the safety comparison. Both heavy-water and gas-cooled reactors have a significantly lower risk of a meltdown — heavy water because the high pressure is distributed over many tubes rather than a single core vessel, and gas-cooled because of the much slower temperature rise in the event of a coolant loss.[6]

The question of how light-water reactors came to dominate has recently been studied by Robin Cowen, in a 1987 Stanford University Ph.D. thesis. The first consumer for nuclear power was the U.S. Navy. In 1949, then Captain Rickover made the pragmatic choice in favor of light-water reactors. He had two good reasons. It was then the most compact technology, an important consideration for submarines, and it was the furthest advanced, suggesting that it would have the quickest route to implementation. In 1954, the first nuclear-powered submarine, *Nautilus*, was launched. The results looked very positive.

At the same time civilian nuclear power became a high priority. The Soviets had exploded their first nuclear bomb in 1949. In response, Atomic Energy Commissioner T. Murray warned, "Once we become fully conscious of the possibility that [energy-poor] nations will gravitate towards the USSR if it wins the nuclear power race, it will be quite clear that this race is no Everest-climbing, kudos-providing contest."[7] General Electric and Westinghouse, with their experience producing light-water reactors for the nuclear-powered submarines, were the natural choice to develop civilian power stations. Considerations of proven reliability and speed of implementation took precedence over finding the most cost-effective and safest technology. Although light-water was first chosen as an interim technology, this gave it enough of a head start down the learning curve that the other options have never had the chance to catch up.

The adoption of QWERTY, gasoline engines, and light-water reactors are but three demonstrations of how history matters in determining today's technology choices. But the historical reasons may be irrelevant considerations in the present. Typewriter-key jamming, hoof-and-mouth disease, and submarine space constraints are not relevant to today's trade-offs between the competing technologies. The important insight from game theory is to recognize early on the potential for future lock-in — once one option has enough of a head start, superior technological alternatives may never get the chance to develop. Thus there is a potentially great payoff in the early stages from spending more time figuring out not only what technology meets today's constraints, but also what options will be the best for the future.

4. FASTER THAN A SPEEDING TICKET

Just how fast should you drive? In particular, should you abide by the speed limit? Again the answer is found by looking at the game where your decision interacts with those of all the other drivers.

If nobody is abiding by the law, then you have two reasons to break it too. First, some experts argue that it is actually safer to drive at the same speed as the flow of traffic.[8] On most highways, anyone who tries to drive at fifty-five miles per hour creates a dangerous obstacle that everyone else must go around. Second, when you tag along with the other speeders, your chances of getting caught are almost zero. The police simply cannot pull over more than a small percentage of the speeding cars. As long as you go with the flow of traffic, there is safety in numbers.

As more people become law-abiding, both reasons to speed vanish. It becomes more dangerous to speed, since this will require weaving in and out of traffic. And your chances of getting caught increase dramatically.

We show this in a chart similar to the one for commuters from Berkeley to San Francisco. The horizontal line measures the percentage of drivers who abide by the speed limit. The lines *A* and *B* show each driver's calculation of his benefit from (*A*) abiding by and (*B*) breaking the law. Our argument says that if no one else is keeping under the limit (the left-hand end), neither should you (line *B* is higher than line *A*); if everyone else is law-abiding (the right-hand end), you should be too (line *A* is higher than line *B*). Once again there are three equilibria, of which only the extreme ones can arise from the process of social dynamics as drivers adjust to one another's behavior.

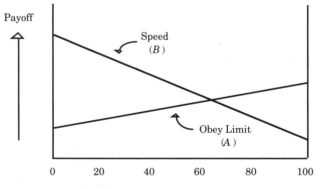

Percent of Drivers Obeying Speed Limit

In the case of the commuters choosing between the two roads, the dynamics converged on the equilibrium in the middle. Here the tendency is toward one of the extremes. The difference arises because of the way interactions work. With commuting, either choice becomes *less* attractive when more of the others follow you, whereas with speeding, additional company makes it *more* attractive.

The general theme of one person's decision affecting the others applies here, too. If one driver speeds up, he makes it a little safer for the others to speed. If no one is speeding, no one is willing to be the first to do so and provide this "benefit" to the others without being "rewarded" for doing so. But there is a new twist: if everyone is speeding, then no one wants to be the only one to slow down.

Can this situation be affected by changing the speed limit? The curves are drawn for a specific speed limit, say 55 m.p.h. Suppose the limit is raised to 65. The value of breaking the limit falls, since beyond a point, higher speeds do become dangerous, and the extra advantage of going 75 instead of 65 is less than the gain of going 65 over 55. Furthermore, above 55 miles an hour, gasoline consumption goes up exponentially with speed. It may be twenty percent more expensive to drive at 65 than at 55, but it could easily be 40 percent more expensive to drive at 75 rather than at 65.

What can lawmakers learn from this if they want to encourage people to drive at the speed limit? It is not necessary to set the speed limit so high that everyone is happy to obey it. The key is to get a critical mass of drivers obeying the speed limit. Thus a short phase of extremely strict enforcement and harsh penalties can change the behavior of enough drivers to generate the momentum toward full compliance. The equilibrium moves from one extreme (where everyone speeds) to the other (where everyone complies). With the new equilibrium, the police can cut back on enforcement, and the compliance behavior is self-sustaining. More generally, what this suggests is that short but intense enforcement can be significantly more effective than the same total effort applied at a more moderate level for a longer time.[9]

5. WHY DID THEY LEAVE?

American cities have few racially integrated neighborhoods. If the proportion of black residents in an area rises above a critical level, it quickly increases further to nearly one hundred percent. If it falls below a critical level, the expected course is for the neighborhood to become all white. Preservation of racial balance requires some ingenious public policies.

Is the de facto segregation of most neighborhoods the product of widespread racism? These days, a large majority of urban Americans would regard mixed neighborhoods as desirable.* The more likely difficulty is that segregation can result as the equilibrium of a game in which each household chooses where to live, even when they all have a measure of racial tolerance. This idea is due to Thomas Schelling.[10] We shall now outline it, and show how it explains the success of the Chicago suburb, Oak Park, in maintaining an integrated neighborhood.

Racial tolerance is not a matter of black or white; there are shades of gray. Different people, black or white, have different views about the best racial mix. For example, very few whites insist on a neighborhood that is 99 or even 95 percent white; yet most will feel out of place in one that is only 1 or 5 percent white. The majority would be happy with a mix somewhere in between.

We can illustrate the evolution of neighborhood dynamics using a chart similar to the one from the QWERTY story. On the vertical axis is the probability that a new person moving into the neighborhood will be white. This is plotted in relationship to the current racial mix. The top right end of the curve shows that once a neighborhood becomes completely segregated, all white, the odds are overwhelming that the next person who moves into the neighborhood will also be white. If

---

* Of course the fact that people have *any* preferences about the racial mix of their neighbors is a form of racism, albeit a less extreme one than total intolerance.

the current mix falls to 95 percent or 90 percent white, the odds are still very high that the next person to move in will also be white. If the mix changes much further, then there is a sharp drop-off in the probability that the next person to join the community will be white; the curve is steep in its middle region. Finally, as the actual percentage of whites drops to zero, so that the neighborhood is now segregated at the other extreme, the probability is very high that the next person to move in will be black.

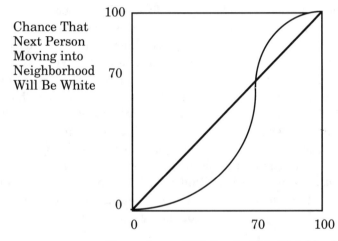

Percentage of Whites in This Neighborhood

In this situation, the equilibrium will be where the racial mix of the population just exactly equals the mix of new entrants to the community. Only in this event are the dynamics stable. There are three such equilibria: two at the extremes where the neighborhood is all white and all black, and one in the middle where there is a mix. The theory so far does not tell us which of the three equilibria is the most likely. In order to answer this question, we need to examine the forces that move the system toward or away from an equilibrium, that is, the social dynamics of the situation.

The social dynamics will always drive the neighborhood to one of the extreme equilibria. Schelling labeled this phenomenon "tipping." Let us see why it occurs.

Suppose the middle equilibrium has 70 percent whites and 30 percent blacks. By chance, let one black family move out and be replaced by a white family. Then the proportion of whites in this neighborhood becomes slightly above 70 percent. Looking at the chart, the probability that the next entrant will also be white is then above 70 percent. The upward pressure is reinforced by the new entrants. Say the racial mix shifts to 75:25 percent. The tipping pressure continues. The chance that a new entrant will be white is above 75 percent, so the expectation is that the neighborhood will become increasingly segregated. This goes on until the mix of new entrants is the same as the mix in the neighborhood. As drawn, that occurs again only when the neighborhood is all white. If the process had started with one white family moving out and one black family moving in, there would have been a chain reaction in the opposite direction, and the odds are that the neighborhood would have become all black.

The problem is that the 70:30 percent mix is not a stable equilibrium. If this mix is somehow disrupted, as chance is sure to do, there is a tendency to move toward one of the extremes. Sadly, from the extremes there is no similar tendency to move back toward the middle. Although segregation is the predicted equilibrium, that does not mean that people are better off at this outcome. Everyone might prefer to live in a mixed neighborhood. But they rarely exist, and even when found tend not to last.

Once again, the source of the problem is the effect of one household's action on the others. Starting at a 70:30 percent mix, when one white family replaces a black family, this may make the neighborhood a little less attractive for future blacks to move in. But it is not assessed a fine for this. By analogy with the road tolls, perhaps there should be a departure tax. But that would be counter to a more basic principle, namely the freedom to live where one chooses. If society wants to prevent tipping, it must look for some other policy measures.

If we cannot fine a departing family for the damage it causes, both to those who remain and those who now might choose not to come, we must take measures that will reduce the incentives for others to follow suit. If one white family leaves, the neighborhood should not become less attractive to another white family. If one black family leaves, the neighborhood should not become less attractive to another black family. Public policy can help prevent the tipping process from gathering momentum.

The racially integrated Chicago suburb of Oak Park provides an ingenious example of policies that work. It uses two tools: first, the town bans the use of "For Sale" signs in front yards, and secondly, the town offers insurance that guarantees homeowners that they will not lose the value of their house and property because of a change in the racial mix.

If by chance two houses on the same street are for sale at the same time, "For Sale" signs would spread this news quickly to all neighbors and prospective purchasers. Eliminating such signs makes it possible to conceal the news that would be interpreted as bad; nobody need know until after a house has been sold that it was even up for sale. The result is that panics are avoided (unless they are justified, in which case they are just delayed). By itself, the first policy is not enough. Homeowners might still worry that they should sell their house while the going is good. If you wait until the neighborhood has tipped, you've waited too long and may find that you've lost most of the value of your home, which is a large part of most people's wealth. Once the town provides insurance, this is no longer an issue. In other words, the insurance removes the *economic* fear that accelerates tipping. In fact, if the guarantee succeeds in preventing tipping, property values will not fall and the policy will not cost the taxpayers anything.

Tipping to an all-black equilibrium has been the more common problem in urban America. But in recent years gentrification, which is just tipping to an all-rich equilibrium, has been on the rise. Left unattended, the free market will often head to these unsatisfactory outcomes. But public policy, combined with an awareness of how tipping works, can help stop the momentum toward tipping and preserve the delicate balances.

6. IT CAN BE LONELY AT THE TOP

Top law firms generally choose their partners from among their junior associates. Those not chosen must leave the firm, and generally move to a lower-ranked one. At the mythical firm Justin-Case, the standards were so high that for many years no new partners were selected. The junior associates protested about this lack of advancement. The partners responded with a new system that looked very democratic.

Here is what they did. At the time of the annual partnership decision, the abilities of the ten junior associates were rated from 1 to 10, with 10 being the best. The junior associates were told their rating privately. Then they were ushered into a meeting room where they were to decide by majority vote the cutoff level for partnership.

They all agreed that everyone making partner was a good idea and certainly preferable to the old days when nobody made partner. So they began with a cutoff of 1. Then some high-rated junior associate suggested that they raise the cutoff to 2. He argued that this would improve the average quality of the partnership. Nine junior associates agreed. The sole dissenting vote came from the least able member, who would no longer make partner.

Next, someone proposed that they raise the standard from

2 to 3. Eight people were still above this standard, and they all voted for this improvement in the quality of the partnership. The person ranked 2 voted against, as this move deprived him of partnership. What was surprising was that the lowest-rated junior associate was in favor of this raising of the standards. In neither case would he make partner. But at least in the latter he would be grouped with someone who has ability 2. Therefore, upon seeing that he was not selected, other law firms would not be able to infer his exact ability. They would guess that he is either a 1 or a 2, a level of uncertainty that is to his advantage. The proposal to raise the standard to 3 passed 9:1.

With each new cutoff level someone proposed raising it by one. All those strictly above voted in favor so as to raise the quality of the partnership (without sacrificing their own position), while all those strictly below joined in support of raising the standard so as to make their failure less consequential. Each time there was only one dissenter, the associate right at the cutoff level who would no longer make partner. But he was outvoted 9:1.

And so it went, until the standard was raised all the way up to 10. Finally, someone proposed that they raise the standard to 11 so that *nobody* would make partner. Everybody rated 9 and below thought that this was a fine proposal, since once more this improved the average quality of those rejected. Outsiders would not take it as a bad sign that they didn't make partner, as nobody makes partner at this law firm. The sole voice against was the most able junior associate, who lost his chance to make partner. But he was outvoted 9:1.

The series of votes brings everybody back to the old system, which they all considered worse than the alternative of promotion for all. Even so, each resolution along the way passed 9:1. There are two morals to this story.

When actions are taken in a piecemeal way, each step of the way can appear attractive to the vast majority of decision-makers. But the end is worse than the beginning for everyone. The reason is that voting ignores the intensity of preferences. In our example, all those in favor gain a very small amount, while the one person against loses a lot. In the series of ten votes, each junior associate has nine small victories and one major loss that outweighs all the combined gains. We saw a similar example in Chapter 1 involving trade tariffs or amendments to the tax reform bill.

Just because an individual recognizes the problem does not mean an individual can stop the process. It is a slippery slope, too dangerous to get onto. The group as a whole must look ahead and reason back in a coordinated way, and set up the rules so as to prevent taking the first steps on the slope. There is safety when individuals agree to consider reforms only as a package rather than as a series of small steps. With a package deal, everyone knows where he will end up. A series of small steps can look attractive at first, but one unfavorable move can more than wipe out the entire series of gains.

In 1989, Congress learned this danger first-hand in its failed attempt to vote itself a 50 percent pay raise. Initially, the pay raise seemed to have wide support in both houses. When the public realized what was about to happen, they protested loudly to their representatives. Consequently, each member of Congress had a private incentive to vote against the pay hike, provided he or she thought that the hike would still pass. The best scenario would be to get the higher salary while having protested against it. Unfortunately (for them) too many members of Congress took this approach, and suddenly passage no longer seemed certain. As each defection moved them further down the slippery slope, there was all the more reason to vote against it. If the pay hike were to fail, the worst possible position would be to go on record supporting the salary hike, pay the political price, and yet not get the raise. At first, there was the potential for a few individuals to selfishly improve their own position. But each defection increased the incentive to follow suit, and soon enough the proposal was dead.

There is a second, quite different moral to the Justin-Case story. If you are going to fail, you might as well fail at a difficult task. Failure causes others to downgrade their expectations of you in the future. The seriousness of this problem depends on what you attempt. Failure to climb Mt. Everest is considerably less damning than failure to finish a 10K race. The point is that when other people's perception of your ability matters, it might be better for you to do things that *increase* your chance of failing in order to reduce its consequence. People who apply to Harvard instead of the local college, and ask the most popular student for a prom date instead of a more realistic prospect, are following such strategies.

Psychologists see this behavior in other contexts. Some individuals are afraid to recognize the limits of their own ability. In these cases they take actions that increase the chance of failure in order to avoid facing their ability. For example, a marginal student may not study for a test so that if he fails, the failure can be blamed on his lack of studying rather than intrinsic ability. Although perverse and counterproductive, there is no invisible hand to protect you in games against yourself.

7. POLITICIANS AND APPLE CIDER

Two political parties are trying to choose their positions on the liberal-conservative ideological spectrum. First the challenger takes a stand; then the incumbent responds.

Suppose the voters range uniformly over the spectrum. For concreteness, number the political positions from 0 to 100, where 0 represents radical left and 100 represents arch-conservative. If the challenger chooses a position such as 48, slightly more liberal than the middle of the road, the incumbent will take a position between that and the middle — say, 49. Then voters with preferences of 48 and under will vote for the challenger; all others, making up just over 51 percent of the population, will vote for the incumbent. The incumbent will win.

If the challenger takes a position above 50, then the incumbent will locate between that and 50. Again this will get him more than half the votes.

By the principle of looking ahead and reasoning backward, the challenger can figure out that his best bet is to locate right in the middle.* At this location, the forces pulling for more conservative or more liberal positions have equal numbers. The best the incumbent can do is imitate the challenger. The two parties take identical stands, so each gets fifty percent of the votes if issues are the only thing that counts. The losers in this process are the voters, who get an echo rather than a choice.

In practice, the parties do not take identical hard positions, but each fudges its stand around the middle ground. This phenomenon was first recognized by Columbia University economist Harold Hotelling in 1929. He pointed out similar examples in economic and social affairs: "Our cities become uneconomically large and the business districts within them are too concentrated. Methodist and Presbyterian churches are too much alike; cider is too homogeneous."[11]

Would the excess homogeneity persist if there were three parties? Suppose they take turns to choose and revise their positions, and have no ideological baggage to tie them down. A party located on the outside will edge closer to its neighbor to chip away some of its support. This will squeeze the party in the middle to such an extent that when its turn comes, it

---

* As with highways, the position in the middle of the road is called the median. When voters' preferences are not necessarily uniform, the challenger locates at the position where fifty percent of the voters are located to the left and fifty percent are to the right. This median is not necessarily the average position. The median position is determined by where there are an equal number of voices on each side, while the average gives weight to how far the voices are away.

will want to jump to the outside and acquire a whole new and larger base of voters. This process will then continue, and there will be *no* equilibrium. In practice, parties have enough ideological baggage, and voters have enough party loyalty, to prevent such rapid switches.

In other cases, locations won't be fixed. Consider three people all waiting for a taxi in Manhattan. The one at the most uptown position will catch the first taxi going downtown, and the one located farthest downtown will catch the first uptown cab. The one in the middle is squeezed out. If the middle person isn't willing to wait, he will move to one of the outside positions. Until the taxi arrives, there may not be an equilibrium; no individual is content to remain squeezed in the middle. Here we have yet another, and quite different, failure of an uncoordinated decision process; it may not have a determinate outcome at all. In such a situation, society has to find a different and coordinated way of reaching a stable outcome.

8. THE STOCK MARKET AND BEAUTY CONTESTS

In often quoted lines, John Maynard Keynes compared the stock market to the newspaper beauty contests of his time.

Professional investment may be likened to those newspaper competitions in which competitors have to pick out the six prettiest faces from one hundred photographs, the prize being awarded to the competitor whose choice most nearly corresponds to the average preference of the competitors as a whole; so that each competitor has to pick, not those faces which he himself finds prettiest, but those which he thinks likeliest to catch the fancy of the other competitors, all of whom are looking at the problem from the same point of view. It is not a case of choosing those which, to the best of one's judgment, are really the prettiest, nor even those which average opinion genuinely thinks the prettiest. We have reached the third degree where we devote our intelligences to anticipating what average opinion expects the average opinion to be.[12]

It matters not who the prettiest woman is in truth. What you care about is trying to predict who everyone else will think is the prettiest or who everyone else will think everyone else will think is prettiest ....

When one hears Keynes' comparison of the stock market to a beauty contest, it is essential to emphasize his beauty contest was no ordinary pageant. In an ordinary pageant the most beautiful contestant should win; the judges need not behave strategically. Similarly, in a stock market, one imagines that the stock with the highest earnings should have the highest price. Keynes' great insight was to explain how strategic play could outweigh reality in determining winners in the stock market and newspaper beauty contests.

In the newspaper contest, readers have to put themselves into all the other readers' shoes simultaneously. At this point their choice of a winner has much less to do with any true or absolute standard of beauty than with trying to find some focal point on which expectations converge. If one contestant was significantly more beautiful than all the others, this could provide the necessary focal point. But the reader's job was rarely that easy. Imagine instead that the hundred finalists were practically indistinguishable except for the color of their hair. Of the hundred, only one is a redhead. Would you pick the redhead?

The task of the reader is to figure out the realized convention without the benefit of communication. "Pick the most beautiful" might be the stated rule, but that could be significantly more difficult than picking the skinniest or the redhead, or the one with an interesting gap between her two front teeth. Anything that distinguishes becomes a focal point and allows people's expectations to converge. For this reason, we should not be surprised that many of the world's most beautiful models do not have perfect features; rather, they are almost perfect but have some interesting flaw that gives their look a personality and a focal point.

Investing in the stock market has many of the same properties. A stock price rises when the demand *at the old price* exceeds the supply.* To make money in the market, your goal is to figure out what stocks other people think are going to appreciate. As always, they are making this calculation by putting themselves into everybody's shoes all at once. When this happens, anything goes.

Stock prices can escalate to absurd levels and then come crashing back to reality. The crash of October 1987 is only a bump compared to some of the speculative bubble crashes in history. From 1634 to 1638 the prices of tulip bulbs in Holland shot up several thousand percent and then wilted away even more quickly. The episode is known to this day as the tulip bulb mania.[13]

The point of all this is that equilibrium can easily be determined by whim or fad. There is nothing fundamental that guarantees the most beautiful contestant will be chosen or the best stock will appreciate the fastest. There are some forces that work in the right direction. High forecast earnings are similar to the beauty contestant's complexion — one of the many necessary but by no means sufficient conditions needed to anchor otherwise arbitrary whims and fads.

9. A RECAPITULATION

In this chapter we described many instances in which the games people play have more losers than winners. Uncoor-

---

* The evening news commentary that the stock market fell owing to heavy selling tends to leave out this condition: remember, for every seller there must be a buyer.

dinated choices interact to produce a poor outcome for society. Let us summarize the problems briefly, and you can then try out the ideas on the case study.

First we looked at games in which each person had an either-or choice. One problem was the familiar multi-person prisoners' dilemma: everyone made the same choice, and it was the wrong one. Next we saw examples in which some people made one choice while their colleagues made another, but the proportions were not optimal from the standpoint of the group as a whole. This happened because one of the choices involved greater spillovers, i.e., effects on others, that the choosers failed to take into account. Then we had situations in which either extreme — everyone choosing one thing or everyone choosing the other — was an equilibrium. To choose one, or make sure the right one was chosen, required social conventions, penalties, or restraints on people's behavior. Even then, powerful historical forces might keep the group locked into the wrong equilibrium.

Turning to situations with several alternatives, we saw how the group could voluntarily slide down a slippery path to an outcome it would collectively regret. In other examples, we found a tendency toward excessive homogeneity. Sometimes there might be an equilibrium held together by people's mutually reinforcing expectations about what others think. In still other cases, equilibrium might fail to exist altogether, and another way to reach a stable outcome would have to be found.

The point of these stories is that the free market doesn't always get it right. There are two fundamental problems. One is that history matters. Our greater experience with gasoline engines, QWERTY keyboards, and light-water nuclear reactors may lock us in to continued use of these inferior technologies. Accidents of history cannot necessarily be corrected by today's market. When one looks forward to recognize that lock-in will be a potential problem, this provides a reason for government policy to encourage more diversity before the standard is set.

Or if we seem stuck with an inferior standard, public policy can guide a coordinated change from one standard to another. Moving from measurements in inches and feet to the metric system is one example; coordinating the use of daylight saving time is another.

Inferior standards may be behavioral rather than technological. Examples include an equilibrium in which everyone cheats on his taxes, or drives above the speed limit, or even just arrives at parties an hour after the stated time. The move from one equilibrium to a better one can be most effectively accomplished via a short and intense campaign. The trick is to get a critical mass of people to switch, and then the bandwagon effect makes the new equilibrium self-sustaining. In contrast, a little bit of pressure over a long period of time would not have the same effect.

The other general problem with laissez faire is that so much of what matters in life takes place outside the economic marketplace. Goods ranging from common courtesy to clean air are frequently unpriced, so there is no invisible hand to guide selfish behavior. Sometimes creating a price can solve the problem, as with the congestion problem for the Bay Bridge. Other times, pricing the good changes its nature. For example, donated blood is typically superior to blood that is purchased, because the types of individuals who sell blood for the money are likely to be in a much poorer state of health. The coordination failures illustrated in this chapter are meant to show the role for public policy. But before you get carried away, check the case below.

10. Case Study #9: A Prescription for Allocating Dentists

In this case study, we explore the coordination problem of how the invisible hand allocates (or misallocates) the supply of dentists between cities and rural areas. In many ways the problem will seem closely related to our analysis of whether to drive or take the train from Berkeley to San Francisco. Will the invisible hand guide the right numbers to each place?

It is often argued that there is not so much a shortage of dentists as a problem of misallocation. Just as too many drivers, left to their own resources, would take the Bay Bridge, is it the case that too many dentists choose the city over the countryside? And if so, does that mean society should place a toll on those who want to practice city dentistry?

For the purposes of this case study, we greatly simplify the dentists' decision problem. Living in the city or in the countryside are considered equally attractive. The choice is based solely on financial considerations — they go where they will earn the most money. Like the commuters between Berkeley and San Francisco, the decision is made selfishly; dentists maximize their individual payoffs.

Since there are many rural areas without enough dentists, this suggests that there is room for an increased number of dentists to practice in rural areas without causing any congestion. Thus rural dentistry is like the train route. At its best, being a rural dentist is not quite as lucrative as having a large city practice, but it is a more certain route to an above-average income. Both the incomes and the value to society of rural dentists stays roughly constant as their numbers grow.

Being a city practitioner is more akin to driving over the Bay Bridge — it is wonderful when you are alone and not so great when the city gets too crowded. The first dentist in an area can be extremely valuable, and maintain a very large practice. But with too many dentists around, there is the potential for congestion and price competition. If the number increases too far, city dentists will be competing for the same patient pool, and their talents will be underutilized. If the population of city dentists grows even further, they may end up earning less than their rural counterparts. In short, as the

number of city practices increases, the value of the marginal
service that they perform falls, as does their income.

We depict this story in a simple chart, again quite similar to
the driving versus train example. Suppose there are 100,000
new dentists choosing between city and rural practices. The
length of the line *AB* represents the 100,000. The number of
new city dentists is the distance to the right of *A*, and the
number of new rural dentists is the distance to the left of *B*.
For example, look at point *C*. As the length *AC* is a quarter of
AB, *C* corresponds to 25,000 new city dentists and 75,000 new
rural dentists.

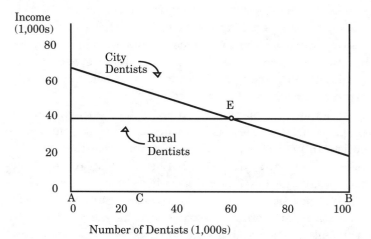

The falling line (city dentists) and the flat line (rural dentists) represent the financial advantages of taking the respec-
tive roads. At point *A*, where everyone chooses rural practices,
city dentists' incomes are above the incomes of those with rural practices. This is reversed at *B*, where everyone chooses
city dentistry.

The equilibrium for career choices is at *E*, where the two
options provide the same financial rewards. To verify this,
suppose that the distribution of career choice results in a point
like *C* to the left of *E*. Since at point *C*, city dentists' incomes

are higher than rural dentists' incomes, we expect that more new dentists should choose city over rural practices. This will move the distribution of city vs. rural to the right of C. The reverse adjustment would take place if we started at a point to the right of E, where city dentists were the lower paid of the two. Only when E is reached will next year's career choices broadly replicate those of this year, and the system will settle down to an equilibrium.

Is this outcome the best for society?

Case Discussion

As in the case of the commuters, the equilibrium does not maximize the combined income of dentists. *But society cares about the consumers of dentistry as well as the practitioners.* In fact, left alone, the market solution at E is the best for society as a whole.

The reason is that there are two side effects created when one more person decides to be a city dentist. The additional city dentist lowers all other dentists' incomes, imposing a cost on the existing city dentists. But this reduction in price is a benefit to consumers. The two side effects exactly cancel each other out. The difference between this story and our commuting example is that no one benefited from the extra commuting time when the Bay Bridge became congested. When the side effect is a change in price (or income), then the purchasers benefit at the producers' cost. There is zero net effect.

From society's viewpoint, a dentist should not worry about lowering colleagues' incomes. Each dentist should pursue the highest-paying practice. As each person makes a selfish choice, we are invisibly led to the right distribution of dentists between city and rural areas. And, the two careers will have equal incomes.*

---

* Or, to the extent that living in a city is worth more than living in a rural area, this differential will be reflected in income differences.

Of course, the American Dental Association may look at this differently. It may place more weight on the loss to city dentists' incomes than on the saving to consumers. From the dental profession's perspective there is indeed a misallocation, with too many dentists practicing in the city. If more dentists took rural practices, then the potential advantages of a city practice would not be "wasted" by competition and congestion. Taken as a whole, the income of dentists would rise if it were possible to keep the number of city dentists below the free-market level. Although dentists cannot place a toll on those who want to practice in the city, it is in the profession's self-interest to create a fund that subsidizes dental students who commit to establish a rural practice.

10

The Strategy of Voting

The foundation of a democratic government is that it respects the will of the people as expressed through the ballot box. Unfortunately, these lofty ideals are not so easily implemented. Strategic issues arise in voting, just as in any other multiperson game. Voters will often have an incentive to misrepresent their true preferences. Neither majority rule nor any other voting scheme can solve this problem, for there does not exist any one perfect system for aggregating up individuals' preferences into a will of the people.*

What this means is that the structure of the game matters. For example, when Congress has to choose between many competing bills, the order in which votes are taken can have a great influence on the final outcome. We begin by looking at the voting process more carefully, figuring out just when an individual's vote matters.

---

* This deep result is due to Stanford University professor Kenneth Arrow. His famous "impossibility" theorem shows that any system for aggregating unrestricted preferences over three or more alternatives into a group decision cannot simultaneously satisfy the following minimally desirable properties: (i) transitivity, (ii) unanimity, (iii) independence of irrelevant alternatives, (iv) non-dictatorship. Transitivity requires that if A is chosen over B and B is chosen over C, then A must be chosen over C. Unanimity requires A to be chosen over B when A is unanimously preferred to B. Independence of irrelevant alternatives requires that the choice between A and B does not depend on whether some other alternative C is available. Non-dictatorship requires that there is no individual who always gets his way and thus has dictatorial powers.

1. THE TIE OF POWER

Recent presidential elections have emphasized the importance of the selection of the vice president. This person will be just a heartbeat away from the presidency. But most candidates for president spurn the suggestion of the second spot on the ticket, and most vice presidents do not seem to enjoy the experience. The prospect of twiddling one's thumbs for four or eight years, waiting for the boss to die, is hardly a fit occupation for anyone.* John Nance Garner, FDR's first VP, expressed this succinctly: "The vice-presidency ain't worth a pitcher of warm spit."

Only one clause of the Constitution specifies any actual activity for the vice president. Article I, Section 3.4 says: "The Vice-President of the United States shall be President of the Senate, but shall have no vote, unless they be equally divided." The presiding is "ceremony, idle ceremony," and most of the time the vice president delegates this responsibility to a rotation of junior senators chosen by the senate majority leader. Is the tiebreaking vote important, or is it just more ceremony?

At first glance, both logic and evidence seem to support the ceremonial viewpoint. The vice president's vote just does not seem important. The chance of a tie vote is small. The most favorable circumstances for a tie arise when each senator is just as likely to vote one way as the other, and an even number of senators vote. The result will be roughly one tie vote in twelve.† Of course senators' votes are far from random. Only when the two parties are roughly equal or when there is an especially divisive issue that splits some of the party lines does the vice president's vote get counted.

---

* No doubt they console themselves by thinking of the even worse plight of Britain's Prince Charles.

† The biggest chance that a fixed group of 50 Senators votes Aye and the remaining 50 vote Nay is $(\frac{1}{2})^{50} \cdot (\frac{1}{2})^{50}$. Multiplying this by the number of ways of finding 50 supporters out of the total 100, we get approximately (1/12).

The most active tiebreaking vice president was our first, John Adams. He cast 29 tiebreaking votes during his eight years. This is not surprising, since his Senate consisted of only 20 members, and a tie was almost three times more likely than it is today, with our 100-member Senate. In fact, over the first 200 years, there have been only 222 occasions for the vice president to vote. More recently, Richard Nixon, under Eisenhower, was the most active vice president, casting a total of 8 tiebreaking votes — out of 1,229 decisions reached by the Senate during the period 1953–61. This fall in tiebreaking votes also reflects the fact that the two-party system is much more entrenched, so that fewer issues are likely to cross party lines.

But this ceremonial picture of the vice president's vote is misleading. More important than how often the vice president votes is the impact of the vote. Measured correctly, the vice president's vote is roughly equal in importance to that of any senator.

One reason that the vice president's vote matters is that it tends to decide only the most important and divisive issues. For example, George Bush, as vice president, voted to save both the administration's chemical weapons program (twice) and the MX missile program. This suggests that we should look more closely at just when it is that a vote matters.

A vote can have one of two effects. It can be instrumental in determining the outcome, or it can be a "voice" that influences the margin of victory or defeat without altering the outcome. In a decision-making body like the Senate, the first aspect is the more important one.

To demonstrate the importance of the vice president's current position, *imagine that the vice president is given a regular vote as President of the Senate.* When does this have any additional impact? For important issues, all 100 senators will try to be present.* If the 100 senators are split 51–49 or more

---

* Or senators on opposite sides of the issue will try to pair off their absences.

lopsidedly, then the outcome is the same no matter which way the vice president votes. *The only time the outcome hinges on the vice president's 101st vote is when the Senate is split 50–50, just the same as now, when the vice president has only a tiebreaking vote.*

We recognize that our account of a vice president's voting power leaves out aspects of reality. Some of these imply less power for the vice president; others, more. Much of a senator's power comes from the work in committees, in which the vice president does not partake. On the other hand, the vice president has the veto power of the president on his side.

Our illustration of the vice president's vote leads to an important moral of wider applicability: anyone's vote affects the outcome only when it creates or breaks a tie. Think how important your own vote is in different contexts. How influential can you be in a presidential election? Your town's mayoral election? Your club's secretarial election?

As with the Senate, the chance that the rest of the electorate reaches a tie, leaving you decisive, is at a maximum when each voter is just as likely to vote one way as the other. Mathematical calculation shows that the chances of a tie are proportional to the square root of the number of voters: increasing the electorate a millionfold reduces the chances of a tie by a factor of a thousand. In the Senate, with 100 voters, we saw that the chance of a tie in the most favorable circumstances was 1 in 12. In a presidential election with 100 million voters, it drops to 1 in 12,000. Because of the electoral college system, there is a greater chance that you will be decisive in affecting the electoral votes of your state. But the fact that the population is rarely split so evenly works the other way, and even a slight advantage for one candidate or the other reduces the chances of a tie drastically. So you might take 1 in 12,000 as an optimistic estimate of your influence in a presidential election. Considering these odds, is it worth your while to vote?

To explore this question, let us take a concrete example. Suppose one candidate, Mr. Soft Heart, has promised to raise the minimum wage from $3.50 to $5.00, and the other, Mr. Hard Head, is opposed to any increase. If you hold a minimum-wage job, work 2,000 hours a year, and expect to keep the job when the wage rises, Mr. Heart will mean $3,000 a year more in your pocket than Mr. Head. Over the four years, this will amount to $12,000. But the chance that your vote will bring this about is only 1 in 12,000. The expected advantage to you from your vote is only a dollar. It is not worth your while to vote if to do so you must sacrifice even 20 minutes of paid working time. Surveys find that most people value their leisure time at about half their wage rate. Therefore voting is not worth 40 minutes of your leisure time.

Even if you are unlikely to change the outcome, you can still add your voice to the crowd. But will it be heard? While it is clear that 100 million to 0 is a landslide, there is no apparent line where the change in one vote causes a landslide to become a simple victory. And yet if enough people change their vote, the landslide will become a tie and then a loss and finally a landslide in the other direction. This absence of a "bright line" dates back to the Greek philosopher Zeno, who tells the paradox in terms of creating a mound from grains of sand one at a time. It seems true that no one grain can turn a non-mound into a mound. And yet, enough grains will turn a molehill into a mountain. A vote is much like a grain of sand. It is hard to imagine how one additional vote will change anyone's perception of the outcome.*

What this tells us is that calculations of personal gains and costs cannot be decisive in motivating people to vote. For the proper functioning of democracy, however, it is very important that people do so. That is why we need social conditioning.

---

* Even though any single individual's opinion of the outcome is ever so slightly changed, a small impact on a large number of people may still add up to something.

From civics classes in elementary school to election-eve appeals to one's patriotic duty, societies work to get out the vote — even if individual voters don't have any major impact on the election.* Where patriotic duty is found insufficient, people are sometimes legally required to vote, as is the case in several countries, including Australia.

2. THE MEDIAN VOTER

So far our emphasis has been on pairwise elections. In such cases there is little strategy other than whether or not to vote. If you vote, you should always vote for the candidate whom you most prefer. Because your vote matters most when it breaks a tie, you want your vote to reflect your preferences honestly.[†] For elections with more than two alternatives, the decision is both whether or not to vote and what to vote for. It is no longer true that one should always vote for one's favorite candidate.

In the 1984 Democratic party primary, supporters of Jesse Jackson had the problem of trying to send a signal with their vote. They could predict that Jackson was unlikely to win. The polls told them that Gary Hart and Walter Mondale were the clear front-runners. There was a great incentive to vote for

---

* A much cheaper and potentially more representative way of deciding elections would be to run a poll. The current practice is a glorified poll; anyone who wants to participate, does so. The theory of statistics tells us that if the vote from a random sample of 10,000 gives one candidate a 5% edge (5,250 or more votes), then there is less than a one-in-a-million chance the outcome will be reversed, *even if 100 million people vote*. If the vote is closer we have to continue expanding the survey size. While this process could greatly reduce the cost of voting, the potential for abuse is also great. The selection of a random voter is subject to a nightmare of problems.

† Again, there is the qualification that you might care about the candidate's margin of victory. Specifically, you might want your candidate to win, but only with a small margin of victory (in order to temper his megalomania, for example). In that case, you might choose to vote against your preferred alternative, provided you were confident that he would win.

those at the head of the pack in order not to waste one's vote. This became an even bigger problem when there were seven candidates competing for the 1988 Democratic party presidential nomination. Supporters didn't want to waste their vote or campaign contributions on a nonviable candidate. Thus polls and media characterizations that pronounced front-runners had the real potential to become self-fulfilling prophecies.

There is another reason why votes may not reflect preferences. One way to help keep your vote from getting lost in the crowd is to make it stand out: take an extreme position away from the crowd. Someone who thinks that the country is too liberal could vote for a moderately conservative candidate. Or she could go all the way to the extreme right and support Lyndon LaRouche. To the extent that candidates compromise by taking central positions, it may be in some voters' interests to appear more extreme than they are. This tactic is effective only up to a point. If you go overboard, you are thought of as a crackpot, and the result is that your opinion is ignored. The trick is to take the most extreme stand consistent with appearing rational.

To make this a little more precise, imagine that we can align all the candidates on a 0 to 100 scale of liberal to conservative. The Young Spartacus League is way on the left, around 0, while Lyndon LaRouche takes the most conservative stance, somewhere near 100.

Voters express their preference by picking some point along the spectrum. Suppose the winner of the election is the candidate whose position is the average of all voters' positions. The way you might think of this happening is that through negotiations and compromises, the leading candidate's position is chosen to reflect the average position of the electorate. The parallel in bargaining is to settle disputes by offering to "split the difference."

Consider yourself a middle-of-the-roader: if it were in your hands, you would prefer a candidate who stands at the position

50 on our scale. But it may turn out that the country is a bit more conservative than that. Without you, the average is 60. For concreteness, you are one of a hundred voters polled to determine the average position.

If you state your actual preference, the candidate will move to $[99 \times 60 + 50]/100 = 59.9$. If, instead, you exaggerate and claim to want 0, the final outcome will be at 59.4. By exaggerating your claim, you are six times as effective in influencing the candidate's position. Here, extremism in the defense of liberalism is no vice.

Of course, you won't be the only one doing this. All those more liberal than 60 will be claiming to be at 0, while those more conservative will be arguing for 100. In the end, everyone will appear to be polarized, although the candidate will still take some central position. The extent of the compromise will depend on the relative numbers pushing in each direction.

The problem with this averaging approach is that it tries to take into account both intensity and direction of preferences. People have an incentive to tell the truth about direction but exaggerate when it comes to intensity. The same problem arises with "split the difference": if that is the rule for settling disputes, everyone will begin with an extreme position.

One solution to this problem dates back to the twenties and Columbia University economist Harold Hotelling. Instead of taking the mean or average position, the candidate chooses the *median* position, the platform where there are exactly as many voters who want the candidate to move left as to move right. Unlike the mean, the median position does not depend on the intensity of the voters' preferences, only their preferred direction. To find the median point, a candidate could start at 0 and keep moving to the right as long as a majority supports this change. At the median, the support for any further rightward move is exactly balanced by the equal number of voters who prefer a shift left.

When a candidate adopts the median position, no voter has

an incentive to distort her preferences. Why? There are only three cases to consider: (i) a voter to the left of the median, (ii) a voter exactly at the median, and (iii) a voter to the right of the median. In the first case, exaggerating preferences leftward does not alter the median, and therefore the position adopted, at all. The only way that this voter can change the outcome is to support a move rightward. But this is exactly counter to his interest. In the second case, the voter's ideal position is being adopted anyway, and there is nothing to gain by a distortion of preferences. The third case parallels the first. Moving more to the right has no effect on the median, while voting for a move left is counter to the voter's interests.

The way the argument was phrased suggested that the voter knows the median point for the voting population, and whether she is to the right or the left of it. Yet the incentive to tell the truth had nothing to do with which of those outcomes occurred. You can think about all three of the above cases as possibilities and then realize that whichever outcome materializes, the voter will want to reveal her position honestly. The advantage of the rule that adopts the median position is that no voter has an incentive to distort her preferences; truthful voting is the dominant strategy for everyone.

The only problem with adopting the median voter's position is its limited applicability. This option is available only when everything can be reduced to a one-dimensional choice, as in liberal versus conservative. But not all issues are so easily classified. Once voters' preferences are more than one-dimensional, there will not be a median. At that point, the possibility of manipulating the system becomes real.

3. NAIVE VOTING

The most commonly used election procedure is simple majority voting. And yet the results of the majority-rule system have paradoxical properties, as was first recognized over two hundred years ago by French Revolution hero the Marquis de Condorcet.

In his honor, we illustrate his fundamental paradox of majority rule using revolutionary France as the setting. After the fall of the Bastille, who would be the new populist leader of France? Suppose three candidates, Mr. Robespierre, Mr. Danton, and Madame Lafarge, are competing for the position. The population is divided into three equally sized groups, left, middle, and right, with the following preferences:

	Left's Ranking	Middle's Ranking	Right's Ranking
1st	Danton	Lafarge	Robespierre
2nd	Lafarge	Robespierre	Danton
3rd	Robespierre	Danton	Lafarge

In a vote of Robespierre against Danton, Robespierre wins two to one. Then in a vote of Robespierre against Lafarge, Lafarge beats Robespierre two to one. But then in a vote of Lafarge against Danton, Danton wins two to one. Thus there is no overall winner. Who ends up on top depends on which vote was the last taken. More generally, this possibility of endless cycles makes it impossible to specify any of the alternatives as representing the will of the people.

Things become even more insidious when voting cycles are embedded in a larger problem. The will of the majority can leave everyone worse off. To show this problem, we update and expand the preferences above. Suppose the Seven Dwarfs are candidates in an election.* The voters are split into three equal factions — call them Left, Middle, and Right. The rankings of the groups are as follows.

---

* Any similarity between this story and the early stages of the 1988 Democratic presidential primaries is purely coincidental.

	Left's Ranking	Middle's Ranking	Right's Ranking
1st	Happy	Grumpy	Dopey
2nd	Sneezy	Dopey	Happy
3rd	Grumpy	Happy	Sleepy
4th	Dopey	Bashful	Sneezy
5th	Doc	Sleepy	Grumpy
6th	Bashful	Sneezy	Doc
7th	Sleepy	Doc	Bashful

Note that the cyclic ordering over Happy, Dopey, and Grumpy is equivalent to the cyclic ordering of Robespierre, Danton, and Madame Lafarge above.

If we start with Happy versus Dopey, Dopey wins. Then Grumpy beats Dopey. And Sneezy beats Grumpy. Next Sleepy beats Sneezy. Then Bashful beats Sleepy, and Doc beats Bashful. This is remarkable. A sequence of majority votes has taken us from Happy, Dopey, and Grumpy all the way to Doc, when every voter agrees that any one of Happy, Dopey, and Grumpy is better than Doc.

How did this happen? The elections were all decided by two-thirds majorities. Those on the winning side gained a position, while those on the losing end went down four slots on average. All voters had four wins and two losses, which on net puts them four places worse than where they started.

At this point you would be justified in objecting that these voters were responsible for their own misfortunes; they voted in a shortsighted way. Each pairwise contest was decided as if it were the only one, instead of being a part of a chain of votes. If the voters had only looked ahead and reasoned backward they never would have allowed themselves to end up with Doc. That's true. But the presence of a voting cycle makes the outcome highly sensitive to the voting procedure. The next section shows how controlling the agenda can determine the outcome.

4. Order in the Court

The way the U.S. judicial system works, a defendant is first found to be innocent or guilty. The punishment sentence is determined only after a defendant has been found guilty. It might seem that this is a relatively minor procedural issue. Yet, the order of this decision-making can mean the difference between life and death, or even between conviction and acquittal. We use the case of a defendant charged with a capital offense to make our point.

There are three alternative procedures to determine the outcome of a criminal court case. Each has its merits, and you might want to choose among them based on some underlying principles.

1. Status Quo: First determine innocence or guilt, then if guilty consider the appropriate punishment.

2. Roman Tradition: After hearing the evidence, start with the most serious punishment and work down the list. First decide if the death penalty should be imposed for this case. If not, then decide whether a life sentence is justified. If, after proceeding down the list, no sentence is imposed, then the defendant is acquitted.

3. Mandatory Sentencing: First specify the sentence for the crime. Then determine whether the defendant should be convicted.

The difference between these systems is only one of agenda: what gets decided first. To illustrate how important this can be, we consider a case with only three possible outcomes: the death penalty, life imprisonment, and acquittal.* This story is based on a true case; it is a modern update of the dilemma faced by Pliny the Younger, a Roman lawyer working under Emperor Trajan around A.D. 100.[1]

The defendant's fate rests in the hands of three judges. Their decision is determined by a majority vote. This is particularly useful since the three judges are deeply divided.

One judge (Judge A) holds that the defendant is guilty and should be given the maximum possible sentence. This judge seeks to impose the death penalty. Life imprisonment is her second choice and acquittal is her worst outcome.

The second judge (Judge B) also believes that the defendant is guilty. However, this judge adamantly opposes the death penalty. Her most preferred outcome is life imprisonment. The precedent of imposing a death sentence is sufficiently troublesome that she would prefer to see the defendant acquitted rather than executed by the state.

The third judge, Judge C, is alone in holding that the defendant is innocent, and thus seeks acquittal. She is on the other side of the fence from the second judge, believing that life in prison is a fate worse than death. (On this the defendant concurs.) Consequently, if acquittal fails, her second-best outcome would be to see the defendant sentenced to death. Life in prison would be the worst outcome.

	Judge A's Ranking	Judge B's Ranking	Judge C's Ranking
Best	Death Sentence	Life in Prison	Acquittal
Middle	Life in Prison	Acquittal	Death Sentence
Worst	Acquittal	Death Sentence	Life in Prison

* Similar results hold even when there are many more outcomes.

Under the status quo system, the first vote is to determine innocence versus guilt. But these judges are sophisticated decision-makers. They look ahead and reason backward. They correctly predict that, if the defendant is found guilty, the vote will be two to one in favor of the death penalty. This effectively means that the original vote is between acquittal and the death penalty. Acquittal wins two to one, as Judge B tips the vote.

It didn't have to turn out that way. The judges might decide to follow the Roman tradition and work their way down the list of charges, starting with the most serious ones. They first decide whether or not to impose a death penalty. If the death penalty is chosen, there are no more decisions to be made. If the death penalty is rejected, the remaining options are life imprisonment or acquittal. By looking forward, the judges recognize that life imprisonment will be the outcome of the second stage. Reasoning backward, the first question reduces to a choice between life and death sentences. The death sentence wins two to one, with only Judge B dissenting.

A third reasonable alternative is to first determine the appropriate punishment for the crime at hand. Here we are thinking along the lines of a mandatory sentencing code. Once the sentence has been determined, the judges must then decide whether the defendant in the case at hand is guilty of the crime. In this case, if the predetermined sentence is life imprisonment, then the defendant will be found guilty, as Judges A and B vote for conviction. But if the death penalty is to be required, then we see that the defendant will be acquitted, as Judges B and C are unwilling to convict. Thus the choice of sentencing penalty comes down to the choice of life imprisonment versus acquittal. The vote is for life imprisonment, with Judge C casting the lone dissent.

You may find it remarkable and perhaps troubling that any of the three outcomes is possible based solely on the order in which votes are taken. Your choice of a judicial system might then depend on the outcome rather than the underlying principles.

5. THE SOPHISTICATES

The problems with majority rule go beyond manipulating the outcome through control of the agenda. Even sophisticated voters who exercise foresight can collectively outsmart themselves. We tell a story that illustrates the point, freely adapting the saga of President Reagan's nominees for the Supreme Court.

Judge Bork was the first nominee. Judges Ginsberg and Kennedy were known to be high on the list, and likely to be nominated should Bork not be confirmed by the Senate. If the Senate turned down all three, the likelihood was that the seat would stay vacant for the next president to fill.

Imagine that the decision rests in the hands of three powerful senators. To avoid impugning the reputation of any actual persons, we will call the three A, B, and C. Their rankings of the four possible outcomes are as follows:

	A's Ranking	B's Ranking	C's Ranking
1st	Kennedy	Ginsberg	Vacant
2nd	Vacant	Kennedy	Bork
3rd	Bork	Vacant	Ginsberg
4th	Ginsberg	Bork	Kennedy

The first thing to observe is that leaving the seat vacant is *unanimously* preferred to nominating Judge Bork. Yet if these are the preferences and the senators correctly predict the order of nominations as Bork, Ginsberg, and Kennedy, the result will be that Bork is confirmed.

We figure out the voting patterns by working backward up the tree.

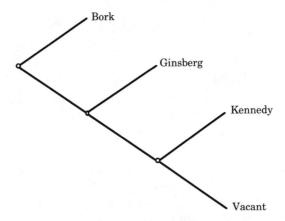

If the vote comes down to appointing Kennedy versus leaving the seat vacant, Kennedy will win. By looking ahead and reasoning backward the senators can predict a victory for Kennedy if Ginsberg is defeated. Therefore, if Bork is turned down the contest becomes Ginsberg or Kennedy. In the Ginsberg versus Kennedy contest, Ginsberg wins two to one.

Reasoning backward again, right at the start the senators should realize that their choice is Bork or Ginsberg. Here, Bork wins two to one. Everyone is looking ahead and correctly figures out the consequences of their action. Yet they collectively end up with a candidate whose nomination, everyone agrees, is worse than leaving the seat vacant.

Now in fact it didn't turn out that way, and there are several reasons. No one was quite certain who the next nominee would be. Preferences changed as more information was learned about the nominees. The senators' preferences may not have been as we represented them. Equally important, we have ignored any possibility for logrolling.

This was a perfect opportunity for logrolling to arise. There were three 2:1 votes. Each of the senators was on the winning side twice and on the losing side once. The gain from each win was worth one position in their ranking, but the loss pushed them down three. It doesn't help to win two small battles and lose the big war. The possibility for mutual gain opens the door for logrolling, and with these preferences we expect Bork would be defeated.

6. All-time Greats

After the White House, election to Cooperstown may be the next most coveted national honor. Membership in the Baseball Hall of Fame is determined by an election. There is a group of eligible candidates — for example, a player with ten years of experience becomes eligible five years after retirement.* The electors are the members of the Baseball Writers Association. Each voter may vote for up to ten candidates. All candidates capturing votes from more than 75 percent of the total number of ballots returned are elected.

One problem with this system is that the electors don't have the right incentives to vote for their true preferences. The rule that limits each voter to ten choices forces the voters to consider electability as well as merit. Some sportswriters may believe a candidate is deserving, but don't want to throw away the vote if the player is unlikely to make the cutoff. This same issue arose for voting in presidential primaries, and it appears in any election in which each voter is given a fixed number of votes to distribute among the candidates.

Two experts in game theory propose an alternative way to

---

* However, if the player has been on the ballot for fifteen years and failed to get elected, then eligibility is lost. For otherwise ineligible players, there is an alternative route to election. An Old Timers' committee considers special cases and sometimes elects one or two candidates a year.

run elections. Steven Brams and Peter Fishburn, one a political scientist and the other an economist, argue that "approval voting" allows voters to express their true preferences without concern for electability.[2] Under approval voting, each voter may vote for as many candidates as he wishes. Voting for one person does not exclude voting for any number of others. Thus there is no harm in voting for a candidate who has no hope of winning. Of course if people can vote for as many candidates as they wish, who gets elected? Like the Cooperstown rule, the electoral rule could specify in advance a percentage of the vote needed to win. Or it could pre-specify the number of winning candidates, and then the positions are filled by those who gather the most votes.

Approval voting has begun to catch on, and is used by many professional societies. How would it work for the Baseball Hall of Fame? Would Congress do better if it used approval voting when deciding which expenditure projects should be included in the annual budget? We look at the strategic issues associated with approval voting when a cutoff percentage determines the winners.

Imagine that election to the different sports halls of fame was decided by approval voting, in which all candidates capturing above a fixed percentage of the votes are elected. At first glance, the voters have no incentive to misstate their preferences. The candidates are not in competition with one another, but only with an absolute standard of quality implicit in the rule that specifies the required percentage of approval. If I think Reggie Jackson should be in the Baseball Hall of Fame, I can only reduce his chances by withholding my approval, and if I think he doesn't belong there, I can only make his admission more likely by voting contrary to my view.

However, candidates may compete against one another in the voters' minds, even though nothing in the rules mandates it. This will usually happen because voters have preferences concerning the size or the structure of the membership. Suppose Dan Marino and John Elway come up for election to the Football Hall of Fame. I think Marino is the better quarterback, although I will admit that Elway also meets the standard for a Hall of Fame berth. However, I think it overridingly important that two quarterbacks not be elected in the same year. My guess is that the rest of the electorate regards Elway more highly and he would get in no matter how I vote, but that Marino's case will be a very close call, and my approval is likely to tip him over. Voting truthfully means naming Marino, which is likely to lead to the outcome in which both are admitted. Therefore I have the incentive to misstate my preference and vote for Elway.

Two players may complement each other, rather than compete, in the voters' minds. I think neither Geoff Boycott nor Sunil Gavaskar belongs in the Cricket Hall of Fame, but it would be a gross injustice to have one and not the other. If in my judgment the rest of the electorate would choose Boycott even if I don't vote for him, while my vote may be crucial in deciding Gavaskar's selection, then I have an incentive to misstate my preference and vote for Gavaskar.

In contrast, a quota rule explicitly places candidates in competition with one another. Suppose the Baseball Hall of Fame limits admission to only two new people each year. Let each voter be given two votes; he can divide them between two candidates or give both to the same candidate. The candidates' votes are totaled, and the top two are admitted. Now suppose there are three candidates — Joe DiMaggio, Marv Throneberry, and Bob Uecker.* Everyone rates DiMaggio at the top, but the electors are split equally between the other two. I know that DiMaggio is sure to get in, so as a Marv Throneberry fan I give my two votes to him to increase his

---

* Marv Throneberry played first base for the '62 Mets, possibly the worst team in the history of baseball. His performance was instrumental to the team's reputation. Bob Uecker is much better known for his performance in Miller Lite commercials than for his play on the baseball field.

chances over Bob Uecker. Of course everyone else is equally subtle. The result: Throneberry and Uecker are elected and DiMaggio gets no votes.

Government expenditure projects naturally compete with one another so long as the total budget is limited, or congressmen and senators have strong preferences over the size of the budget. We will leave you to think which, if any, is the DiMaggio project, and which ones are the Throneberrys and Ueckers of federal spending.

7. "LOVE A LOATH'D ENEMY"

Incentives to distort one's preferences appear in other situations, too. One instance occurs when you can move first and use this opportunity to influence others.[3] Take for example the case of charitable contributions by foundations. Suppose there are two foundations, each with a budget of $250,000. They are presented with three grant applications: one from an organization helping the homeless, one from the University of Michigan, and one from Yale. Both foundations agree that a grant of $200,000 to the homeless is the top priority. Of the two other applications, the first foundation would like to see more money go to Michigan, while the second would prefer to fund Yale. Suppose the second steals a march and sends a check for its total budget, $250,000, to Yale. The first is then left with no alternative but to provide $200,000 to the homeless, leaving only $50,000 for Michigan. If the two foundations had split the grant to the homeless, then Michigan would have received $150,000, as would Yale. Thus the second foundation has engineered a transfer of $100,000 from Michigan to Yale through the homeless. In a sense, the foundation has distorted its preferences — it has not given anything to its top charity priority. But the strategic commitment does serve its true interests. In fact, this type of funding game is quite common.* By acting first, small foundations exercise more influence over which secondary priorities get funded. Large foundations and especially the federal government are then left to fund the most pressing needs.

This strategic rearranging of priorities has a direct parallel with voting. Before the 1974 Budget Act, Congress employed many of the same tricks. Unimportant expenditures were voted on and approved first. Later on, when the crunch appeared, the remaining expenditures were too important to be denied. To solve this problem, Congress now votes first on budget totals and then works within them.

When you can rely on others to save you later, you have an incentive to distort your priorities by exaggerating your claim and taking advantage of the others' preferences. You might be willing to gain at the expense of putting something you want at risk, if you can count on someone else bearing the cost of the rescue.

The principle of forcing others to save you can turn the outcome all the way around, from your worst to your best alternative. Here we show how this is done using the votes of a corporate board of trustees facing a hostile takeover. Their immediate problem is how to respond. Four options have been proposed, each with its own champion.

The founding president is looking for a way to keep the company intact. His first preference is to initiate a poison-pill provision into the company charter. The poison pill would be designed to prevent any outside party from attaining control without board approval.

---

* One explicit example is the strategic game played between the Marshall and Rhodes Scholarships. The Marshall Fund's objective is to have the maximum influence over who is given a scholarship to study in England. If someone has the potential to win both a Marshall and a Rhodes, the Marshall Fund prefers to have the person study as a Rhodes Scholar; that brings the person to England at no cost to the Marshall Fund and thus allows the Marshall Scholarship to select one more person. Hence the Marshall Fund waits until the Rhodes Scholarships have been announced before making its final selections.

The two young members of the board feel the situation is more desperate. They believe that a takeover is inevitable and are concentrating on finding a way to make the present transaction more acceptable. Their preferred action is to look for a white knight, a buyer who is acceptable to management and the board. The management representation on the board suggests a third possibility. The present managers would like the opportunity to buy the company through a management buyout, an MBO.

The fifth member of the board is an outside director. He is cautiously optimistic about the present raider and argues that there is time to see how the offer develops.

After these four options have been discussed, everyone ends up with a clear picture of where the others stand (or sit) on the four proposals. For example, the founder is a man of action; his worst outcome is the Wait & See position. The two young board members agree with the fifth that the MBO option is unattractive; whenever management competes with an outside bidder it opens the door to conflict of interest and insider trading, for managers are the ultimate insiders. The complete set of preferences is presented below.

	Founder's Ranking	Two Young Directors' Rankings	Management's Ranking	Outside Director's Ranking
1st	Poison Pill	White Knight	MBO	Wait & See
2nd	MBO	Poison Pill	Poison Pill	White Knight
3rd	White Knight	Wait & See	Wait & See	Poison Pill
4th	Wait & See	MBO	White Knight	MBO

Faced with these options, the board must make a decision. Everyone recognizes that the voting procedure may well influence the outcome. Even so, they decide there is a natural order to the decision-making process: begin by comparing the active courses of action and then decide whether the best one is worth doing. They first compare an MBO with a White Knight, and the more preferred alternative is then compared with the Poison Pill option. Having found the best active response, they decide whether this is worth doing by comparing it with Wait & See.

This voting problem is represented by the tree below.

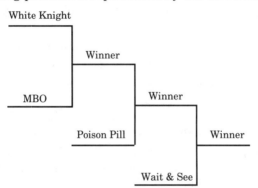

This tree should remind you of a tennis tournament in which some players are seeded. We are seeding "Wait & See" all the way into the finals, "Poison Pill" into the semifinals, and giving no seed to "MBO" and "White Knight."

Boxing and chess both work this way, too. There is a series of challenges that you must win in order to go against the presiding world champion. The U.S. presidential election process also works this way. When there is an incumbent president, that person is typically a shoo-in for his party's nomination. The opposing party runs a primary to decide who will go against the incumbent in the final elections. The primary process, the ensuing party nomination, and the presidential election can be thought of as a series of elimination elections. But back to the boardroom.

We suppose that the five board members have enough foresight to realize the consequences of their actions in successive rounds, and vote according to their true preferences. Backward reasoning makes this problem easy to solve. You can work out the solution and see that the White Knight option wins (or you can jump to the next paragraph), but that is not the point of this story. We are interested in showing how the founder can improve the outcome from his perspective by making a commitment to distorted preferences.

How is it that the White Knight option wins under foresighted voting? The last election must be Wait & See versus something. In this final election everyone has an incentive to vote honestly, since this will determine the actual outcome. The three possibilities are easy to calculate:

- Wait & See vs. Poison Pill, *Poison Pill* wins 4–1.

- Wait & See vs. MBO, *Wait & See* wins 3–2.

- Wait & See vs. White Knight, *White Knight* wins 3–2.

Now we go back one previous round. The contest will be either Poison Pill vs. White Knight or Poison Pill vs. MBO. In the first case, both Poison Pill and White Knight are preferred to Wait & See. So whatever wins the second round will be implemented. The board members prefer White Knight to Poison Pill, 3–2.

In the second case, a vote for MBO is in reality a vote for Wait & See. Board members can anticipate that if MBO beats Poison Pill for the active course, it will lose out in the next comparison with Wait & See. So when deciding between Poison Pill and MBO, board members will act as if deciding between Poison Pill and Wait & See, with the result that Poison Pill wins 4–1. Thus the first-round comparison is truly between Poison Pill and White Knight. White Knight is chosen by a 3–2 margin and is then selected in each of the subsequent comparisons.

Once the founder recognizes what will happen, there is a strategy he can employ to get his most preferred option, the Poison Pill. Look what happens if the founder "adopts" the preferences of the outside board member. Of course it is essential that this change of preferences is credible and is made known to all the other voters. Suppose the founder simply gives his vote to the outside director and leaves the meeting.

At first glance this seems nothing short of crazy; the adopted preferences are almost the opposite of his true ones. But look at the effect. The votes will now go as follows:

- Wait & See vs. Poison Pill, *Poison Pill* wins 3–2.
- Wait & See vs. MBO, *Wait & See* wins 4–1.
- Wait & See vs. White Knight, *Wait & See* wins 3–2.

The only active option that can beat Wait & See is Poison Pill. Right from the start the board members should predict that if Poison Pill ever loses, the outcome will be Wait & See. Yet both MBO and White Knight supporters prefer Poison Pill to Wait & See. They are forced to vote for Poison Pill as it is their only viable alternative; thus Poison Pill wins.

By transferring his support to the opposition, the founder is able to make a credible threat that it is either Poison Pill or Wait & See. As a result, all but the die-hard Wait & See supporters dump the White Knight option (which can no longer beat Wait & See) in favor of the Poison Pill. Superficially, this transfer of a vote doubles the strength of the Wait & See supporters. Actually, it leads to an outcome that is worse from their viewpoint — Poison Pill rather than White Knight. In voting, strength can be weakness. Of course, if the outside director sees through the game, he should refuse to accept the founder's proxy.

If you regard this story as farfetched, something quite like it did occur in the 1988 Wisconsin presidential primary. The Republican governor of the state said that of the Democratic candidates, Jesse Jackson was the most interesting. Many commentators thought this was a Machiavellian attempt to get Republicans to cross over and vote for Jackson in the Democratic primary, thereby helping produce a more easily beatable opponent for Bush in the November election. Apparently,

Michael Dukakis was sufficiently easy for George Bush to beat, even without this help.

8. CASE STUDY #10: ALL OR NOTHING

Gin and vermouth: some prefer them straight, while others only drink them mixed, i.e., a martini. We've seen examples of both types of preferences. In election to the Football Hall of Fame, some would be happy with either Elway or Marino, but not both, while in cricket others find only the martini combination of Boycott and Gavaskar palatable.

Is the budget approval process all that different? How can it be improved? One suggestion is to give the president the power of a line-item veto.

We ask the Congress, once again: Give us the same tool that 43 governors have, a line-item veto, so we can carve out the boondoggles and pork — those items that would never survive on their own.

— Ronald Reagan, State of the Union Address, January 27, 1987.

Yet, it is possible that this may be a tool the president is better off without. How could that be?

Case Discussion

One reason is that without a line-item veto, the president is committed to taking what the Congress gives him; he cannot modify it piecemeal to better suit his preferences. Consequently, compromises made in Congress will be honored without fear that the president will pick and choose what segments to keep. Once Congress predicts they will lose all of the parts that would not survive on their own, the process of agreeing on a budget will become much more contentious, and a consensus compromise may not be found. Congress may be much less willing to serve the president a martini if he can remix it before presenting it to the nation.

Thus a president with a line-item veto might end up with less power, simply because the Congress is less willing (or able) to put proposals on his desk. A simple example helps illustrate the point. President Reagan wanted funds for Star Wars. Unfortunately for Reagan, the Republican party did not control the Congress. The Democrats' approval had to be bought. The budget offered the Democrats a package of social programs that made the defense spending tolerable. The willingness of the Democrats to approve the budget was contingent on the complete package. If they thought that Reagan could use a line-item veto to cut the social programs (in the name of pork), they would be unwilling to give him the Star Wars funds.

The debate about the effectiveness of the line-item veto for reducing deficits is best settled by looking at the experience at the state level. Columbia University economist Douglas Holtz-Eakin has examined the historical evidence:

> Gubernatorial veto power is quite old. The President of the Confederacy had (but did not exercise) item veto power during the Civil War and 28 states (out of a total of 45) adopted a line item veto between 1860 and 1900. By 1930, 41 of the 48 states had a provision for line item veto power. The governors of Iowa and West Virginia acquired line item veto power in 1969.[4]

And yet, after looking at all these cases, Professor Holtz-Eakin was unable to see any reduction in the budget deficits of states whose governor had the line-item veto.

11

Bargaining

A newly elected trade union leader went to his first tough bargaining session in the company boardroom. Nervous and intimidated by the setting, he blurted out his demand: "We want ten dollars an hour or else." "Or else what?" challenged the boss. The union leader replied, "Nine dollars fifty."

Few union leaders are so quick to back down, and bosses need the threat of Japanese competition, not their own power, to secure wage concessions. But the situation poses several important questions about the bargaining process. Will there be an agreement? Will it occur amicably, or only after a strike? Who will concede and when? Who will get how much of the pie that is the object of the haggling?

In Chapter 2, we sketched a simple story of two children arguing over the division of an ice-cream pie. Because the pie melted while the exchange of offers and counteroffers went on, the two sides were motivated to reach an immediate agreement. Yet the agreed division was based on what would happen if either side let the pie melt. The example illustrated the strategic principle of looking ahead and reasoning back. Many realities of the bargaining process were sacrificed in order to make that principle stand out. This chapter uses the same principle, but with more attention to issues that arise during bargaining in business, politics, and elsewhere.

We begin by recapitulating the basic idea in the context of union-management negotiation over wages. To look ahead and reason back, it helps to start at a fixed point in the future, so let us think of an enterprise with a natural conclusion, such as a hotel in a summer resort. The season lasts 101 days. Each day the hotel operates, it makes a profit of $1,000. At the beginning of the season, the employees' union confronts the management over wages. The union presents its demand. The management either accepts this, or rejects it and returns the next day with a counteroffer. The hotel can open only after an agreement is reached.

First suppose bargaining has gone on for so long that even if the next round leads to an agreement, the hotel can open for only the last day of the season. In fact bargaining will not go on that long, but because of the logic of looking ahead and reasoning back, what actually happens is governed by a thought process that starts at this logical extreme. Suppose it is the union's turn to present its demand. At this point the management should accept anything as being better than nothing. So the union can get away with the whole $1,000.*

Now look at the day before the last, when it is the management's turn to make an offer. It knows that the union can always reject this, let the process go on to the last day, and get $1,000. Therefore the management cannot offer any less. And the union cannot do any better than get $1,000 on the last day, so the management need not offer any more on the day before. Therefore the management's offer at this stage is clear: of the $2,000 profit over the last two days, it asks half. Each side gets $500 per day.

Next let the reasoning move back one more day. By the same logic, the union will offer the management $1,000, and ask for $2,000; this gives the union $667 per day and the management $333. We show the full process in the following table:

---

* We could make the more realistic assumption that the management will need some minimal share such as $100, but that will only complicate the arithmetic, and won't change the basic idea of the story.

Table 1: Successive Rounds of Wage Bargaining

Days to Go	Offer by	Union's Share Total	Union's Share Per Day	Management's Share Total	Management's Share Per Day
1	Union	$1,000	$1,000	$0	$0
2	Management	1,000	500	1,000	500
3	Union	2,000	667	1,000	333
4	Management	2,000	500	2,000	500
5	Union	3,000	600	2,000	400
...					
100	Management	50,000	500	50,000	500
101	Union	51,000	505	50,000	495

Each time the union makes an offer, it has an advantage, which stems from its ability to make the last all-or-nothing offer. But the advantage gets smaller as the number of rounds increases. At the start of a season 101 days long, the two sides' positions are almost identical: $505 versus $495. Almost the same division would emerge if the management were to make the last offer, or indeed if there were no rigid rules like one offer a day, alternating offers, etc.[1] The appendix to this chapter shows how this framework generalizes to include negotiations in which there is no predetermined last period. Our restrictions to alternating offers and a known finite horizon were simply devices to help us look ahead. They become innocuous when the time between offers is short and the bargaining horizon is long — in these cases, looking ahead and reasoning backward leads to a very simple and appealing rule: split the total down the middle.

What is more, the agreement occurs on the very first day of the negotiation process. Because the two sides look ahead to predict the same outcome, there is no reason why they should fail to agree and jointly lose $1,000 a day. Not all instances of union-management bargaining have such a happy beginning. Breakdowns in negotiations do occur, strikes or lockouts happen, and settlements favor one side or the other. By refining our example and ringing some changes on its premises, we can explain these facts.

1. THE HANDICAP SYSTEM IN NEGOTIATIONS

One important element that determines how the pie will be split is each side's cost of waiting. Although both sides may lose an equal amount of profits, one party may have other alternatives that help partially recapture this loss. Suppose that the members of the union can earn $300 a day in outside activities while negotiations with the hotel management go on. Now each time the management's turn comes, it must offer the union not only what the union could get a day later, but also at least $300 for the current day. The entries in our table change in the union's favor; we show this in a new table. Once again the agreement occurs at the season opening and without any strike, but the union does much better.

Table 2: Successive Rounds of Wage Bargaining

Days to Go	Offer by	Union's Share		Management's Share	
		Total	Per Day	Total	Per Day
1	Union	$1,000	$1,000	$0	$0
2	Management	1,300	650	700	350
3	Union	2,300	767	700	233
4	Management	2,600	650	1,400	350
5	Union	3,600	720	1,400	280
...					
100	Management	65,000	650	35,000	350
101	Union	66,000	653	35,000	347

The result can be seen as a natural modification of the principle of equal division, to allow for the possibility that the parties start the process with different "handicaps," as in golf. The union starts at $300, the sum its members could earn on the outside. This leaves $700 to be negotiated, and the principle is to split it evenly, $350 for each side. Therefore the union gets $650 and the management only $350.

In other circumstances the management could have an advantage. For example, it might be able to operate the hotel using scabs while the negotiations with the union go on. But because those workers are less efficient or must be paid more, or because some guests are reluctant to cross the union's picket lines, the management's profit from such operation will be only $500 a day. Suppose the union members have no outside income possibilities. Once again there will be an immediate settlement with the union without an actual strike. But the prospect of the scab operation will give the management an advantage in the negotiation, and it will get $750 a day while the union gets $250.

If the union members have an outside income possibility of $300 *and* the management can operate the hotel with a profit of $500 during negotiations, then only $200 remains free to be bargained over. The management gets $600 and the union gets $400. The general idea is that the better a party can do by itself in the absence of an agreement, the higher will be its share of the pie that is the subject of the bargaining.

2. "This Will Hurt You More Than It Hurts Me"

When a strategic bargainer observes that a better outside opportunity translates into a better share in a bargain, he will look for strategic moves that improve his outside opportunities. Moreover, he will notice that what matters is his outside opportunity *relative* to that of his rival. He will do better in the bargaining even if he makes a commitment or a threat that lowers both parties' outside opportunities, so long as that of the rival is damaged more severely.

In our example, when the union members could earn $300 a day on the outside while the management could make a profit of $500 a day using scab labor, the result of the bargaining was $400 for the union and $600 for the management. Now suppose the union members give up $100 a day of outside income to intensify their picketing, and this reduces the management's profit by $200 a day. Then the bargaining process gives the union a starting point of $200 ($300 minus $100) and the management $300 ($500 minus $200). The two starting points add up to $500, and the remaining $500 of daily profit from regular operation of the hotel is split equally between them. Therefore the union gets $450 and the management gets $550. The union's threat of hurting both (but hurting the management more) has earned it an extra $50.

The major league baseball players used just such a tactic in their wage negotiations in 1980. They went on strike during the exhibition season, returned to work at the start of the regular season, and threatened to strike again starting on Memorial Day weekend. To see how this "hurt the team owners more," note that during the exhibition season the players got no salaries, while the owners earned revenue from vacationers and locals. During the regular season the players got the same salary each week. For the owners, the gate and television revenues are low initially and rise substantially during and after the Memorial Day weekend. Therefore the loss of the owners *relative* to that of the players was highest during the exhibition season and again starting Memorial Day weekend. It seems the players knew the right strategy.[2]

The owners gave in just before the second half of the threatened baseball strike. But the first half actually occurred. Our theory of looking ahead and reasoning back is clearly incomplete. Why is it that agreements are not always reached before any damage is done — why are there strikes?

3. Brinkmanship and Strikes

Before an old contract expires, the union and the firm begin the negotiations for a new labor contract. But there is no sense of urgency during this period. Work goes on, no output is sacrificed, and there is no apparent advantage to achieving an agreement sooner rather than later. It would seem that each party should wait until the last moment and state its demand just as the old contract is about to expire and a strike looms. That does happen sometimes, but often an agreement is reached much sooner.

In fact, delaying agreement can be costly even during the tranquil phase when the old contract still operates. The process of negotiation has its own risk. There can be misperception of the other side's impatience or outside opportunities, tension, personality clashes, and suspicion that the other side is not bargaining in good faith. The process may break down despite the fact that both parties want it to succeed.

Although both sides may want the agreement to succeed, they may have different ideas about what constitutes success. The two parties do not always look forward and see the same end. They may not have the same information or share the same perspective, so they see things differently. Each side must make a guess about the other's cost of waiting. Since a side with a low waiting cost does better, it is to each side's advantage to claim its cost is low. But these statements will not be taken at face value; they have to be proven. The way to prove one's waiting costs are low is to begin incurring the costs and then show you can hold out longer, or to take a greater risk of incurring the costs — lower costs make higher risks acceptable. It is the lack of a common view about where the negotiations will end that leads to the beginning of a strike.

The situation is tailor-made for the exercise of brinkmanship. The union could threaten an immediate breakdown of talks followed by a strike, but strikes are very costly to union members as well. While time for continued negotiation remains, such a dire threat lacks credibility. But a smaller threat can remain credible: tempers and tensions are gradually rising, and a breakdown may occur even though the union doesn't really want it to. If this bothers the management more than it bothers the union, it is a good strategy from the union's perspective. The argument works the other way around too; the strategy of brinkmanship is a weapon for the stronger of the two parties — namely, the one that fears a breakdown less.

Sometimes wage negotiations go on after the old contract has expired but without a strike, and work continues under the terms of the old contract. This might seem to be a better arrangement, because the machinery and the workers are not idle and output is not lost. But one of the parties, usually the union, is seeking a revision of the terms of the contract in its favor, and for it the arrangement is singularly disadvantageous. Why should the management concede? Why should it not let the negotiations spin on forever while the old contract remains in force de facto?

Again the threat in the situation is the probability that the process may break down and a strike may ensue. The union practices brinkmanship, but now it does so after the old contract has expired. Time for routine negotiations is past. Continued work under an expired contract while negotiations go on is widely regarded as a sign of union weakness. There must be some chance of a strike to motivate the firm to meet the union's demands.

When the strike happens, what keeps it going? The key to commitment is to reduce the threat in order to make it credible. Brinkmanship carries the strike along on a day-by-day basis. The threat never to return to work would not be credible, especially if the management comes close to meeting the union's demands. But waiting one more day or week is a credible threat. The losses to the workers are smaller than their potential gains. Provided they believe they will win (and soon), it is worth their while to wait. If the workers are correct in their beliefs, management will find it cheaper to give in and in fact should do so immediately. Hence the workers' threat would cost them nothing. The problem is that the firm may not perceive the situation the same way. If it believes the workers are about to concede, then losing just one more day's or week's profits is worth getting a more favorable contract. In this way, both sides continue to hold out, and the strike continues.

Earlier, we talked about the risk of brinkmanship as the chance that both sides would fall together down the slippery slope. As the conflict continues, both sides risk a large loss with a small but increasing probability. It was this increasing exposure to risk that induced one side to back down. Brinkmanship in the form of a strike imposes costs differently, but the effect is the same. Instead of a small chance of a large loss, there is a large chance, even certainty, of a small loss when a strike begins. As the strike continues unresolved, the small loss grows, just as the chance of falling off the brink increases. The way to prove determination is to accept more risk or watch strike losses escalate. Only when one side discovers that the other is truly the stronger does it decide to back down. Strength can take many forms. One side may suffer less from waiting, perhaps because it has valuable alternatives; winning may be very important, perhaps because of negotiations with other unions; losing may be very costly, so that the strike losses look smaller.

This application of brinkmanship applies to the bargaining between nations as well as that between firms. When the United States tries to get its allies to pay a greater share of the defense costs, it suffers from the weakness of negotiating while working under an expired contract. The old arrangement in which the Americans bear the brunt of the burden continues in the meantime, and the U.S. allies are happy to let the negotiations drag on. Can — and should — the United States resort to brinkmanship?

Risk and brinkmanship change the process of bargaining in a fundamental way. In the earlier accounts of sequences of offers, the prospect of what would come later induced the parties to reach an agreement on the very first round. An integral aspect of brinkmanship is that sometimes the parties do go over the brink. Breakdowns and strikes can occur. They may be genuinely regretted by both parties, but may acquire a momentum of their own and last surprisingly long.

4. SIMULTANEOUS BARGAINING OVER MANY ISSUES

Our account of bargaining has so far focused on just one dimension, namely the total sum of money and its split between the two sides. In fact there are many dimensions to bargaining: the union and management care not just about wages but health benefits, pension plans, conditions of work, and so on. The United States and its NATO allies care not just about total defense expenditures, but how they are allocated. In principle, many of these are reducible to equivalent sums of money, but with an important difference — each side may value the items differently.

Such differences open up new possibilities for mutually acceptable bargains. Suppose the company is able to secure group health coverage on better terms than the individual workers would obtain on their own — say, $1,000 per year instead of $2,000 per year for a family of four. Now the workers would rather have health coverage than an extra $1,500 a year in wages, and the company would rather offer health coverage than an extra $1,500 in wages, too.[3]

It would seem that the negotiators should throw all the issues of mutual interest into a common bargaining pot, and exploit the difference in their relative valuations to achieve outcomes that are better for everyone. This works in some instances; for example, broad negotiations toward trade liberalization in the General Agreement on Tariffs and Trade (GATT) have had better success than ones narrowly focused on particular sectors or commodities.

But joining issues together opens up the possibility of using one bargaining game to generate threats in another. For example, the United States may have had more success in extracting concessions in negotiations to open up the Japanese market to its exports if it threatened a breakdown of the military relationship, thereby exposing Japan to a risk of Soviet or Chinese aggression. The United States had no interest in actually having this happen; it would be merely a threat that would induce Japan to make the economic concession. Therefore, Japan would insist that the economic and military issues be negotiated separately.

5. CASE STUDY #11: 'TIS BETTER TO GIVE THAN TO RECEIVE?

Recall our bargaining problem in which a hotel's management and its labor were negotiating over how to divide the season's profits. Now, instead of labor and management alternating offers, imagine that *only* the management gets to make offers, and labor can only accept or reject.

As before, the season lasts 101 days. Each day the hotel operates, it makes a profit of $1,000. Negotiations start at the beginning of the season. Each day, the management presents its offer, which is either accepted or rejected by labor. If accepted, the hotel opens and begins making money. If rejected, the negotiations continue until either an offer is accepted or the season ends and the entire profits are lost.

Table 3 illustrates the declining potential profits as the season progresses. If both labor and management's only concern is to maximize its own payoff, what do you expect will happen (and when)?

Table 3: Wage Bargaining — Management Makes All Offers

Days to Go	Offer by	Total Profits to Divide	Amount Offered to Labor
1	Management	$ 1,000	?
2	Management	2,000	?
3	Management	3,000	?
4	Management	4,000	?
5	Management	5,000	?
...			
100	Management	100,000	?
101	Management	101,000	?

Case Discussion

In this case, we expect the outcome to differ radically from 50:50. Because management has the sole power to propose, it is in the much stronger bargaining position. Management should be able to get close to the entire amount and reach agreement on the first day.

To predict the bargaining outcome, we start at the end and work backward. On the last day there is no value in continuing, so labor should be willing to accept any positive amount, say $1.00. On the penultimate day, labor recognizes that rejecting today's offer will bring only $1.00 tomorrow; hence, they prefer to accept $2.00 today. The argument continues right up to the first day. Management proposes to give labor $101, and labor, seeing no better alternative in the future, accepts.

Table 4: Wage Bargaining — Management Makes All Offers

Days to Go	Offer by	Total Profits to Divide	Amount Offered to Labor
1	Management	$ 1,000	$ 1
2	Management	2,000	2
3	Management	3,000	3
4	Management	4,000	4
5	Management	5,000	5
...			
100	Management	100,000	100
101	Management	101,000	101

This story clearly exaggerates management's true bargaining power. Postponing agreement, even by one day, costs management $999 and labor only $1. To the extent that labor cares not only about its payments but also how these payments compare to management's, this type of radically unequal division will not be possible. But that does not mean we must return to an even split. Management still has all the bargaining power. Its goal should be to find the minimally acceptable amount to give to labor so that labor prefers getting that amount over nothing, even though management may get more. For example, in the last period, labor might be willing to accept $334 while management gets $666 if labor's alternative is zero. If so, management can perpetuate that 1:2 split throughout each of the 101 days and capture two-thirds of the total profit. The value of this technique for solving bargaining problems is that it suggests some of the different sources of bargaining power. Splitting the difference or even division is a common but not universal solution to a bargaining problem. Look forward and reason backward provides a reason why we might expect to find unequal division. In particular, it suggests that in the case of making offers, " 'Tis better to give than to receive."

6. APPENDIX: PATIENCE IS ITS OWN REWARD

It is possible to apply backward reasoning even when problems lack a fixed endpoint.* This is an important feature of most bargaining problems. Let us look therefore at a more typical setting, such as a steel company. A strike is in progress. If it is settled, the company can make an operating profit of $3 million each week. The union and the management are bargaining over the division of this sum. Negotiation sessions are held weekly, and the two sides alternate in making offers.

Every week that goes by without an agreement, the two sides together sacrifice $3 million. As usual, time is money. An immediate settlement is in their joint best interest. But on what terms? Intuition suggests that the party that is more impatient for a settlement will make the earlier or the larger concessions. A more detailed look at the process confirms this intuition, and converts it into more precise predictions about the two parties' shares.

Time is money in many different ways. Most simply, a dollar received earlier is worth more than the same dollar received later, because it can be invested and earn interest or dividends in the meantime. If the rate of return on investments is 5 percent a year, then a dollar received right now is worth $1.05 received a year later.

The same idea applies to our union and management, but there are some additional features that may add to the impatience factor. Each week the agreement is delayed, there is a risk that old, loyal customers will develop long-term relationships with other suppliers, and the firm will be threatened with permanent closure. The workers and the managers will have to move to other jobs that pay less well, the union lead-

---

* This approach was pioneered by the economist Ariel Rubinstein, and the solution we discuss is often called the Rubinstein bargaining solution in his honor. One example of how to do this is provided in the case study "The Limits to Charity" offered in Chapter 13.

ers' reputation will suffer, and the management's stock options will become worthless. An immediate agreement is better than one a week later precisely to the extent of the probability that this will come to pass in the course of that week.

Of course the union and the management may assess the risks and their consequences differently. Just to make things precise, suppose the union regards $1.00 right now as equivalent to $1.01 a week later, and for the management the figure is $1.02. In other words, the union's weekly "interest rate" is 1 percent; the management's, 2 percent. The management is twice as impatient as the union.

This difference in the two sides' impatience has a dramatic effect on their bargaining settlement: the two sides' shares are in inverse proportion to their rates of interest, so the union gets two-thirds ($2 million per week) and the management one-third ($1 million per week).

The fact that the greater share in bargaining agreements goes to the more patient side is very unfortunate for the United States. Our system of government, and its coverage in the media, foster impatience. When negotiations with other nations on military and economic matters are making slow progress, interested lobbyists seek support from congressmen, senators, and the media, who pressure the administration for quicker results. Our rival nations in the negotiations know this very well, and are able to secure greater concessions from us.

12

Incentives

Why have socialist economic systems failed so miserably?
The best laid Five Year Plans of Stalin and his successors
"gang agley" because the workers and the managers lacked
adequate incentives. Most importantly, the system offered no
reward for doing a good job rather than a merely adequate
one. People had no reason to show initiative or innovation,
and every reason to cut corners wherever they could — fulfill-
ing quantity quotas and slacking on quality, for example.

A market economy has a better natural incentive mechanism, namely the profit motive. A company that succeeds in
cutting costs, or introducing a new product, makes a greater
profit; one that lags behind stands to lose money. But even
this does not work perfectly. Each employee or manager in a
company is not fully exposed to the chill wind of competition in
the market, and the top management of the firm has to devise
its own internal carrots and sticks to obtain the desired standards of performance from those below. When two firms join
forces for a particular project, they have the added problem
of designing a contract that will share the incentives between
them in the right way.

1. HOW TO REWARD WORK EFFORT

We bring out the important ideas for the design of incentive
schemes through a series of examples. Imagine yourself as the

owner of a high-tech company in California trying to develop and market a new computer chess game, Wizard 1.0. If you succeed, you will make a profit of $200,000 from the sales. If you fail, you make nothing. Success or failure hinges on what your expert player-programmer does. She can either put her heart and soul into the work, or just give it a routine shot. With high-quality effort, the chances of success are 80 percent, but for routine effort, the figure drops to 60 percent.

Chess programmers can be hired for $50,000, but they like to daydream, and will give only their routine effort for this sum. For high-quality effort, you have to pay $70,000. What should you do?

	Chance of Success	Average Revenue	Salary Payments	Average Profit = Revenue – Salary
Low-Quality Effort	60%	$120,000	$50,000	**$70,000**
High-Quality Effort	80%	$160,000	$70,000	**$90,000**

A routine effort will get you $200,000 with a 60 percent chance, which comes out to $120,000 on average. Subtracting the $50,000 salary leaves an average profit of $70,000. The corresponding calculation if you hire a high-effort expert is 80 percent of $200,000 minus $70,000, that is, $90,000. Clearly you do better to hire a high-effort expert at the higher salary.

But there is a problem. You can't tell by looking at the expert's working day whether she is making routine effort or quality effort. The creative process is mysterious. The drawings on your programmer's pad may be the key to a great graphics display that will ensure the success of Wizard 1.0, or just doodles of pawns and bishops to accompany her daydreaming. Knowing that you can't tell the difference between routine effort and quality effort, what is to prevent the expert from accepting the salary of $70,000 appropriate for high effort, but making routine effort just the same? Even if the project fails, that can always be blamed on chance. After all, even with genuine quality effort, the project can fail 20 percent of the time; this was just that kind of bad luck.

When you can't observe the quality of effort, you have to base your reward scheme on something you can observe. In the present instance that can be only the ultimate outcome, namely success or failure of the programming effort. This does have a link to effort, albeit an imperfect one — higher quality of effort means a greater chance of success. This link can be exploited to generate an incentive scheme.

What you do is offer the expert a remuneration that depends on the outcome: a larger sum upon success and a smaller sum in the event of failure. The difference, or the bonus for success, should be just enough to make it in the employee's own interest to provide high-quality effort. In this case, the bonus must be big enough so that the expert expects a high effort will raise her earnings by $20,000, from $50,000 to $70,000. Hence the bonus for success has to be at least $100,000: a 20 percent increase in the chance of getting a $100,000 bonus provides the necessary $20,000 expected payment for motivating high-quality effort.

It remains to find the separate sums to be paid in the event of success or failure. That needs a little calculation. The answer is that you should pay the employee $90,000 for success, and she should pay you a fine of $10,000 in the event of failure. With this incentive scheme, the programmer's incremental reward for success is $100,000, the minimum necessary for inducing quality effort. The average payment to her is $70,000 (an 80 percent chance of $90,000 and a 20 percent chance of minus $10,000). This leaves you, the owner, an average profit of $90,000 (an 80 percent chance of $200,000 minus the average salary of $70,000). This is exactly what you could have gotten if you could observe quality of effort by direct supervision. The incentive scheme has done a perfect job; the unobservability of effort hasn't made any difference.

In essence, this incentive scheme sells 50 percent of the firm to the programmer in exchange for $10,000 and her effort. Her net payments are then either $90,000 or −$10,000, and with so much riding on the outcome of the project it becomes in her interest to supply high-quality effort in order to increase the chance of success (and her profit share of $100,000). The only difference between this contract and the fine/bonus scheme is in the name. While the name may matter, we see there is more than one way to achieve the same effect.

But these solutions may not be possible, either because assessing a fine on an employee may not be legal or because the worker does not have sufficient capital to pay the $10,000 for her 50 percent stake. What do you do then? The answer is to go as close to the fine solution or equity-sharing as you can. Since the minimum effective bonus is $100,000, the worker gets $100,000 in the event of success and nothing upon failure. Now the employee's average receipt is $80,000, and your profit falls to $80,000. With equity-sharing, the worker has only her labor and no capital to invest in the project. But she still has to be given a 50 percent share to motivate her to supply high-quality effort. So the best you can do is sell her 50 percent of the company for her labor alone. The inability to enforce fines or get workers to invest their own capital means that the outcome is less good from your point of view — in this case, by $10,000. Now the unobservability of effort makes a difference.

Another difficulty with the fine/bonus scheme or equity-sharing is the problem of risk. The worker's incentives arise from her taking a $100,000 gamble. But this large risk may not be evaluated by the statistical average of the outcomes. In this case, the worker has to be compensated both for supplying high-quality effort and for bearing risk. The bigger the risk, the bigger the compensation. This extra compensation is another cost of a firm's inability to monitor its workers' efforts.

Often the best solution is a compromise; risk is reduced by giving the worker less than ideal incentives and consequently this motivates less than an ideal amount of effort.

In other instances you may have other indicators of the quality of effort, and you can and should use them when designing your incentive scheme. Perhaps the most interesting and common situation is one in which there are several such projects. Even though success is only an inexact statistical indicator of the quality of effort, it can be made more precise if there are more observations. There are two ways in which this can be done. If the same expert works for you on many projects, then you can keep a record of her string of successes and failures. You can be more confident in attributing repeated failure to poor effort quality rather than the working of chance. The greater accuracy of your inference allows you to design a better incentive scheme. The second possibility is that you have several experts working on related projects, and there is some correlation in the success or failure of the projects. If one expert fails while others around her are succeeding, then you can be more confident that she is a shirker and not just unlucky. Therefore rewards based on relative performance — in other words, prizes — will generate suitable incentives.

When an employer designs incentives to motivate a worker, the problems are only one-sided. More complicated and more interesting are the problems of joint ventures in which each side has to provide the right incentives to motivate the other.

2. How to Organize a Joint Venture

In the late 1960s, Benson and Hedges launched their new 100-millimeter-long cigarettes with a memorable television commercial, in which "Hedges" described his search for "Benson." Hedges had the idea for an extra-long cigarette, and was sure that it would be a success if he could use the great tobacco from an obscure brand called Benson's. After many adventures, he found Benson. "I can see it now," he exclaimed, "Hedges and Benson 100s!" Of course, he concluded, "Benson saw it a little different."

By combining their resources, Benson and Hedges could increase their total profit. They had to agree on its division. Presumably Benson won that round. Now we want to think of what happens next.

Once their partnership agreement is made and the new brand is launched, the two are to a considerable extent stuck with each other. Neither can return to the old independent pursuit without sacrificing some profit. Hedges' innovation has become tied in the public's mind to one particular brand of tobacco, and Benson has lost his previous brand identification and customer base. Knowing this, each would be tempted to reopen the partnership agreement and extract a little more advantage at the expense of the other, threatening to walk out of the whole deal if the demand is refused.

But if the two are good strategists, this does not come as a surprise. Each can foresee the possibility, and becomes reluctant to enter into a deal that leaves him open to such future exploitation. The whole profitable scheme is threatened. The solution is to provide, in the original deed of partnership, enforceable penalty clauses that remove the temptation to renege. This chapter is about the design of such clauses.

The issue arises in personal partnerships just as in business ones. Imagine a working couple, both of whom dislike cooking but cannot afford to eat out more than once a week. They start with an implicit or explicit understanding that they will split the cooking chores equally — three days a week each. But the wife, say, knows that the husband is not likely to walk out just because she cuts her share down to two days. She is tempted to discover essential work that demands her presence at the office for an extra hour on some days, making it impossible for her to get home in time to fix dinner even though it is her turn. The husband in turn should look ahead to this and try to arrange the initial deal in such a way that the wife's future temptation is reduced.

Of course the personal and long-term aspects of a marriage often suffice to ensure that the parties do not try such tricks, or that they resolve such disputes amicably when they do arise. Business partnerships are less influenced by personal emotions, and the dollar amounts of the temptation to cheat are often higher. Therefore the kinds of contracts we will discuss are more relevant in this setting, even though the marriage analogy sometimes makes for more striking and amusing stories.

What are the essential features of this class of situations? First, these situations involve projects that require simultaneous participation by two or more people or firms. Each side must make some investment up front — a stake it stands to lose if the relationship is terminated — or else the other side's walking out will be no threat at all. Second, there must be some uncertainty about subsequent events that acts as a justification for reopening of the agreement, or else a simple clause that provides large punitive damages for any breach will serve the purpose.

In fact both these conditions exist to some degree in many actual instances. We will highlight them by constructing an example that is modeled on a real case, but isolates some features of it for emphasis.

When IBM chose Microsoft's operating system (MS-DOS) for its first generation of personal computers, this was a big factor in Microsoft's growth and profits. In turn, the future development of IBM's family of computers was constrained by their dependence on features of MS-DOS. Let us stylize this example.

Suppose the development of a computer system involves separate development of a compatible pair of hardware and software components. Two firms, each specializing in one area, are contemplating this project. The initial exploration will require $2.2 million of investment in the hardware part, and $1.1 million in the software. This initial investment will reveal the additional costs of completing the development. For the moment, the prospective partners know only the low, middle, and high values of the likely costs. Suppose these are $18, $24, and $30 million for the hardware and $9, $12, and $15 million for the software. The finished computer system is expected to generate operating profits of $39 million.

The Unified Decision

Before we ask what kind of contract these two firms can agree to, and abide by, let us pose a simpler question. Suppose instead of two separate firms specializing in hardware and software, there is just one integrated firm. Its management is appraising a project with two components, hardware and software, whose costs and revenues are exactly as above. How will the management proceed?

The decision involves two stages. The first is whether to go ahead with the exploration; the second, depending on what the exploration has shown, is whether to proceed with the further development. As usual, the management must look ahead and reason back, that is, start thinking about the second stage first.

With three possible values of the cost for each component, there are nine cases that can arise. Each is equally likely; thus the probability of each is 1/9. The chart shows the total costs for each of these cases. The initial exploration reveals which of these cases is going to arise. At that point the exploration costs have already been incurred, and the only question is whether further development is worthwhile, that is, whether the operating profits will cover the costs of development.

Development Costs -- Hardware + Software (in millions of dollars)

Software

	Low (9)	Middle (12)	High (15)
Low (18)	27	30	33
Middle (24)	33	36	39
High (30)	39	42	45

Hardware

In two of the cases, namely, those in which the hardware costs turn out to be at the high end and the software costs are either medium or high, the total development costs exceed the $39 million operating profit. If the initial exploration reveals that one of these cases is going to arise, the project should be canceled. In two other cases, one in which high hardware costs combine with low software costs and one in which medium hardware costs combine with high software costs, the operating profits only just cover the development costs. The management has no preference between going ahead and canceling; let us suppose it goes ahead, perhaps because it can thus show its concern for the workers so long as no actual loss is entailed.

We can show the net profit (operating profit minus development cost) in each of these nine cases. The two entries at the bottom right are zero because cancellation is possible. Without this option, these cases would have entailed the losses shown in parentheses.

Profits (in millions of dollars)

Software

		Low (9)	Middle (12)	High (15)
	Low (18)	12	9	6
Hardware	Middle (24)	6	3	0
	High (30)	0	0 (– 3)	0 (– 6)

The nine entries add up to $36 million, but since each case has a probability of only 1/9, their statistical average is only 36/9 = $4 million.

Now look at the first stage of decision, namely whether or not to undertake the initial exploration. This costs $3.3 million, and the expected profit is $4 million. Therefore the decision is to go ahead. Without the option of cancellation, the statistical average of subsequent profits would have been only $3 million, and the whole project would have been rejected. The possibility of divorce if things don't work out makes it easier to enter into a marriage in the first place.

Contracts

Let us abandon the fiction of an integrated firm, and see how separate software and hardware firms tackle the same decision. The range of costs for the hardware firm is exactly twice that for the software firm, so the answer would seem simple. Let each bear its own exploration costs. Go ahead with the development except in the two cases identified in the chart above. If the project continues, reimburse each firm for its development costs, and then split the remaining sum (the net profit) between them in the ratio of two (for hardware) to one (for software).

Unfortunately this won't work. Suppose the hardware firm's initial exploration reveals that its development costs are going to be low. Then it benefits by lying and claiming to have middle costs. Whether the firm lies or tells the truth, the project will always proceed. But exaggerating costs results in an extra $6 million cost reimbursement but only a $4 million reduction in profit-sharing. This is true no matter what the software firm announces. Thus claiming middle costs when actual costs are low is a dominant strategy for the hardware firm.

The software firm has a similar temptation; it wants to pretend to have high costs. But when they both engage in such pretense, the development stage will never show an operating profit, and when both of them know this at the exploration stage, they will decide not to proceed with the project at all.

How can a firm lie about its costs? In fact it is very easy to overstate costs. Each firm probably has several lines of business with common overhead costs, and can apply a disproportionate share of the overhead to this project. A firm can actually increase its costs — for example, by paying the managers inflated salaries and padding other expenses. When the padded costs must be paid out of one's own revenue, there is no temptation to do so. But when the costs are reimbursed from a joint revenue pool, each partner firm is tempted to cheat the other. "Cost plus" contracts awarded by governments suffer large overruns for the same reason.*

Let us therefore think of an alternative. Simply split the operating profit between them in the ratio of two (for hardware) to one (for software), and have each firm bear its own

---

* In fact the design of defense contracts would have provided the best example for this chapter, but for the fact that the analogue of the operating profit is too elusive in the case of defense to allow any numerical examples. How does one value national defense?

development costs. Now there is no incentive to pad costs. But we have lost the procedure for making the right cancellation decision. The software firm gets $13 million of the operating profit. When its costs are high ($15 million), it wants to cancel the development, even though continuation would be jointly profitable if the hardware firm's costs were low at the same time. On the other hand, if the software firm's costs are medium ($12 million), it wants to go ahead, even though cancellation would be jointly preferable if the hardware firm's costs were high at the same time. Should the contract allow cancellation at the request of one party (divorce on demand), or should both parties have to concur (divorce by mutual consent only)? Either rule will lead to undesirable outcomes in some of the cases. This is the dilemma of designing an ideal contract — how to combine efficient go-ahead decisions with the incentive to truthfully reveal private information about costs or revenues.

Paying What It Costs

We begin by focusing on the incentives for the hardware firm. The simplest solution is to have the hardware firm reimburse the software firm for its costs and keep all the remaining profits if it decides to proceed. Whenever the joint costs are less than the profit opportunity, the hardware firm will decide to proceed — it gets the total revenue minus its own development costs minus the cost reimbursement to the software firm. This incentive scheme gives the hardware firm the incentive to make the efficient decision.

How does the hardware firm know the software firm's cost? Both sides could simultaneously announce their costs and agree that the project proceeds only if the sum of the announced costs is below the profit opportunity. Since the hardware firm keeps all the profits after reimbursing the software firm for its development costs, it wants to proceed whenever these residual profits exceed its true costs. The only way to ensure this outcome is for the hardware firm to announce the truth. If the software firm exaggerates its costs, then the go-ahead decisions won't always be correct. But the hardware firm still wants to make a truthful announcement no matter which strategy the software firm follows: truth-telling is the hardware firm's dominant strategy.

To see this, consider each of the cases. The hardware firm knows that the software firm could announce one of three numbers. If that number is $9 million (the low end), the project will go ahead no matter what cost figure the hardware firm announces, and its revenue will be $39 - 9 = \$30$ million, enough to cover any of its costs. Next suppose the software firm says $12 million. If the hardware firm's true costs are $18 million (low) or $24 million (middle), truthful revelation will let the project proceed and result in $27 million, which still covers the true cost of $18 or $24 million. Pretending the costs are high results in cancellation, which passes up a profitable opportunity. On the other hand, if the hardware firm's costs are truly $30 million (high), and it pretends they are low or medium, the project goes ahead and the hardware firm gets $27 million, which is a net loss of $3 million.

To sum up, inflating costs has no effect on profits when the project goes ahead, but can result in cancellation and missed profitable opportunities. Deflating costs makes no difference when the project is canceled, but may result in a go-ahead decision exactly when it means a loss. Therefore truth-telling is the dominant strategy for the hardware firm. The incentive scheme alters the strategic environment for the hardware firm to the point where its moral is "Neither an inflator nor a deflator be."

A different point of view sheds useful new light on the incentive mechanism. When the hardware firm tries to get a go-ahead decision, it is asking the software firm to incur some cost. Such costs inflicted on others are called *externalities*, and the purpose of incentive schemes is to induce people to take into account the externalities they impose on others. This is just what happens when the hardware firm receives as payment the operating profit minus the software firm's cost. When the project goes ahead, the hardware firm's total cash flow equals the operating profit, minus the software firm's costs, minus its own costs. Therefore the hardware firm is just as concerned to reduce costs for the software firm as it is for itself. In other words, it is acting in the joint interest, or has internalized the externality.

Thus we have solved the hardware firm's incentive problem. The exact same trick also solves the software firm's incentive problem, if the situation is set up the other way around — i.e., the software firm gets the total profits minus its own costs and the costs announced by the hardware firm. As above, the project proceeds whenever profits exceed the sum of the two announced costs. A parallel argument shows that a truthful announcement is the dominant strategy for the software firm.

But all is not yet well. We still have to combine the two incentive schemes so that they can operate simultaneously. Otherwise we only get truth-telling by one side and then no guarantee of any efficiency in the outcomes. The problem with running both incentive schemes simultaneously is that in every case in which the project goes ahead, the total payments exceed the total revenues! All that is available for payout is the operating profit. But the combined schemes pay out twice the operating profit, minus the sum of the two costs. The shortfall equals the operating profit minus the sum of the two costs, and this is positive whenever the project goes ahead.

One way to get around this problem is for the two firms to bank some suitable sum up front and use this to cover shortfalls. If the firms bank the statistical average of the expected shortfalls, they will come out ahead in some cases and lose in others, but break even on the average. In our example the banked amount works out at $4 million.

But it is possible to do even better. We can devise a contract that (1) gives both firms the incentive to reveal their costs truthfully, (2) always ensures efficient go-ahead or cancellation decisions, and (3) guarantees that the contract breaks even on a case-by-case basis, not just on the average.

The principle behind the efficient contract is to get firms to take into account the costs they impose on others by their actions. We just saw that when each firm pays the other's cost, they are each motivated to announce the truth and make an efficient go-ahead decision. But this leads to a problem with budget balancing. So instead of paying the actual cost of the other firm, each can pay the expected or statistical average of the costs its action will impose. When each firm declares a low cost, this increases the chance that the project will proceed and correspondingly the chance that the other firm will have to bear some production costs. To make each firm take into account the average externality it will inflict on the other type of firm, it should receive the statistical average of the project's operating profit minus the average of the costs of the other type of firm it will be dealing with when the project goes ahead. If the firm inflates its own cost, it risks canceling the project more frequently and getting smaller receipts, while if it deflates costs this leads to a higher "externality" payment for the expected costs imposed on the other firm.

Two examples will clarify this. If the hardware firm declares its costs to be low ($18 million), then the project will go ahead no matter what the costs of the software firm, which can be $9, $12, or $15 million, each with a one-third chance. The statistical average is $12 million. This is the sum subtracted from the operating profit of $39 million in calculating the hardware firm's receipt. If the hardware firm declares high cost ($30 million), then the project will go ahead only if the software firm declares low cost ($9 million), which happens one-third of the time. So the hardware firm should receive one third of $39 minus $9 million, or $10 million. The chart below shows the receipt figures so calculated. In each cell the receipts of the hardware firm are shown in the bottom left and the receipts for the software firm are in the top right.

Receipt Calculations ---First Stage (in millions of dollars)

Software

		Low (9)		Middle (12)		High (15)
		15		12		12
Low (18)	27		27		27	
		15		12		12
Middle (24)	27		27		27	
		15		12		12
High (30)	10		10		10	

Hardware

But the receipts so calculated do not balance the budget on a case-by-case basis. For example, in the bottom left case the project collects a revenue of $39 million but pays out only $25 million, while in the two other cases in the bottom row there is no revenue generated (because the project does not go ahead) but there is a payout of $22 million. Therefore a second stage of the calculation must adjust the payouts and achieve balance. This must be done without upsetting the firms' incentives to reveal their true costs. We can change each firm's receipts in response to what the other firm says; for example, we can add or subtract any number from the hardware firm's receipts in the first column without altering its incentive to give one answer or the other. Each column of the hardware firm's receipts and each row of the software firm's receipts can be adjusted this way. We can also rearrange the hardware firm's payoffs along each row so long as their statistical average is preserved, and similarly for the software firm along each column. All these adjustments give us more than enough freedom to ensure case-by-case balance. We offer one possible answer in Scheme 1.

**Scheme 1 with Correct Incentives and
Budget Balance (in millions of dollars)**

Software

		Low (9)	Middle (12)	High (15)
Hardware	Low (18)	15 24	12 27	12 27
	Middle (24)	15 24	12 27	12 27
	High (30)	6 33	3 −3	3 −3

This has the nice property that the hardware firm's receipts, averaged over all nine possibilities, are $20.33 million, while those of the software firm are $10 million; the ratio of 2:1 is almost exactly the ratio of their general cost structure, and therefore the scheme seems to offer the fairest division of the returns between the two. But in the cases in which the project is canceled, the hardware firm must pay the software firm $3 million. This can be a cause of disputes after the fact. An alternative scheme, Scheme 2 that follows, has zero payments when there is a cancellation. This might be easier to enforce. But it gives the hardware firm an overall better deal: an average of $23.33 million as against only $7 million for the software firm, a ratio of more than three to one.

**Scheme 2 with Correct Incentives and Budget
Balance (in millions of dollars)**

Software

		Low (9)	Middle (12)	High (15)
		12	9	9
Hardware	Low (18)	27	30	30
		12	9	9
	Middle (24)	27	30	30
		3	0	0
	High (30)	36	0	0

If one side, when terminating a partnership, is required to make the other side whole, then this side will have just the right incentive to maintain the partnership. Sometimes it will be dissolved, but the gain to one side is not at the expense of the other.

The idea of paying the cost you impose on others is useful in many contexts. It even helps us understand bidding strategy in auctions.

3. THE STRATEGY OF AUCTIONS

Many production or supply contracts, especially government ones but sometimes also private ones, are awarded by a sealed-bid auction. Each firm submits in a sealed envelope the price for which it is willing to do the job. Then all the bids are compared, and the lowest bidder wins, and receives the price that she bid.

Imagine yourself as a bidder for such a contract, say con-

struction of a stretch of highway. Your cost (which includes
the normal return you require on investment) is $10 million.
You do not know the costs of your competitors, and may not
even know their identities. But you have reason to believe
that their costs will range somewhere between $5 million and
$15 million. The best of them will have a cost figure that is
equally likely to lie anywhere between the extremes — one
chance in ten for each million in this range. What bid should
you submit?

You will never submit a bid that is lower than your cost. For
example, suppose you bid $9 million. This makes no difference
if you don't win, but if you do win, you will be paid a price that
is less than your cost.* You will be paving the way to your own
bankruptcy.

What about submitting a bid that is higher than your cost?
Suppose all the others bid honestly, and see what happens if
you submit the bid of $11 million. You must consider three
possibilities separately. Five times out of ten, some rival will
have bid less than $10 million, and your inflated bid will make
no difference at all. Four times out of ten, the best rival bid
will exceed $11 million. You could have won the contract with
a bid of either $10 million or $11 million, but the higher bid
gets you $1 million more profit. There is one chance in ten that
the best rival bid falls between $10 million and $11 million.
Now your overstatement costs you the contract. But at $10
million the price only just covered your costs, so the contract
was only barely worth having anyway.

Putting the three cases together, you see that submitting
an inflated bid is a good strategy for you; in the language of
game theory, it dominates truthful bidding. The other participants are thinking along the same lines. Therefore all bids
get inflated.

---

* Here we are supposing that the bid is a firm commitment, and that you
cannot later renegotiate a higher price. In the next section we will look at
contracts with renegotiation.

When the bids reveal the true costs, society can make an accurate cost-benefit analysis of the road, and the decision to build it will be economically efficient. Are there other bidding schemes that remove the strategic temptation to inflate the bids?

Yes. One simple scheme awards the contract to the lowest bidder, but pays her a price equal to the second-lowest bid, rather than her own. Let us see how this works. Suppose again that your cost is $10 million, and that you are thinking of bidding $11 million. As before, there are three cases to consider. If the best rival bid is under $10 million, then your strategy makes no difference. If the best rival bid is more than $11 million, you still win the contract, but now the price you get equals the best rival bid, so the inflation has not gained you anything. If the best rival bid falls between $10 and $11 million, your strategy has cost you the contract, when the truth would have gotten you at least a little profit, namely the excess of the best rival bid over $10 million.

To sum up, inflating your bid gains you nothing in two of the cases, and loses a little in one case. Therefore you have a dominant strategy, namely submitting a bid that equals your cost.

We can look at it in another way, and thereby shed some useful new light on the scheme. When you inflate your bid from $10 million to $11 million, you are inflicting a cost on society, namely creating the possibility that the contract will go to a firm that has a higher cost — uses up more resources — than yours. Here again, this cost inflicted by one person on others is called an externality. A good incentive scheme must induce you to take into account the true social cost of your action, including any externality you impose on others. This can be done by charging you the costs, or paying you a reward for avoiding them. In the present instance, the second method is the one at work. By not inflating your

bid, you save society the risk of an unnecessarily costly un-
dertaking, and are rewarded with a price equal to the higher
cost.

This is just like the first incentive scheme we described for
the joint venture. In this case, the efficient solution is to have
the firm with the lowest cost get the contract. By taking on the
project, it saves the firm with the next lowest costs from incurring its costs. This savings is a positive externality. When the
winning bidder is paid for incurring this externality, it has the
incentive to announce the truth, and efficient decisions will be
made. But the ability to elicit true costs from the bidders does
not come for free. The Department of Transportation has to
pay the lowest bidder more than his own cost, namely the cost
of the next lowest bidder.

Items can be sold as well as purchased using this type
of auction. Each person places his bid in a sealed envelope,
and the highest bidder is sold the item at the second highest
bidder's price. Developed by Columbia University economist
William Vickrey, this procedure is sometimes called a Vickrey auction or a philatelist auction (stamp journals use this
procedure to auction stamps through the mail). Once again,
each person should bid his or her true valuation. Bidding
more than one's value risks winning the auction when it is not
worthwhile, while underbidding never saves you money but
risks losing the prize when you were still willing to pay the
second highest bid.

In fact, this one-step procedure should lead to exactly the
same outcome as a traditional English auction. In the English
auction, all the bidders are in the same room and an auctioneer calls out successively higher prices. The bidding progresses
until only one bidder is left — going once, going twice, sold.
The penultimate bidder should drop out only when the price
exceeds his valuation. Thus the person who values the item
most highly should win the prize, and he pays a price equal to

the value of the next highest bidder.* But that is exactly the outcome of the Vickrey auction!

Compare the Vickrey auction to the more standard way to run a sealed-bid auction — the highest bidder wins the prize and pays his bid, or if the auction is used to sell a contract, the lowest bidder is awarded the contract and is paid his bid. Which scheme works better for the seller (or buyer)?

It is remarkable but true that, on average, the two schemes lead to exactly the same outcomes. In the case of a government collecting bids for a road project, the seeming budgetary advantage of paying the lowest bid rather than the next lowest bid disappears when we understand how the bidders respond to it strategically, namely by inflating their bids. The lowest bidder wins and is paid an amount equal to his own bid, but that will be an inflated bid. A complete mathematical analysis of the problem shows that the budgetary effect of the bid inflation under the conventional method is exactly the same as that of paying the winner the bid of the next bidder. Therefore the scheme we described does not cost any more than the conventional one. The intuitive reason for this equivalence is that both types of auctions should always lead to an efficient outcome: the person with the lowest costs should always win. But efficiency arises only when people take account of the externality they impose on others. Thus a firm's optimal bid is the expected cost on the next best competitor conditional on winning the auction. This is just like the balanced-budget version of the joint-venture incentive; in this case, the winning firm bids the expected or average externality rather than the actual externality.

---

* Actually, there is typically some minimum bidding increment. Since the price moves upward in jumps, the expected selling price in an English auction is the minimum bid above the value of the second highest bidder. The difference in selling price between an English and Vickrey auction is thus limited to the size of the bidding unit.

4. CASE STUDY #12: THE RISK OF WINNING

One of the more unusual features of a Vickrey sealed-bid auction is that the winning bidder does not know how much she will have to pay until the auction is over and she has won. Remember, in a Vickrey auction the winning bidder pays only the second highest bid. In contrast, there is no uncertainty in the more standard sealed-bid auction, in which the winner pays her bid. Since everyone knows her own bid, no one has any doubts as to how much she will have to pay if she wins.

The presence of uncertainty suggests that we might want to consider the effect of risk on the participants' bidding strategies. The typical response to uncertainty is negative: the bidders are worse off in a Vickrey auction because they do not know how much they will have to pay if they have submitted the winning bid. Is it reasonable that a bidder will respond to this uncertainty or risk by lowering her bid below the true valuation?

Case Discussion

It is true that the bidders dislike the uncertainty associated with how much they might have to pay if they win. Each is in fact worse off. Yet, in spite of the risk, participants should still bid their true valuations. The reason is that a truthful bid is a dominant strategy. As long as the selling price is below the valuation, the bidder wants to buy the good. The only way to ensure that you win whenever the price is below your value is to bid the true value.

In a Vickrey auction, bidding the true valuation doesn't make you pay more — except when someone else would have outbid you, in which case you would have wanted to raise your bid until the selling price exceeded your valuation. The risk associated with a Vickrey auction is limited; the winner is never forced to pay an amount greater than her bid. While there is uncertainty about what the winner will pay, this uncertainty is only over the degree of good news. Even though the good news might be variable, the best strategy is to win the auction whenever it's profitable. That means bidding your true value. You never miss a profitable opportunity and whenever you win you pay less than your true value.

13

Case Studies

1. THE OTHER PERSON'S ENVELOPE IS ALWAYS GREENER

The inevitable truth about gambling is that one person's gain must be another person's loss. Thus it is especially important to evaluate a gamble from the other side's perspective before accepting. For if they are willing to gamble, they expect to win, which means they expect you to lose. Someone must be wrong, but who? This case study looks at a bet that seems to profit both sides. That can't be right, but where's the flaw?

There are two envelopes, each containing an amount of money; the amount of money is either $5, $10, $20, $40, $80, or $160 and everybody knows this. Furthermore, we are told that one envelope contains exactly twice as much money as the other. The two envelopes are shuffled, and we give one envelope to Ali and one to Baba. After both the envelopes are opened (but the amounts inside are kept private), Ali and Baba are given the opportunity to switch. If both parties want to switch, we let them.

Suppose Baba opens his envelope and sees $20. He reasons as follows: Ali is equally likely to have $10 or $40. Thus my expected reward if I switch envelopes is $(10 + 40)/2 = \$25 > \$20$. For gambles this small, the risk is unimportant, so it is in my interest to switch.

By a similar argument, Ali will want to switch whether she

sees $10 (since she figures that he will get either $5 or $20, which has an average of $12.50) or $40 (since she figures to get either $20 or $80, which has an average of $50).

Something is wrong here. Both parties can't be better off by switching envelopes since the amount of money to go around is not getting any bigger by switching. What is the mistaken reasoning? Should Ali and/or Baba offer to switch?

Case Discussion

A switch should never occur if Ali and Baba are both rational and assume that the other is too. The flaw in the reasoning is the assumption that the other side's willingness to switch envelopes does not reveal any information. We solve the problem by looking deeper and deeper into what each side thinks about the other's thought process. First we take Ali's perspective about what Baba thinks. Then we use this from Baba's perspective to imagine what Ali might be thinking about him. Finally, we go back to Ali and consider what he should think about how Baba thinks Ali thinks about Baba. Actually, this all sounds much more complicated than it is. Using the example, the steps are easier to follow.

Suppose that Ali opens his envelope and sees $160. In that case, she knows that she has the greater amount and hence is unwilling to participate in a trade. Since Ali won't trade when she has $160, Baba should refuse to switch envelopes when he has $80, for the only time Ali might trade with him occurs when Ali has $40, in which case Baba prefers to keep his original $80. But if Baba won't switch when he has $80, then Ali shouldn't want to trade envelopes when she has $40, since a trade will result only when Baba has $20. Now we have arrived at the case in hand. If Ali doesn't want to switch envelopes when she has $40, then there is no gain from trade when Baba finds $20 in his envelope; he doesn't want to trade his $20 for $10. The only person who is willing to trade is someone who finds \$5 in the envelope, but of course the other side doesn't want to trade with him.

2. THE LAST SHALL BE FIRST

The U.S. government had a major problem trying to motivate several million teenagers to register for the military draft. Large-scale civil disobedience would make it impossible to punish everyone who violated the law. Still, the government had a big advantage: it set the rules.

To see the advantage of moving first, imagine that the government is only allowed to punish *one* person who fails to register. How can they use this single threat to induce everyone to register?

Case Discussion

The government announces that it will go after evaders in alphabetical order. The person with surname Aaron knows that he would be singled out for punishment if he failed to register. The certainty of punishment is then enough to motivate him to register. Then the Abrams conclude that since all of the Aarons will surely register, it is they who will be punished. And so on down the line right through to the Zhukovs and the Zweibels.

A lawyer might argue that it is unconstitutional to single out people for punishment because of the alphabetical ordering of their names. But nothing is special about the alphabet. The key point is that the order of punishment is pre-specified. A randomly chosen and announced order of birthdates, or social security numbers, does just as well. A few selective punishments go a long way in keeping everyone in line, and are much cheaper than offering market wages to attract an equal number and quality of recruits.

For example, if Congress mistook appearances for reality, it might forbid the Draft Board to use alphabetical order as the means by which they choose who gets punished first, leaving open other equivalent methods. What is needed to stop the practice is to forbid the *pre-announcement* of any order.

When the participants in a game are ranked in some order, it is often possible to predict what the person at one end will do. This knowledge influences the action of the next person, which in turn influences the third, and so on down the line.

The story we have told is a bit extreme. By the time we get to the Zhukovs, someone will surely not register and then be punished. The Zhukovs don't really have to worry. With so many individuals, one expects a small amount of slippage. The point is that the number of punishments available need not be anywhere near the number of people to motivate. The capacity (and willingness) to jail a thousand protestors can deter several million would-be's.

3. THE THREE-WAY DUEL

Three antagonists, Larry, Mo, and Curly, are engaged in a three-way duel. There are two rounds. In the first round, each player is given one shot: first Larry, then Mo, and then Curly. After the first round, any survivors are given a second shot, again beginning with Larry, then Mo, and then Curly.

For each duelist, the best outcome is to be the sole survivor. Next best is to be one of two survivors. In third place is the outcome in which no one gets killed. Dead last is that you get killed.

Larry is a poor shot, with only a 30 percent chance of hitting a person at whom he aims. Mo is a much better shot, achieving 80 percent accuracy. Curly is a perfect shot — he never misses.

What is Larry's optimal strategy in the first round? Who has the greatest chance of survival in this problem?

Although backward reasoning is the safe way to solve this problem, we can jump ahead a little by using some forward-looking arguments. We start by examining each of Larry's options in turn. What happens if Larry shoots at Mo? What happens if Larry shoots at Curly?

If Larry shoots at Mo and hits, then he signs his own death warrant. It becomes Curly's turn to shoot, and he never misses. Curly will not pass at the chance to shoot Larry, as this leads to his best outcome. Larry shooting at Mo does not seem to be a very attractive option.

If Larry shoots at Curly and hits, then it is Mo's turn. Mo will shoot at Larry. [Think about how we know this to be true.] Hence, if Larry hits Curly, his chance of survival is less than 20 percent (the chance that Mo misses).

So far, neither of these options looks to be very attractive. In fact, Larry's best strategy is to fire up in the air! In this case, Mo will shoot at Curly, and if he misses, Curly will shoot and kill Mo. Then it becomes the second round and it is Larry's turn to shoot again. Since only one other person remains, he has at least a 30 percent chance of survival, since that is the probability that he kills his one remaining opponent.

The moral here is that small fish may do better by passing on their first chance to become stars. We see this every four years in presidential campaigns. When there is a large number of contenders, the leader of the pack often gets derailed by the cumulative attacks of all the medium-sized fish. It can be advantageous to wait, and step into the limelight only after the others have knocked each other and themselves out of the running.

Thus, your chances of survival depend on not only your own ability but also whom you threaten. A weak player who threatens no one may end up surviving if the stronger players kill each other off. Curly, although he is the most accurate, has the lowest chance of survival — only 14 percent. So much for survival of the fittest! Mo has a 56 percent chance of winning. Larry's best strategy turns his 30 percent accuracy into a 41.2 percent chance of winning.[1]

Today's duels are more likely to be fought between takeover specialist T. Boone Pickens and the target management over who will end up with control of the board of directors. Our next case presents the story of a firm that tried to preempt a takeover duel through the use of a poison pill. But things don't always come out as planned, especially if you don't think far enough ahead.

4. THE SHARK REPELLENT THAT BACKFIRED

In recent years, corporations have adopted many new and innovative ways, often called shark repellents, to prevent outside investors from taking over their company. Without commenting on the efficiency or even morality of these ploys, we present a new and as yet untested variety of poison pill and ask you to consider how to overcome it.

The target company is Piper's Pickled Peppers. Although now publicly held, the old family ties remain, as the five-member board of directors is completely controlled by five of the founder's grandchildren. The founder recognized the possibility of conflict between his grandchildren as well as the threat of outsiders. To guard against both family squabbles and outsider attacks, he first required that the board of director elections be staggered. This trick means that even someone who owns 100 percent of the shares cannot replace the entire board — rather, only the members whose terms are expiring. Each of the five members had a staggered five-year term. An outsider could hope to get at most one seat a year. Taken at face value, it appeared that it would take someone three years to get a majority and control of the company.

The founder was worried that his idea of staggered terms

would be subject to change if a hostile party wrested control of the shares. A second provision was therefore added. The procedure for board election could be changed *only* by the board itself. Any board member could make a proposal without the need for a seconder. But there was a major catch. The proposer would be required to vote for his own proposal. The voting would then proceed in clockwise order around the boardroom table. To pass, a proposal needed at least 50 percent of the total board (absences were counted as votes against). Given that there were only five members, that meant at least 3 out of 5. Here's the rub. Any person who made a proposal to change either the membership of the board or the rules by how that membership was determined would be deprived of his position on the board and his stock holdings *if his proposal failed*. The holdings would be distributed evenly among the remaining members of the board. In addition, any board member who voted for a proposal that failed would also lose his seat on the board and his holdings.

For a while this provision proved successful in fending off hostile bidders. But then Sea Shells by the Sea Shore Ltd. bought 51 percent of the shares in a hostile takeover attempt. Sea Shells voted herself one seat on the board at the annual election. But it did not appear that loss of control was imminent, as she was one lone voice against four.

At their first board meeting, Sea Shells proposed a radical restructuring of the board membership. This was the first such proposal that the board had ever voted on. Not only did the Sea Shells proposal pass, amazingly, it passed unanimously! As a result, Sea Shells got to immediately replace the entire board. The old directors were given a lead parachute (which is still better than nothing) and then were shown the door.

How did she do it? Hint: It was pretty devious. Backward reasoning is the key. First work on a scheme to get the resolution to pass, and then you can worry about unanimity. To ensure that the Sea Shells proposal passes, start at the end and make sure that the final two voters have an incentive to vote for the proposal. This will be enough to pass the resolution, since Sea Shells starts the process with a first yes vote.

Case Discussion

Many proposals do the trick. Here's one of them. Sea Shells' restructuring proposal has the following three cases:

- If the proposal passes unanimously, then Sea Shells chooses an entirely new board. Each board member replaced is given a small compensation.

- If the proposal passes 4 to 1, then the person voting against is removed from the board, and no compensation is made.

  If the proposal passes with a vote of 3 to 2, then Sea Shells transfers the entirety of its 51 percent share of Peter's Pickled Peppers to the other two yes voters in equal proportion. The two no voters are removed from the board with no compensation.

At this point, backward reasoning finishes the story. Imagine that the vote comes down to the wire: the last voter is faced with a 2–2 count. If he votes yes, it passes and he gets 25.5 percent of the company's stock. If it fails, Sea Shells' assets (and the other yes-voter's shares) are distributed evenly among the three remaining members, so he gets $(51 + 12.25)/3 = 21.1$ percent of the company's stock. He'll say yes.

Everyone can thereby use backward reasoning to predict that if it comes down to a 2–2 tie-breaking vote, Sea Shells will win when the final vote is cast. Now look at the fourth voter's dilemma. When it is his turn to vote, there are either

(i) 1 yes vote (by Sea Shells),

(ii) 2 yes votes, or

(iii) 3 yes votes.

If there are three yes votes, the proposal has already passed. The fourth voter would prefer to get something over nothing, and therefore votes yes. If there are two yes votes, he can predict that the final voter will vote yes even if he votes no. The fourth voter cannot stop the proposal from passing. Hence, again it is better to be on the winning side, so he will vote yes. Finally, if he sees only one yes vote, then he would be willing to bring the vote to a 2–2 tie. He can safely predict that the final voter will vote yes, and the two of them will make out very nicely indeed.

The first two Piper's board members are now in a true pickle. They can predict that even if they both vote no, the last two will go against them and the proposal will pass. Given that they can't stop it from passing, it is better to go along and get something.

This case demonstrates the power of backward reasoning. Of course it helps to be devious too.

5. WINNING WITHOUT KNOWING HOW

Chapter 2 introduced games in which players move in sequence and which always ends after a finite number of moves. In theory, we could examine every possible sequence of moves and thereby discover the best strategy. This is relatively easy for tic-tac-toe and impossible (at present) for chess. In the game below, the best strategy is unknown. Yet, even without knowing what it is, the very fact that it exists is enough to show that it must lead to a win for the first player.

ZECK is a dot-game for two players. The object is to force your opponent to take the last dot. The game starts with dots arranged in any rectangular shape, for example a 7 × 4:

```
. . . . . . .
. . . . . . .
. . . . . . .
. . . . . . .
```

Each turn, a player removes a dot and with it *all* remaining dots to the northeast. If the first player chooses the fourth dot in the second row, this leaves his opponent with

```
            . . .

            . . .

          . . . . . . .

          . . . . . . .
```

Each period at least one dot must be removed. The person who is forced to take the last dot loses.

For any shaped rectangle with more than one dot, the first player must have a winning strategy. Yet this strategy is not currently known. Of course we look at all the possibilities and then figure it out for any particular game, such as the 7 × 4 above — but we don't know the best strategy for all possible configurations of dots. How can we show who has the winning strategy without knowing what it is?

Case Discussion

If the second player has a winning strategy, that means that for *any* opening move of the first player, the second has a response that puts him in a winning position. Imagine that the first player just takes the upper right-hand dot.

```
          . . . . . .

          . . . . . . .

          . . . . . . .

          . . . . . . .
```

No matter how the second player responds, the board will be left in a configuration that the first player could have created in his first move. If this is truly a winning position, the first player should have and could have opened the game this way. There is nothing the second player can do to the first that the first player can't do unto him beforehand.

6. A SEASON FOR EVERYTHING AND EVERYTHING IN ITS SEASON

Consider the problem faced by the former United States Football League (USFL) in deciding whether to play in the fall or the spring. The fall market is the biggest, and consequently, the USFL's ideal would be to have a monopoly in the fall and have the National Football League (NFL) move to the spring. But, if the NFL remains in the fall, the USFL does better to take a monopoly in the spring. The worst possible outcome for the USFL would be if both leagues moved to a spring schedule.

The NFL, even with its stronger reputation, still prefers that the USFL play during its off season. However, its reputation is strong enough and the fall market is sufficiently bigger than the spring that the NFL prefers to go head-to-head against the USFL in the fall than take the spring by itself.

To make these ideas more precise, suppose that there are 100 million people who would watch football in the fall, and 50 million in the spring. If one league has a monopoly during a season, it gets the entire market for that season. If the two go head-to-head during a season, the NFL gets a 70 percent share and the USFL a 30 percent share during that season; the potential viewers for the other season go unserved.

The following table gives the viewer figures for both leagues for the four possible combinations of their choices. To save space, we have combined the tables of their separate yields into one. In each box, the bottom left entry is the USFL's market, and the top right is the NFL's market.

Table of Market Sizes for [USFL, NFL]

NFL

	Fall	Spring
USFL Fall	70 30	50 100
Spring	100 50	35 15

What do we expect to happen?

Case Discussion

The USFL does not have a dominant strategy. Its best move is always to play during the NFL's off season. Clearly this is not independent of what the NFL does. The NFL, however, does have a dominant strategy. It prefers the fall season independent of the USFL's choice; observe that the numbers in its first column, 70 and 100, are uniformly bigger than the corresponding numbers, 50 and 35, in the second column.

What should happen in this game? The NFL should pick its dominant strategy, namely the fall. The USFL, by putting itself in the NFL's cleats, should be able to predict that the NFL will play in the fall. Then, the USFL should choose the spring.

These predictions remain true for a wide range of potential fall and spring market sizes. Given a 70:30 market split between the NFL and USFL, the fall market can be anywhere from 43 percent to 233 percent bigger than the spring market and the same predictions fall out. Given this robustness of our result, we conclude that the USFL's move to a fall schedule was a mistake, and one that may very well have cost them their existence.

7. HE WHO LASTS LAST LASTS BEST?

Managers generally take a rosy view of time: markets expand, better technologies become available, information improves. But where there is growth, there is also decay. More than 10 percent of the United States' manufacturing output was accounted for by industries whose real output had shrunk during the 1970s. These declining industries range from core manufacturing such as steel, tire, and rubber to fibers and chemicals, to baby foods and vacuum tubes. The reasons for the decline are varied, ranging from technological progress (transistors over vacuum tubes) to improved foreign competition (steel) to regulation (chemicals) to changing demographics (baby foods).

In these declining industries, someone must reduce capacity in order for the industry to remain profitable. Each firm would like its competitors to shoulder the reduction; that way they can capture the remaining market by themselves.[2] This case examines the question of whether survivability is related to size. In declining markets, do Davids cut Goliaths down to size or do they get stepped on?

We look at competition between David and Goliath, both producers in the declining slingshot industry. David is a small producer. He manufactures one slingshot per quarter. Goliath is twice David's size. He produces two slingshots per quarter. The two competitors have no flexibility in choosing output. If they are in, they are in; once they stop, they can't come back.*

---

* In fact, these assumptions are appropriate for industries in which the marginal cost of producing up to historical capacity is low. For these industries, fixed costs dominate and result in tremendous pressure to fill up excess capacity. In alumina refining, for instance, operating below full capacity

Their battle has some of the same characteristics as *Time* versus *Newsweek*. Each quarter they decide whether to produce or to exit, without knowing their competitor's coeval choice. But then they find out last period's move and get to repeat the battle next quarter (provided neither exited).

The price chart on the next page details the market price (net of cost) depending on how much is produced. Starting in the first quarter of 1988, if David is a monopolist, he can expect to make $3 on his one slingshot. If David exits and leaves Goliath as a monopolist, Goliath gets a lower unit price since his output is bigger; in this case, he gets $2 per slingshot. (Of course, $2 on two slingshots is better than $3 on David's one.) If both David and Goliath produce, they are said to be duopolists. In that case they saturate the market, and the price (net of cost) falls to 50 cents.

The declining market is evident from the price chart. The first column shows the price net of cost if David captures the market for himself. The second column details the price net of cost if Goliath is a monopolist. The third column details the price net of cost if both firms continue to produce in a duopoly.

In each quarter after January 1988, the price falls by 25 cents for any output level brought to market. As can be seen from the chart, the pressure to exit begins in the third quarter of 1988, when the duopolists first lose money. By January 1990, Goliath is no longer profitable even as a monopolist. A year later, even David can no longer expect to make any money.

---

utilization is technically inefficient in that it alters product characteristics. Operating below 70 percent capacity is infeasible because a minimal amount of chemicals has to be fed through the machinery to keep it running. A strategy of frequently shutting down and starting up is not a viable option either. After each shutdown, corrosive chemicals accumulate in the machinery (e.g., caustic soda in the digestors). Start-up requires cleaning out the machinery and readjusting and "debottlenecking" it — a process that sometimes takes over a year. In effect, then, alumina refineries face a choice between operating at close to full capacity and shutting down permanently.

Table of Price (Net of Cost)

	David Alone	Goliath Alone	David & Goliath
Jan. 1988	3.00	2.00	0.50
Apr.	2.75	1.75	0.25
July	2.50	1.50	0.00
Oct.	2.25	1.25	−0.25
Jan. 1989	2.00	1.00	−0.50
Apr.	1.75	0.75	−0.75
July	1.50	0.50	−1.00
Oct.	1.25	0.25	−1.25
Jan. 1990	1.00	0.00	−1.50
Apr.	0.75	−0.25	−1.75
July	0.50	−0.50	−2.00
Oct.	0.25	−0.75	−2.25
Jan. 1991	0.00	−1.00	−2.50
Apr.	−0.25	−1.25	−2.75
July	−0.50	−1.50	−3.00
Oct.	−0.75	−1.75	−3.25

Over the twelve quarters from 1988 to 1991 the slingshot industry will become extinct. But when do the firms exit? Who gives up first? When do they exit?

This problem can be solved using the technique of sequentially eliminating dominated strategies. To get you started, note that staying past January 1990 is a dominated strategy for Goliath, as he forevermore loses money, irrespective of whether David stays or exits. Now work backward and ask what you would do if you were David and it was the third quarter of 1989 and Goliath was still producing.*

Case Discussion

In this problem, it does not matter how much money you make, just how long you can make it. The firm that can hang on the longest can force out its more profitable rival as soon as duopoly profits begin to turn negative.

As suggested in the hint, if David can hold on until the third quarter of 1989 he is home free. From then on, the worst possibility is that Goliath stays in the market through the fourth quarter of 1989. This will cost David $2.25 in duopoly losses. But when 1990 comes, Goliath must exit, since he suffers losses either as a duopolist or as a monopolist. Thus, David can count on making $2.50 in monopoly profits during the 1990s, which is enough to tide him over any possible losses during the final two quarters of 1989.

Now, the power of backward reasoning picks up steam. Given that David is committed to staying upon reaching July 1989 (exiting is a dominated strategy), Goliath can expect to earn only losses from July 1989 onward. Thus, he will exit immediately if he ever finds himself as a duopolist on that date. That means that David can expect to make the $2.50 as a monopolist in 1990 and $2.75 as a monopolist in the final two quarters of 1989. This windfall of $5.25 more than covers the maximum duopoly losses up until that date ($1.50), and

---

* In calculating the value of the worst-case scenario, you can simplify the mathematics by assuming a zero interest rate; profits (losses) tomorrow and today are equally valuable.

therefore David should never exit before January 1991. Given that David is committed to staying, Goliath should leave as soon as duopoly profits turn negative, July 1988.

Note that Goliath cannot make the same commitment to stay in the market for the same length of time. That commitment breaks down first in January 1990, and then the guaranteed exit by January 1990 translates into a forced exit by July 1989. The slippery slope for Goliath brings him back all the way to October 1988, the first instance when the market isn't big enough for the two of them.

This simple story of fighting for market share in declining industries may help explain the observation that large firms are often the first to exit. Charles Baden Fuller, an expert in the decline of British markets, reports that when the demand for U.K. steel casing fell by 42 percent over the period 1975–1981, executives of the two largest firms, F. H. Lloyd and the Weir Group, "felt that they had borne the brunt of the costs of rationalization; they accounted for 41 percent of the industry output in 1975, but for 63% of the capacity that was withdrawn over the 1975–1981 period, reducing their combined market share to 24 percent."

Remember that size is not always an advantage: in judo and here in exit strategies, the trick is to use your rival's bigger size and consequently inflexibility against him.

8. NOBLESSE OBLIGE

An important feature of OPEC is that its members are of unequal size. Saudi Arabia is potentially a much larger producer than any of the others. Do large and small members of a cartel have different incentives to cheat?

We keep matters simple by looking at just one small country, say Kuwait. Suppose that in a cooperative condition, Kuwait would produce 1 million barrels per day, and Saudi

Arabia would produce 4. For each, cheating means producing 1 million extra barrels a day. So Kuwait's choices are 1 and 2; Saudi Arabia's, 4 and 5. Depending on the decisions, total output on the market can be 5, 6, or 7. Suppose the corresponding profit margins (price minus production cost per barrel) would be $16, $12, and $8 respectively. This leads to the following profit table. In each box, the bottom left number is the Saudi profit, and the top right number is the Kuwaiti profit, each measured in millions of dollars per day.

**Profits (Millions of Dollars / Day)
for [Saudi Arabia, Kuwait]**

Kuwait
Production

		1	2
Saudi Arabia Production	4	64 16	48 24
	5	60 12	40 16

Kuwait has a dominant strategy: cheat by producing 2. Saudi Arabia also has a dominant strategy, but this is the co-operative output level of 4. The Saudis cooperate even though Kuwait cheats. The prisoners' dilemma has vanished. Why?

Case Discussion

Saudi Arabia has an incentive to cooperate for purely selfish reasons. If they produce a low output, the market price rises and the profit margins go up for *all* members of OPEC. If they had only a small share in OPEC's total output, they would not find it profitable to provide this "public service" to the whole cartel. But if their share is large, then a large part of the benefit of the higher profit margin comes to them, and it may be worth the cost of suffering some reduction in volume. This is what happens for the illustrative numbers we chose above.[3] Here is another way out of the prisoners' dilemma: find a large benefactor who acts cooperatively and tolerates others' cheating.

The same thing happens in many alliances. In many countries, a large political party and one or more small parties must form a governing coalition. The large party commonly takes the responsible positions and makes the compromises that hold the alliance together, while the small parties insist on their special concerns and get their often extreme way. The influence of small religious parties in Israel's coalition government is a prime example. Another example arises in the NATO alliance; the United States provides a disproportionate amount of the defense expenditure whose benefits go to Western Europe and Japan. Mancur Olson has aptly labeled this phenomenon "the exploitation of the great by the small."

9. Fill 'er Up

Many gasoline stations advertise only the price of their *leaded* gasoline. What makes this peculiar is that very few of their customers actually buy leaded gasoline; only cars manufactured before 1976 are able to use leaded gas.

It is clear how this practice began. Originally, there was only one type of gasoline. It wasn't until 1911, when Lewis and Jacob Blaustein invented a way to boost gasoline octane without using lead additives, that unleaded gas even became available. Another sixty years passed before it became the standard.

Now stations continue to advertise the price of a product bought by few customers. The stations display only one number to catch the eye of the passing motorist and continue to use the one they used before. Most motorists must infer the unleaded price they need to know from the leaded price. Why does this practice persist?

Case Discussion

What would happen if one gasoline station decided to advertise its unleaded gas price in big numbers? Motorists find it too difficult to read anything but the numbers. As a result, they assume it is the leaded gas price being advertised. Typically, unleaded gas is about five cents a gallon more expensive at the pumps, and drivers therefore would mistakenly add about a nickel to make their guess of the unleaded price. This maverick gasoline station puts itself at a disadvantage, as motorists overestimate its price. Interestingly enough, unleaded gas is cheaper wholesale. This suggests that leaded gas plays the role of a loss leader.*

A maverick station advertising its unleaded price puts itself at a further disadvantage: it competes on its bread-and-butter product. It is much better to engage in price wars on goods that account for only a small fraction of sales. A price war with unleaded gas threatens the profitability of the whole station.

The bottom line is that stations go on advertising the leaded price. This locked-in equilibrium is different in one respect from that of the QWERTY typewriter keyboard in Chapter 9: there we could find no winners from the status quo; here the gas stations benefit from the lack of competition over the price of unleaded gas. But the consumers are stuck in a bad equilibrium, and no gas station has any incentive to change it.

---

* Economists can offer a second reason why leaded gasoline sells for less: it is bought by a different set of customers. You might not be surprised to see smaller markups on products bought by people who drive old cars than on products bought by people who drive new cars. A new owner of a $30,000 BMW is less likely to balk at a ten cent markup than someone driving a beat-up '74 Pinto.

If society wants to improve matters for consumers, one way would be to legislate a change in the convention; require that if only one price is posted, this price must be that of unleaded. A second solution is to require that gasoline stations advertise in big numbers all of their basic grades, leaded, unleaded, and super unleaded. Soon enough this will all be moot; the sale of leaded gas is being phased out, so stations will have to advertise the price of their unleaded gas — its the only type they will be selling.

10. BAY BRIDGE

The morning traffic from Oakland to San Francisco across the Bay Bridge gets backed up from 7:30 to 11:00 A.M. Until the jam clears at 11:00, each additional car that enters the traffic makes all those who come later wait just a little longer. The right way to measure this cost is to sum up the additional waiting times across everyone who is delayed. What is the total waiting-time cost imposed by one additional car that crosses the bridge at 9:00 A.M.?

You may be thinking you don't know enough information. A remarkable feature to this problem is that the externality can be calculated based on the little amount you've been told. You don't need to know how long it takes the cars to cross the toll plaza, nor the distribution of cars that arrive after 9:00. The answer is the same whether the length of the traffic jam stays constant or varies widely until it clears.

Case Discussion

The trick is to see that all that matters is the sum of the waiting time. We are not concerned with who waits. (In other circumstances, we might want to weigh the waiting times by the monetary value of time for those caught in the jam.) The simplest way to figure out the total extra waiting time is to shuffle around who waits, putting all the burden on one person. Imagine that the extra driver, instead of crossing the bridge at 9:00 A.M., pulls his car over to the side and lets all the other drivers pass. If he passes up his turn in this way, the other drivers are no longer delayed by the extra car. Of course, he has to wait two hours before the traffic clears and the road is clear. But these two hours exactly equal the total waiting time imposed on all the other drivers if he were to cross the bridge rather than wait on the sidelines. The reason is straightforward. The total waiting time is the time it takes for everyone to cross the bridge. Any solution that involves everyone crossing the bridge gives the same total waiting time, but distributed differently. Looking at the solution in which the extra car does all the extra waiting is the easiest way to add up the new total waiting time.

11. THE TRAGEDY OF THE COMMONS

In an important and influential article, University of California biologist Garrett Harding described how untrammeled choices of individuals could lead to disaster for society:

> Picture a pasture open to all. It is to be expected that each herdsman will try to keep as many cattle as possible on this commons. ... Therein is the tragedy. Each man is locked into a system that compels him to increase his herd without limit, in a world that is limited. Ruin is the destination toward which all men rush, each pursuing his own best interest in a society that believes in the freedom of the commons.[4]

He discussed overpopulation, pollution, excessive fishing, and depletion of exhaustible resources in these terms. He concluded that people worldwide must recognize the necessity of restricting individual freedom in these choices, and accept some "mutual coercion mutually agreed upon."

We are asking you to identify the nature of the problem. Try to relate it to one or more of the examples we gave in this chapter. You can then identify alternative solutions and examine their merits.

Case Discussion

Depending upon the circumstances, the tragedy of the commons could be a many-person prisoners' dilemma (each person grazes too many cows) or a spillover problem (too many people choose to become herdsmen).

The economist's favorite solution would be the establishment of property rights. This is what actually happened in the fifteenth and sixteenth centuries in England: the common land was enclosed and claimed by the local aristocrats or landlords. When land is private property, the invisible hand will shut the gate to just the right extent. The owner will charge grazing fees to maximize his rental income, and this will cut back the use. This will enhance overall economic efficiency, but alter the distribution of income; the grazing fees will make the owner richer, and the herdsmen poorer.

This approach is not feasible in some instances. Property rights over the high seas are hard to define and enforce in the absence of an international government, as is control over air that moves from one country to another carrying pollutants. For this reason, whaling and acid rain must be handled by more direct controls, but securing the necessary international agreements is no easy matter either.

Population is an even harder problem, as Harding noted. The right of decision about one's family, including its size, is enshrined in the United Nations' Universal Declaration of Human Rights and in many countries' bills of rights. Countries like China and India that have at times used some coercion in their population-control efforts have evoked widespread disapproval.

Sometimes, when the group is small enough, voluntary cooperation solves the problem. When two oil or gas producers have wells that tap into the same underground deposit, each has the incentive to speed up his uptake, to get more of the resource before the other does. When both of them follow this policy, the excessive speed of depletion can actually lower the total amount that can be recovered from the deposit. In practice, drillers recognize the problem and seem able to reach production-sharing arrangements that keep at the proper level the total flow from all wells tapping one deposit. All's well that ends well?

12. WHAT PRICE A DOLLAR?

Professor Martin Shubik of Yale University designed the following game of entrapment. An auctioneer invites bids for a dollar. Bidding proceeds in steps of five cents. The highest bidder gets the dollar, but *both* the highest *and* the second highest bidders pay their bids to the auctioneer.[5]

Professors have made tidy profits — enough for a lunch or two at the faculty club — from unsuspecting undergraduates playing this game in classroom experiments. Suppose the current highest bid is 60 cents and you are second with 55. The leader stands to make 40 cents, but you stand to lose your 55. By raising to 65, you can put the boot on the other foot. The logic is no different when the leading bid is $3.60 and yours is $3.55. If you do not raise the bidding still further, the "winner" loses $2.60, but you lose $3.55.

How would you play this game?

Case Discussion

This is an example of the slippery slope. Once you start sliding, it is hard to recover. It is better not to take the first step unless you know where you are going.

The game has one equilibrium, in which the first bid is a

dollar and there are no further bids. But what happens if the bidding starts at less than a dollar. The escalation has no natural limit other than the amount of money in your wallet. At least, the bidding must stop when you run out of money. That is all we need to apply Rule 1: Look forward and reason backward.

Imagine that Eli and John are the two students in Shubik's auction of a dollar. Each has $2.50 in his wallet, and each knows the other's cash supply.[6] To keep things simple, bidding takes place in dime units.

To start at the end, if Eli ever bids $2.50, he'll win the dollar (and be down $1.50). If he bids $2.40, then John must bid $2.50 in order to win. Since it is not worth spending a dollar to win a dollar, an Eli bid of $2.40 will win if John's current bid is at $1.50 or less.

The same argument works if Eli bids $2.30. John can't bid $2.40 and expect to win, because Eli would counter with $2.50. To beat $2.30, John needs to go all the way up to $2.50. Hence a $2.30 bid beats $1.50 and below. So does a $2.20 bid, a $2.10 bid, all the way down to a $1.60 bid. If Eli bids $1.60, John should predict that Eli won't give up until the bidding reaches $2.50. Eli's dollar sixty is already lost; but it is worth his while to spend another ninety cents to capture the dollar.

The first person to bid $1.60 wins, because that establishes a credible commitment to go up to $2.50. In our mind, we should think of $1.60 as the same sort of winning bid as $2.50. In order to beat $1.50, it suffices to bid $1.60, and nothing less will do. That means $1.50 will beat all bids at 60 cents and below. Even a bid of 70 cents will beat all bids at 60 cents and below. Why? Once someone bids 70 cents, it is worthwhile for them to go up to $1.60 and be guaranteed victory. With this commitment, no one with a bid of 60 cents or less finds it worthwhile to challenge.

We expect that either John or Eli will bid 70 cents and the bidding will end. Although the numbers will change, the conclusion does not depend on there being just two bidders. Given that budgets differ, backward reasoning can still find the answer. But it is critical that everyone know everyone else's budget. When budgets are unknown, as one would expect, an equilibrium will exist only in mixed strategies.

Of course there is a much simpler and more profitable solution for the students: collusion. If the bidders agree among themselves, a designated person will bid a dime, no one else will bid at all, and the class will share the profit of ninety cents.

You may take this story as proof of the folly of Yale undergraduates. But is the escalation of the superpowers' nuclear arms arsenals all that different? Both incurred costs in the trillions of dollars in quest of the "dollar" of victory. Collusion, which means peaceful coexistence, is a much more profitable solution.

13. THE KING LEAR PROBLEM

Tell me, my daughters, —
Since now we will divest us both of rule,
Interest of territory, cares of state, —
Which of you shall we say doth love us most?
That we our largest bounty may extend
Where nature doth with merit challenge.
    — Shakespeare, *King Lear*

King Lear was worried about how his children would treat him in his old age. Much to his regret, he discovered that children do not always deliver what they promise.

In addition to love and respect, children are also motivated by the possibility of an inheritance. Here we look at how a strategic use of inheritance can manipulate children to visit their parents.

Imagine that parents want their children each week to each

visit once and phone twice. To give their children the right incentives, they threaten to disinherit any child who fails to meet this quota. The estate will be evenly divided among all the children who meet this quota. (In addition to motivating visits, this scheme has the advantage of avoiding the incentive for children to suffocate their parents with attention.)

The children recognize that their parents are unwilling to disinherit all of them. As a result, they get together and agree to cut back the number of visits, potentially down to zero.

The parents call you in and ask for some help in revising their will. Where there is a will, there is a way to make it work. But how? You are not allowed to disinherit all of the children.

Case Discussion

As before, any child who fails to meet the quota is disinherited. The problem is what to do if all of them are below the quota. In that case, give *all* of the estate to the child who visits the most. This will make the childrens' reduced visiting cartel impossible to maintain. We have put the children into a multiperson dilemma. The smallest amount of cheating brings a massive reward. A child who makes just one more phone call increases his or her inheritance from an equal share to 100 percent. The only escape is to go along with the parents' wishes. (Obviously, this strategy fails with only children. There is no good solution for couples with an only child. Sorry.)

14. *United States* v. *Alcoa*

An established firm in an industry stands to gain by keeping out new competition. Then it can raise prices to monopoly levels. Since monopoly is socially harmful, the antitrust authorities try to detect and prosecute firms that employ strategies to deter rivals from entering the business.

In 1945, the Aluminum Corporation of America (Alcoa) was convicted of such a practice. An appellate panel of Circuit Court judges found that Alcoa had consistently installed more refining capacity than was justified by demand. In his opinion, Judge Learned Hand said:

> It was not inevitable that it [Alcoa] should always anticipate increases in the demand for ingot and be prepared to supply them. Nothing compelled it to keep doubling and redoubling its capacity before others entered the field. It insists that it never excluded competitors; but we can think of no more effective exclusion than progressively to embrace each new opportunity as it opened and to face every newcomer with new capacity already geared into a great organization.

This case has been debated at length by scholars of antitrust law and economics.[7] Here we ask you to consider the conceptual basis of the case. How could the construction of excess capacity deter new competitors? What distinguishes this strategy from others? Why might it fail?

Case Discussion

An established firm wants to convince potential new competitors that the business would not be profitable for them. This basically means that if they entered, the price would be too low to cover their costs. Of course the established firm could simply put out the word that it would fight an unrelenting price war against any newcomers. But why would the newcomers believe such a verbal threat? After all, a price war is costly to the established firm too.

Installing capacity in excess of the needs of current production gives credibility to the established firm's threat. When such capacity is in place, output can be expanded more quickly and at less extra cost. It remains only to staff the equipment and get the materials; the capital costs have already been incurred and are bygones. A price war can be fought more easily, more cheaply, and therefore more credibly.

This makes sense in the logic of strategy, but will such a device work in practice? There are at least two qualifications that limit its success. First, if there are many firms already in the industry, then discouraging newcomers gives more profit to all of them. Will any one firm bear the costs of capacity when it gets only a part of the benefit? This is a standard prisoners' dilemma. If one firm is large enough, it may in its own interest provide such a service to the rest of the industry. Otherwise the firms must collude in building capacity; this may be hard to hide from the antitrust authorities.

In the Alcoa case, one may not regard the dilemma of who will install capacity as a serious problem, because Alcoa had a 90 percent share of the primary aluminum ingot market. But — and this is the second qualification — is that the relevant market? Even if there are no other producers of primary ingots, secondary production from scrap is a source of competition. So is Alcoa's own future production. Many aluminum-based products are highly durable. If Alcoa puts more aluminum on the market in the future, then the values of these durable goods will decrease. If the company cannot credibly guarantee the users that it will restrict its own future output, then they will fear such losses, and therefore reduce the price they are willing to pay for aluminum now. This is just like IBM's problem of pricing mainframe computers. The solution of renting is much harder here: you can't rent aluminum as such; Alcoa would have to extend its operations into all sorts of aluminum-based products.

15. Two Wrongs Keep Things Right

Parents often face a difficult problem punishing their children for bad behavior. Children have an uncanny sense that the parents' threat to punish may not be credible. They recognize that the punishment may hurt the parents as much as the children (although for very different reasons). The standard parental dodge to this inconsistency is that the punishment is for the child's own good. How can parents do a better job at making their threat to punish bad behavior credible?

Case Discussion

With two parents and one child, we have a three-person game. Teamwork can help the parents make an honest threat to punish a misbehaving child. Say the son misbehaves, and the father is scheduled to carry out the punishment. If the son attempts to rescue himself by pointing out the "irrationality" of his father's actions, the father can respond that he would, given the choice, prefer not to punish his son. But, were he to fail in carrying out the punishment, that would be breaking an agreement with his wife. Breaking that agreement would be worse than the cost of punishing the child. Thus the threat to punish is made credible.

Even single parents can play this game, but the argument gets much more convoluted, as the punishment agreement must be made with the child. Once again, say the son misbehaves, and his father is scheduled to carry out the punishment. If the son attempts to rescue himself by pointing out the "irrationality" of his father's actions, the father can respond that he would, given the choice, prefer not to punish his son. But, were he to fail in carrying out the punishment, then this would be a misdeed on his part, a misdeed for which he should be punished. Thus, he is punishing his son only to prevent getting punished himself. But who is there to punish him? It's the son! The son replies that were his father to forgive him, he too would forgive his father and not punish his father for failing to punish him. The father responds that were his son to fail to punish him for being lenient, this would be the *second* punishable offense done by the son in the same day! And so on and so forth do they keep each other honest. This may seem a little farfetched, but no less convoluted than most arguments used to justify punishing kids who misbehave.

16. WINNING THE HOME STRETCH

Chapter 1 told the story of how to keep the lead in the America's Cup race. Since each boat could observe the other, it was relatively straightforward for Dennis Conner to follow John Bertrand's course. How to stay ahead gets more complicated when the moves are simultaneous: prediction rather than observation is needed.

In duplicate bridge, a team is evaluated by how well it does playing a particular hand when compared to a second team that plays the same hand against a different set of opponents. Imagine that you are playing for Team A, and going into the final hand you are leading Team B, Goren and Zeck.

Your hand is almost but not quite perfect. You are guaranteed to make 6 no trump. You figure that you have a 50 percent chance of making 7 no trump, but then so do Goren and Zeck, since they are playing the same hand in the other room.* If you bid 7 and make it, that guarantees that you win the tournament. Even if you bid 7 and fail, if Goren and Zeck have made the same bid and also failed you still win. If both sides bid 6, you are guaranteed to win, since you went into the final round with the lead. If you bid 6 and they bid 7 and make it, they will overtake you and win.

What should you do to maximize your chance of winning? What do you think Goren and Zeck will do? How likely are you to win?

---

* It is important in this problem that your chance of making 7 no trump is independent of Goren and Zeck's chances, even though both teams are playing the same cards. This could happen if you will make 7 only if the lead is clubs and make 6 otherwise. Based on the cards, the lead is equally likely to be clubs or diamonds; in this case, your chance of making 7 will be independent.

Case Discussion

You are looking to maximize your chance of winning. The following table gives your probability based on who does what.

Your Team's Chance of Winning

Goren and Zeck

	7 No Trump	6 No Trump
7 No Trump	0.75	0.50
6 No Trump	0.50	1.0

Your Team (rows): 7 No Trump, 6 No Trump

Where did these numbers come from? When both teams bid 7 no trump, you will win unless you fail and they make it, which is a one-in-four possibility; hence you have a three-fourths chance of winning. When you alone bid 7 no trump, you win if you make it and lose if you don't; it's a fifty-fifty proposition. When you bid 6 and they bid 7, you win only if they fail; again it's a fifty-fifty proposition. When neither of the teams bids 7, you are guaranteed a victory.

Now that the table is filled out, calculating the equilibrium strategy is easy. Using the Williams method we find that 7 no trump should be bid two-thirds of the time and 6 no trump the other third.* If we take ratios by column rather than row and recognize that your chance of winning is the same as Goren and Zeck's chance of losing, then we find that they should play 7 no trump with probability 2/3 and 6 no trump with probability 1/3.

---

* In equilibrium, the ratio of 7 no trump to 6 no trump is $(1-0.5):(0.75-0.5)$ or 2:1.

What are your chances of winning the tournament? You can expect to win two out of three times that you are in this situation. For example, if you bid 7 no trump, then with probability 2/3 Goren and Zeck will also be playing 7 no trump, so your chance of winning is 0.75, and with 1/3 probability Goren and Zeck will bid 6 no trump, so that you win with chance 0.5: the weighted average is (2/3)(3/4) + (1/3)(1/2) = 2/3. You can verify that bidding 6 no trump leads to the same chance of winning.

In contrast, suppose you ignored the idea of mixing and always bid 7 no trump in this situation. If Goren and Zeck figured this out then they would never bid 7 no trump and your chance of winning would be reduced to 0.5. The advantage of following your equilibrium mixture is that you can't be outfoxed by your rivals.

17. BRINKMANSHIP AND THE JURY

On March 25, 1988, Judge Howard E. Bell, presiding over the Robert Chambers "Preppy Murder" trial, was facing a tough problem. According to *New York Times* reports, "The 12-member jury was falling apart. Desperate notes came out from individual jurors asking to be removed from the case. One man burst into tears in front of the judge and said his emotional health had been destroyed by the strain. At noon, two notes came out at the same time — one from the jury forewoman saying that the panel was 'at an impasse'; the other from an individual juror saying there was no impasse and that a verdict was still possible."

A hung jury would be a defeat for all parties. Jennifer Levin's family would have to suffer through a second trial, and Robert Chambers would have to bear several more months of uncertainty before being able to either get on with his life or start serving his sentence. Although there might be little else they could agree on, both sides wanted a verdict.

After nine days of deliberating, there was increasing evidence that if the jury did in fact come up with a decision, there would be no way to predict the decision beforehand. "Jurors said later that the votes were swinging wildly between convicting and acquitting Mr. Chambers of the most serious charge of second-degree murder."

How can Judge Bell use brinkmanship to help both parties?

Case Discussion

The prosecutor, Ms. Fairstein, and the Levin family would prefer to see a guarantee that Chambers get some sentence and be found guilty, than leave the outcome in the hands of an increasingly random jury, or worse, risk getting no result and having to go through a retrial.

The defense side, Chambers's attorney Mr. Litman and the Chambers family, also had reason to fear: an increasingly difficult-to-predict jury decision or retrial could both be worse than reaching a settlement plea bargain.

Judge Bell uses the risk of the jury actually reaching a decision or becoming hopelessly deadlocked as the threat to get both sides to negotiate. The judge has no control over how long the jury takes to make up its mind. As the defense and prosecution are negotiating a settlement, there is the constant risk that the jury will reach a decision or a permanent impasse.

There is no clear line saying that after ten days, six hours there will be a mistrial or a decision. Instead it is a slippery slope. Judge Bell has an incentive to keep the jury together and use this to pressure the two parties to reach terms. Even if the judge knows that the jury is at a permanent impasse, he might want to keep this from the two lawyers. He can tell the jury to play Monopoly for a day or two.

If the outcome were known, then the risk would be resolved and the two parties would lose their incentive to compromise. It is only because the two sides feel differently about the risk that they are brought together to seek a common middle ground.

When a case is brought before a jury, we create a risk that is beyond our control. Initially, we may think we know how the jury will decide, and the risk is manageable. But as the deliberations proceed, the uncertainty about the decision becomes overwhelming. The two opposing sides begin to have more similar beliefs about what the jury will decide, and then they can eliminate the risk by providing their own verdict.

Whether Judge Bell knowingly engaged in brinkmanship or not, he helped perpetuate a slippery slope that made everyone look for the safe high ground in a plea bargain.

18. THE FREEDOM TO MEDDLE

Liberal or libertarian social philosophies have a basic tenet that everyone has the right to make certain decisions without outside interference. Can social decisions be made in conformity with this principle?

Consider an issue that most people would place in this domain of individual sovereignty — the color of one's bedroom walls. Take two people, Rosencrantz and Guildenstern, and two colors, red and green. There are four possible color combinations. Write RG for the case in which Rosencrantz's bedroom walls are red and Guildenstern's are green, GR the other way round, RR when both walls are red, and GG when both are green.

One way to interpret the libertarian principle is, "For any choice in which the alternatives differ only in the color of one person's walls, that person's preference should be accepted by society."[8] Suppose Rosencrantz is a nonconformist; he wants his walls to be a different color from Guildenstern's. However, Guildenstern is a conformist; he wants his walls to be the same color as Rosencrantz's. With these preferences, there is no decision that abides by this libertarian principle — just try the different possibilities.[9]

You might think the problem is that each person's preference was, properly speaking, not for the color of his own walls as such, but for a color the same as, or the opposite of, the other person's. Allowing such preferences to rule the society's choice is tantamount to too much meddling in each other's affairs. Therefore let us create a second scenario, and restrict the sense of libertarianism: "If a person has an unconditional preference for the color of his own walls, and two alternatives differ only in this color, then that person's preference should be accepted by society."

Suppose Rosencrantz has an unconditional preference for his bedroom walls being red — he prefers RX to GX whether X, the color of Guildenstern's walls, equals R or G. While Rosencrantz prefers his own walls red, he also has a meddlesome interest and is even more strongly concerned that Guildenstern's walls be red. Thus his ranking of the four possibilities is RR best, GR second, RG third, and GG last. Guildenstern has a similar preference for green: GG best, GR second, RG third, RR last.

Ranking of Outcomes in Second Scenario by [Rosencrantz, Guildenstern]

	Guildenstern's Wall	
	Red	Green
Rosencrantz's Wall Red	4 / 1	3 / 3
Green	2 / 2	1 / 4

Show that the libertarian principle can lead to an outcome that is worse from both of their viewpoints than some other outcome. What can make libertarianism workable?

Case Discussion

The libertarian principle leads the players into a prisoners' dilemma. Rosencrantz's unconditional preference for having red bedroom walls is the analogue of a dominant strategy. Whichever color Guildenstern picks, Rosencrantz does better choosing red. Under libertarianism, society allows him this choice. Similarly, Guildenstern has his bedroom walls green as a dominant strategy. Once again, a liberalist society gives him this choice.

Putting their individual choices together leads to the outcome RG. But both Rosencrantz and Guildenstern prefer GR to RG. As in the prisoners' dilemma, we have another example where both players' following their dominant strategy leads them to a mutually inferior outcome.

One solution might be to restrict the sense of libertarianism still further. Thus the social decision might accept Rosencrantz's preference for red over green walls only if it is even less meddlesome, in the sense that he prefers both RG and RR over both GR and GG. This works, but only in the sense that since preferences are not actually of this kind, libertarianism doesn't apply in this situation. Philosophers have debated this problem endlessly, and devised further restrictions on libertarian rights.[10] But most of these proposals impose libertarianism as an outside requirement on the social decisions of people who continue to have meddlesome preferences about what others do. A truly lasting and workable solution requires general agreement over which matters belong to the domain of privacy, and agreement to abandon our preferences (become indifferent) about one another's choices in such matters. In other words, libertarianism should be ingrained in our private preferences if it is to succeed as a social norm.

19. A MEDALLION FOR THE MAYOR

In 1987, New York City mayor Ed Koch succeeded in increasing the number of licensed taxicabs in Manhattan. Over the previous fifty years, the population of Manhattan increased by 3 million people, while the number of taxicabs grew by 100. One sign of the shortage is that the right to legally operate a taxi (called a medallion) sold in the open market for just over $125,000 in 1987. At the same time, taxis were rented out for two twelve-hour shifts daily at about $60 per shift (or $45,000 per year).

If the city just auctioned off the 100 new medallions, they could bring in $12.5 million. The problem is that all the new owners should be worried that the city has discovered something too good to be true. Why won't they try to auction off 100 more new medallions next year? If the city can't promise to refrain from increasing the number of medallions until the point where they become worthless, nobody will pay very much for them in the first place.

Mayor Koch has called you in as a consultant. He wants advice on how to raise revenue when he increases the number of taxis. He is looking for a way to commit himself (and future administrations) not to keep diluting the value of the old medallions by continually printing new ones. The Taxi and Limousine Commission is in shambles, and nobody trusts a politician's word alone. What do you suggest?

Case Discussion

The trick is simply to rent rather than sell the new medallions. That way, nobody is paying for any future value which might later be appropriated. The mayor has an incentive to restrict the number of rental medallions, because if he rents too many, the total rent will fall, potentially all the way to zero if the medallions become worthless.

Note that this is really just an application of making commitments step by step. Here the steps are not the number of medallions but rather the length of time for which the medallions are good. People are willing to trust the mayor for a week or a year. It takes time to pass new legislation. And the most that is at risk is one year's value of a medallion. Rather than sell this year's medallion, next year's medallion, and all future medallions rolled up into one eternal medallion, the mayor can restore credibility by selling these commodities one at a time. The simple way to do this is just to rent rather than sell.

20. ARMS ACROSS THE OCEAN

In the United States many homeowners own guns for self-defense. In Britain almost no one owns a gun. Cultural differences provide one explanation. The possibility of strategic moves provides another.

In both countries, a majority of homeowners prefer to live in an unarmed society. But they are willing to buy a gun if they have reason to fear that criminals will be armed. Many criminals prefer to carry a gun as one of the tools of their trade.

The table below suggests a possible ranking of outcomes. Rather than assign specific monetary payoffs to each possibility, the outcomes are ranked 1, 2, 3, and 4 for each side.

Ranking of Outcomes [Homeowners, Criminals]

		Criminals	
		No Guns	Guns
Homeowners		[1, 2]	[4, 1]
No Guns			
Guns		[2, 4]	[3, 3]

If there were no strategic moves, we would analyze this as a game with simultaneous moves, and use the techniques from Chapter 3. We first look for dominant strategies. Since the criminals' grade in column 2 is always higher than that in a corresponding row in column 1, criminals have a dominant strategy: they prefer to carry guns whether or not homeowners are armed.

Homeowners do not have a dominant strategy; they prefer to respond in kind. If criminals are unarmed, a gun is not needed for self-defense.

What is the predicted outcome when we model the game as one with simultaneous moves? Following Rule 2, we predict that the side with a dominant strategy uses it; the other side chooses its best response to the dominant strategy of its opponent. Since guns is the dominant strategy for criminals, this is their predicted course of action. Homeowners choose their best response to guns; they too will own a gun. The resulting equilibrium is ranked [3,3], the third best outcome for both parties.

In spite of their conflicting interests, the two sides can agree on one thing. They both prefer the outcome in which neither side carries guns [1,2] to the case in which both sides are armed [3,3]. What strategic move makes this possible and how could it be credible?

Case Discussion

Imagine for a moment that criminals are able to preempt the simultaneity and make a strategic move. They would commit not to carry guns. In this sequential game, homeowners do not have to predict what criminals will do. They would see that the criminals' move has been made, and they are not carrying guns. Homeowners then choose their best response to the criminals' commitment; they too go unarmed. This outcome is ranked [1, 2], an improvement for *both* sides.

It is not surprising that criminals do better by making a

commitment.* But homeowners are better off, too. The reason for the mutual gain is that both sides place a greater weight on the others' move than their own. Homeowners can reverse the criminals' move by allowing them to make an unconditional move.†

In reality, homeowners do not constitute one united player, and neither do criminals. Even though criminals as a class may gain by taking the initiative and giving up guns, any one member of the group can get an additional advantage by cheating. This prisoners' dilemma would destroy the credibility of the criminals' initiative. They need some way to bond themselves together in a joint commitment.

If the country has a history of very strict gun-control laws, guns will be unavailable. Homeowners can be confident that criminals will be unarmed. Britain's strict control of guns allows criminals to commit to work unarmed. This commitment is credible, as they have no alternative. In the United States, the greater prevalence of guns denies criminals an ability to commit to work unarmed. As a result, many homeowners are armed for self-defense. Both sides are worse off.

Clearly this argument oversimplifies reality; one of its implications is that criminals should support gun-control legislation. Even in Britain, this commitment is difficult to maintain. The continuing political strife over Northern Ireland has had

---

* Could the criminals have done even better? No. Their best outcome is the homeowners' worst. Since homeowners can *guarantee* themselves 3 or better by owing guns, no strategic move by criminals can leave homeowners at 4. Hence, a commitment to go unarmed is the best strategic move for criminals. What about a commitment by the criminals to carry arms? This is their dominant strategy. Homeowners would anticipate this move anyway. Hence, it has no strategic value. By analogy with warnings and assurances, a commitment to a dominant strategy could be called a "declaration": it is informational rather than strategic.

† What happens if homeowners preempt and let the criminals respond? Homeowners can predict that for any unconditional choice of action on their part, criminals will respond by going armed. Hence, homeowners will want to go armed, and the result is no better than with simultaneous moves.

the indirect effect of increasing the availability of guns to the criminal population. As a consequence, the criminals' commitment not to carry guns has begun to break down.

In looking back, note that something unusual happened in the transition from a simultaneous-move to a sequential-move game. Criminals chose to forego what was their dominant strategy. In the simultaneous-move game it was dominant for them to carry guns. In the sequential-move game, they chose not to. The reason is that in a sequential-move game, their course of action affects the homeowners' choice. Because of this interaction, they can no longer take the homeowners' response as beyond their influence. They move first, so their action affects the homeowners' choice. Carrying a gun is no longer a dominant strategy in the sequential representation of the game.

21. THE LIMITS TO CHARITY

Many public goods, such as educational television, are financed primarily through private contributions. Since everyone benefits from the provision, there is an implicit bargaining problem over who will make the contributions and who will get a free ride. A look at the similarities between fund-raising and bargaining can help design a more effective fund-raising campaign.

In a bargaining problem, labor and management face pressure to compromise because of the potential for lost profits if a strike occurs. The incentive for compromise is similar to the the incentive to contribute. Public TV fund-raising campaigns try to make their viewers recognize a cost if contributions are not forthcoming. They threaten that shows may be canceled. More immediately, the station may interrupt scheduled broadcasts until a certain fund-raising goal is met. The desired programs are held hostage; the ransom is the next target level.

Just as the workers want the best deal possible, public television stations want to raise as much money as possible. But if they try to push beyond what is feasible, they risk alienating their viewers. The programs can be kept hostage only so long before they are given up.

The maximum level of potential contributions will of course depend on the number of viewers and how much they value the programming. If there are N potential contributors and each has a benefit B, the best one might hope is that the fund-raising will be successful whenever the target level T is less than the combined benefits, NB. Is that true? To answer this question, we look at a simple case in which there are only two potential contributors. The fund-raising goal is $10,000 and each values a successful campaign at $7,500. Then it should work, shouldn't it? The problem is that neither side wants to give $7,500 and let the other contribute only $2,500 and get all the surplus. Here we have a bargaining problem. The total combined value is $15,000 and the cost is only $10,000. How do the two parties divide the $5,000 surplus?

Again we use the idea of alternating offers to keep matters simple. In the present context, the two contributors are asked in sequence to make a donation pledge. The solicitation continues until the goal is met. We expect both individuals will make more than one pledge. They should employ the strategy of moving in small steps. This ensures that neither gets too far ahead of the other and thus contributes an unfair share. But there is a cost of moving slowly, and this must be balanced against the potential for exploitation.

The cost of moving slowly is that the contributors are impatient and would prefer to see the goal reached sooner rather than later. A benefit of B today is worth δB if we must wait until tomorrow before the benefit is received, where $\delta < 1$. This is just like lost interest on money; the difference in value between today and tomorrow is $B(1 - \delta)$, and if you think of these lost benefits as interest forgone, then think of $1 - \delta$ as the interest rate. Finally, remember that the contributions are made in the form of a pledge; they need be paid only after the fund-raising goal is met. Now all the facts are on the table. How much money can the campaign raise?

Case Discussion

This problem was recently solved by economists Anat Admati and Motty Perry. A remarkable feature of their answer is that the total contributions do not depend on the interest-rate variable δ. Even more surprising is that it is possible to raise an amount equal to the total valuation of all the contributors. Hence if the project is worthwhile, it should be possible to raise the money.

As always, we start at the end and work backward. While there is no natural time period for an ending, there is a contribution level that ends the implicit bargaining: if the fund-drive target is T, then the problem is over when T has been contributed. When the pledged amount is close enough to T, then the person whose turn it is should cap it off rather than wait another round. How close is close enough? The best that one can hope for by waiting is that the other person will make up the difference. Hence unless you bring the contribution to T, you can do no better than δV, the full value of the project one period later. On the other hand, if you contribute an amount x today, then you get the value $V - x$, the value today net your contribution. It is worthwhile bringing the total contributions up to T provided the amount needed is

$$x \leq (1 - \delta)V;$$

the contribution must be less than the interest lost.

Now both parties can look ahead and reason that once the contributions are up to $T - (1 - \delta)V$, the goal will be reached one period later. If the total pledge is close enough to this amount, then it is worthwhile to bring it up to that total and speed up the completion of the campaign. Note that there is no incentive to contribute an amount that brings the total above that level, for that just reduces the next party's contribution without any savings to yourself. Nor are you willing to bring the pledge total all the way to T, since that involves more money than the cost of delaying completion by one period. Thus if you make a contribution of y that brings the total to $T-(1-\delta)V$, your payoff is $\delta(V-y)$: one period later you get the payoff V and pay your pledge y. Alternatively, you can wait a period and switch positions. Then the other person makes a contribution that brings you up to $T-(1-\delta)V$, in which case it becomes worth your while to contribute $x = (1-\delta)V$. Your payoff is

$$\delta^2[V - (1-\delta)V] = \delta^3 V;$$

this is the value of completing the campaign in two periods net the contribution you make. Comparing the value of contributing to waiting, we see that it is worthwhile contributing rather than suffering an extra period of delay provided

$$y \le (1 - \delta^2)V.$$

Note that our calculations did not take into account the amount that each person has already contributed. The reason is that the contributors are always looking forward to how much more they should contribute; their previous pledges are not a relevant part of this calculation since they will be paid one way or the other and thus net out of any cost-benefit calculation.

So far we have figured out how much money will be raised in the last two periods. Applying the same reasoning allows us to go back further and calculate how long the campaign will take to reach its goal and how much people are willing to contribute at each stage so as not to delay the process. The total potential for contributions is the sum of these amounts. They are

$$(1 - \delta)V + (1 - \delta^2)V + \delta(1 - \delta^2)V + \delta^2(1 - \delta^2)V + \ldots = 2V$$

Note that the first two terms were the contributions from the last two periods as calculated above. What is remarkable is that the total potential for contributions does not depend on the interest rate δ. This maximum amount equals the sum of the two contributors' valuations. It is possible to get individuals to contribute their full value of the project. This suggests that the outcome of the fund-raising drive is a good reflection of how much the contributors value the project.

22. THE LIMITS TO REDISTRIBUTION

The political systems of many countries have economic equality as a central tenet of their policy. Almost all governments use some form of redistributive taxation. For example, the United States had top rates of income tax exceeding 70 percent in the 1960s and 1970s, while in Sweden the marginal tax rate could exceed 100 percent. But in the last decade the idea has taken hold that high tax rates destroy incentives to work. Thus in the 1980s, the top rates were reduced dramatically, both by the United States and even by the more egalitarian government of Sweden.

The prime motivation to lower taxes was the deleterious effect of taxes on work incentives. While there is now a greater incentive to accumulate wealth, there is also greater inequality of income. Of course there are many causes of inequality, and a tax on income is a blunt tool for attacking the symptom, not the cause. Think about the different causes of inequality and how they influence the design of an ideal tax system. What are the problems of implementing this ideal system? How does it compare with the present system?

Case Discussion

We begin by looking at some of the causes of economic inequality. First, there is luck. This can be of two kinds. Some people are born with some innate talent or advantage over others. Even among those who start equal in these respects, fortune favors the endeavors of some more than others. Many people think there is something unfair about inequality that arises from luck, and taxation that equalizes such advantages finds fairly broad support.

Then there is effort; some people just work harder or longer than others. When people express agreement with the claim that taxation destroys incentives, they usually mean the incentive to supply effort. Who would work hard if the government stands ready to take away a large part of the result? Many people also think it morally right that one should be able to keep the fruits of one's own effort, although die-hard egalitarians argue that one should be willing to share the gains with others.

Let us suppose that the government wants to collect at least a part of the economic fruit of each citizen's effort, without destroying incentives. If the tax collectors can observe each individual's effort, there is no problem. The tax schedule for each person can be expressed directly in terms of his effort, and a really punitive tax levied for any amount of effort smaller than the ideal.

In fact it is very difficult to monitor the effort of millions of workers. They may have to clock in and clock out every day, but they can take things easy and lower the quality of their work. Even the Soviet-type economies, which have very severe penalties at their disposal, have found it impossible to improve the quality of work without offering material incentives. This has led them into a vicious circle in which the workers say of the government: "We pretend to work, and they pretend to pay us."

In practice, effort must be judged by an indirect indicator, usually the income that results from the effort. But this indicator is not perfect; a high income may be the result of a large amount or a high quality of effort, or it may be due to a stroke of luck. Then the tax system can no longer be finely tuned to eliciting the right effort from each person. Instead of a harsh punishment for shirking, the tax schedule would have to impose a harsh punishment for realizing low income, and that will punish the unlucky along with the shirkers. There is a fundamental conflict between the egalitarian and the incentive effects of the tax system, and the schedule must strike a balance between them.

Next consider differences in natural talent. The egalitarian might think it perfectly legitimate to tax away the economic gains that arise for this reason. But ability to do so depends on locating the talented, and inducing them to exercise that talent despite the knowledge that the resulting income will be taxed away. The problem is made all the worse because much effort is required to bring even the best of talent to full fruition. Once again, pursuit of egalitarianism is limited because it requires the society to make poor use of its talent pool.

The best example of the difficulty of identifying and then taxing the fruits of talent occurs in the treatment of top artists and sport stars in the Soviet Union and other communist countries. The avowed policy of these countries is that all the winnings of the sport stars, or receipts from performances of the artists in the West, go to the state, and the individuals get only salaries and expenses. One would think that such people would give their best anyway, motivated by their personal pride and the pleasure that comes from doing one's best. In practice, the salaries and other perks place these individuals far above the average standard of living in their countries. Even then, many of them defect to the West. Recently, some top Soviet tennis players have started to negotiate the percentage of their winnings they may keep, an unusual instance of bargaining about an income tax schedule.

Finally, even after a tax schedule that attempts to strike the right balance between equality and incentives has been established, the administration must think about its enforcement strategy. The ultimate economic result of effort or luck, namely a person's income or wealth, is not easily observed by the government. The payers of items like wages, salaries, interest, and dividends are required to report them to the tax authorities. But to a considerable extent, governments must ask individuals to report their own incomes. The reports can be audited, but that is a costly process, and in practice only a small percentage of tax returns can be audited. How should these be chosen?

In our discussion of the advantages of mixed strategies, we pointed out that fixed and publicly known rules on auditing have a serious flaw. People who are thinking of understating income or inflating their deductions will make sure to stay just outside the audit criteria, and those who cannot avoid an audit will be honest. Exactly the wrong people will be audited. Therefore some randomness in the auditing strategy is desirable. The probability of an audit should depend on the various items on a tax return. But how?

If all people were otherwise identical, then the ones with low incomes would be the ones who had bad luck. But anyone can report a low income and hope to be taken for a victim of bad luck. This seems to imply that the probability of an audit should be higher for the tax returns reporting lower incomes.

But people are not otherwise identical, and these differences are often much bigger than those of luck. A tax return reporting an income of $20,000 is more likely to be from an honest factory worker than a cheating lawyer. Luckily, the tax authorities do have independent information about a person's occupation. Therefore a better rule is, the probability of an audit should be high for a return in which the reported income is low compared to what one would expect for someone in that occupation. Similarly, audits should target those returns claiming deductions that are high compared with what one would expect given other aspects of the return. And that is in fact done.

23. FOOLING ALL THE PEOPLE SOME OF THE TIME: THE LAS VEGAS SLOTS

Any gambling guide should tell you that slot machines are your worst bet. The odds are way against you. To counter this perception and encourage slot machine play, some Las Vegas casinos have begun to advertise the payback ratio for their machines — the fraction of each dollar bet returned in prize money. Going one step further, some casinos guarantee that they have machines that are set to a payback ratio greater than 1! These machines actually put the odds in your favor. If you could only find those machines and play them, you would expect to make money. The trick, of course, is that they don't tell you which machines are which. When they advertise that the average payback is 90 percent and that some machines are set at 120 percent, that also means that other machines must be set somewhere below 90 percent. To make it harder for you, there is no guarantee that machines are set the same way each day — today's favorable machines could be tomorrow's losers. How might you go about guessing which machines are which?

Case Discussion

Since this is our final case, we can admit that we do not have the answer — and even if we did, we probably wouldn't share it. Nonetheless, strategic thinking can help make a more educated guess. The trick is to put yourself into the casino owners' shoes. They make money only when people play the disadvantageous machines at least as much as the favorable machines.

Is it really possible that the casinos could "hide" the machines which are offering the favorable odds? If people play the machines that pay out the most, won't they find the best ones? Not necessarily, and especially not necessarily in time! The payoff of the machine is in large part determined by the chance of a jackpot prize. Look at a slot machine that takes a quarter a pull. A jackpot prize of $10,000 with a 1 in 40,000 chance would give a payoff ratio of 1. If the casino raised the chance to 1 in 30,000, then the payoff ratio would be very favorable at 1.33. But people watching others play the machine would almost always see a person dropping quarter after quarter with no success. A very natural conclusion would be that this is one of the least favorable machines. Eventually, when the machine pays its jackpot prize, it could be retooled and then set at a lower rate.

In contrast, the least favorable machines could be set to pay back a large fraction of the money with a very high chance, and basically eliminate the hope of the big jackpot. Look at a machine set with a payback of 80 percent. If it provided a $1 prize on roughly every fifth draw, then this machine would make a lot of noise, attracting attention and possibly more gamblers' money.

Perhaps the experienced slot players have figured all this out. But if so, you can bet that the casinos are just doing the reverse. Whatever happens, the casinos can find out at the end of the day which machines were played the most. They can make sure that the payoff patterns that attract the most play are actually the ones with the lower payoff ratio. For while the difference between a payoff ratio of 1.20 and 0.80 may seem large — and determines the difference between making money and losing money — it can be extremely hard to distinguish based on the number of experiments any one slot player has to make. The casinos can design the payoffs to make these inferences harder and even go the wrong way most of the time.

The strategic insight is to recognize that unlike the United Way, the Las Vegas casinos are not in the business to give out money. In their search for the favorable machines, the majority of the players can't be right. For if the majority of the people were able to figure it out, the casino would discontinue their offer rather than lose money. Hence, don't wait in line. You can bet that the most heavily played machines are not the ones with the highest payback.

Notes

1 TEN TALES OF STRATEGY

1. Their research is reported in "The Hot Hand in Basketball: On the Misperception of Random Sequences," *Cognitive Psychology* 17 (1985): 295–314.

2. *New York Times*, Sept. 22, 1983, p. B19.

3. These quotes are from Martin Luther's speech at the Diet of Worms on April 18, 1521, as described in Roland Bainton, *Here I Stand: A Life of Martin Luther* (New York: Abingdon-Cokesbury).

4. Don Cook, *Charles de Gaulle: A Biography* (New York: Putnam, 1982).

5. David Schoenbrun, *The Three Lives of Charles de Gaulle* (New York: Athenaeum, 1966).

6. Gary Hufbauer, Diane Berliner, and Kimberley Ann Elliott, *Trade Protection in the United States: 31 Case Studies* (Washington, D.C.: Institute for International Economics, 1985).

2 ANTICIPATING YOUR RIVAL'S RESPONSE

1. *Robert Frost's Poems*, ed. Louis Untermeyer (New York: Washington Square Press, 1971).

2. He can move one of eight pawns forward either one square or two, or he can move one of the two knights in one of two ways (to the squares labeled rook-3 or bishop-3).

3 SEEING THROUGH YOUR RIVAL'S STRATEGY

1. Alfred, Lord Tennyson, *In Memoriam* (New York: W. W. Norton, 1973) pp. 19–20. Even better is Samuel Butler's play on Tennyson: "Tis better to have loved and lost than never to have lost at all," from *The Way of All Flesh* (New York: E. P. Dutton, 1952) p. 385.

2. Quoted from "Game Theory: Reagan's Move," *New York Times*, April 15, 1981, p. D2.

3. Researchers at the frontiers of game theory worry about the limitations of the Nash equilibrium concept. They have developed games where intuitively obvious outcomes are not Nash equilibria and vice versa. But these issues do not affect most applications of game theory. Readers who are curious about the limits of Nash equilibrium can find excellent discussions in Ken Binmore's forthcoming text *Fun and Games* (Lexington, Mass.: D.C. Heath) and David Kreps's *Game Theory and Economic Modelling* (Oxford: Oxford University Press, 1990).

4 RESOLVING THE PRISONERS' DILEMMA

1. Reported in the *Wall Street Journal*, December 4, 1986.

2. Robert Axelrod, *The Evolution of Cooperation* (New York: Basic Books, 1984).

3. This case study summarizes his paper "Issues in the Coordination of Monetary and Fiscal Policy" in *Monetary Issues in the 1980's* (Kansas City: Federal Reserve Bank of Kansas City, 1983).

5 STRATEGIC MOVES

1. *Institutional Investor* (June 1979).

2. The terminology, and much of the analysis, was pioneered by Thomas Schelling in *The Strategy of Conflict* (Cambridge, Mass.: Harvard University Press, 1960).

3. Oscar Wilde, *Lady Windermere's Fan* (London: Methuen, 1909).

4. "Economic Scene," *New York Times* April 10, 1981, p. D2 and April 15, 1981, p. D2.

5. The Sun Tzu translation is from Lionel Giles, *Sun Tzu on the Art of War*.

6. See John Newhouse, *The Sporty Game* (New York: Alfred A. Knopf, 1983).

7. We chose the particular numbers for costs and profits to make the points in the simplest way; other numbers can produce different outcomes. For more on this topic see Avinash Dixit and Albert

Kyle, "The Use of Protection and Subsidies for Entry Promotion and Deterrence," *American Economic Review* (March 1985): 139–52.

6 CREDIBLE COMMITMENTS

1. *Bartlett's Familiar Quotations* (Boston, Mass.: Little, Brown & Co., 1968), p. 967.

2. Dashiell Hammett, *The Maltese Falcon* (San Francisco: Pan Books, Ario Press, 1983), p. 15.

3. Hobbes, *Leviathan* (London: J. M. Dent & Sons, 1973), p. 71.

4. John F. Kennedy speaking on July 25, 1961. The quote is taken from Fred Ikle's book, *How Nations Negotiate* (New York: Harper and Row, 1964), p. 67.

5. *Wall Street Journal*, August 7, 1986.

6. *Wall Street Journal*, January 2, 1990, p. B1.

7. Even so, Mr. Russo might find it difficult to renegotiate with a large number of people simultaneously. If even one person fails to agree, the renegotiation is held up.

8. This example is from his commencement address to the Rand Graduate School, later published as "Strategy and Self-Command," in *Negotiation Journal* (October 1989).

9. Prescott, *The History of the Conquest of Mexico*, vol. 1 (London: Gibbings and Co., 1896), Chapter 8.

10. Ibid.

11. This interpretation and further mathematical analysis of strategic commitment may be found in Jeremy Bulow, John Geanakoplos, and Paul Klemperer's paper "Multimarket Oligopoly: Strategic Substitutes and Complements," *Journal of Political Economy* 93 (1985): 488–511.

12. This description and quote comes from Michael Porter, *Cases in Competitive Strategy* (New York: Free Press, 1983).

13. *Pudd'nhead Wilson's Calendar* (New York: W. W. Norton, 1980), Chapter 15, p. 73.

14. Thomas Schelling, *The Strategy of Conflict* (Cambridge, Mass.: Harvard University Press, 1960), p. 200.

15. For a fascinating account of incentives used to motivate soldiers, see John Keegan's book *The Face of Battle* (New York: Viking Press, 1976).

16. See Fisher, McGowan, and Greenwood's account in *Folded, Spindled, and Mutilated* (Cambridge, Mass.: MIT Press, 1983).

17. Ronald Coase, "Durability and Monopoly," *Journal of Law and Economics* 15 (April 1972).

7 UNPREDICTABILITY

1. *New York Times*, October 12, 1986, pp. 5.1–2.

2. David Halberstam, *The Summer of '49* (New York: Morrow, 1989).

3. *The Compleat Strategyst*, rev. ed. (New York: McGraw-Hill, 1966).

4. For a more detailed account of this story, see Christopher Andrew's book *Her Majesty's Secret Service* (New York: Penguin, 1986).

5. This story is taken from Sigmund Freud's *Jokes and Their Relationship to the Unconscience* (New York: W. W. Norton, 1963).

6. John McDonald, *Strategy in Poker, Business, and War* (New York: W. W. Norton, 1950), p. 30.

8 BRINKMANSHIP

1. For a detailed account of the crisis, see Elie Abel, *The Missile Crisis* (New York: J. B. Lippincott, 1966). Graham Allison offers a wonderful game-theoretic analysis of the Cuban missile crisis in his book *Essence of Decision: Explaining the Cuban Missile Crisis* (Boston: Little, Brown & Co., 1971); we shall refer to this at several points in this chapter.

2. The evidence is in Graham Allison's *Essence of Decision*, pp. 129–30.

3. Allison, *Essence of Decision*, p. 131. He attributes it to Elie Abel's reconstruction of the meeting.

4. See Schelling's book *Arms and Influence* (New Haven, Conn.: Yale University Press, 1966), p. 70.

5. These excerpts are taken from the book on which the movie was based: Dashiell Hammett's *The Maltese Falcon* (San Francisco: Pan Books, Ario Press, 1983), p. 169.

6. See Graham Allison's *Essence of Decision.*

7. This hypothetical scenario was painted in an episode of the British television comedy series, "Yes, Prime Minister."

8. "Inadvertent Nuclear War?" *International Security* 7 (1982): 28–54.

9. Both quotes are from a *New York Times Magazine* (December 15, 1985, pp. 31–69) article on then Navy Secretary Lehman.

9 COOPERATION AND COORDINATION

1. This estimate for the advantage of DSK over QWERTY is based on work by David Rumelhart, a psychology professor at Stanford University.

2. The sad facts of this story come from Stanford economist W. Brian Arthur, "Competing Technologies and Economic Prediction," *Options*, International Institute for Applied Systems Analysis, Laxenburg, Austria, April 1984. Additional information is provided by Paul David, an economic historian at Stanford, in "Clio and the Economics of QWERTY," *American Economic Review*, Papers and Proceedings, May 1985.

3. See W. Brian Arthur, Yuri Ermoliev, and Yuri Kaniovski's paper "On Generalized Urn Schemes of the Polya Kind." Originally published in the Soviet journal *Kibernetika*, it has been translated and reprinted in *Cybernetics* 19 (1983): 61–71. Similar results are shown through different mathematical techniques by Bruce Hill, David Lane, and William Sudderth in their paper "A Strong Law for Some Generalized Urn Processes," published in *Annals of Probability* 8 (1980): 214–26.

4. W. Brian Arthur, "Competing Technologies and Economic Prediction," *Options*, International Institute for Applied Systems Analysis, Laxenburg, Austria (April, 1984): 10–13.

5. See R. Burton's 1976 paper "Recent Advances in Vehicular Steam Efficiency," *Society of Automotive Engineers* Preprint 760340, and W. Strack's paper "Condensers and Boilers for Steam-powered Cars," NASA Technical Note, TN D-5813 (Washington, D.C., 1970). While the overall superiority may be in dispute among engineers, a strong

advantage of steam or electric powered cars is the reduction in pollution emissions.

6. These comparisons are catalogued in Robin Cowen's 1988 New York University working paper "Nuclear Power Reactors: A Study in Technological Lock In." The expert engineer sources for these conclusions include Hugh McIntyre's 1975 *Scientific American* article "Natural-Uranium Heavy-Water Reactors," Harold Agnew's 1981 *Scientific American* article "Gas-Cooled Nuclear Power Reactors," and Eliot Marshall's 1984 *Science* article "The Gas-Cooled Reactor Makes a Comeback."

7. The quote is from M. Hertsgaard's book *The Men and Money Behind Nuclear Energy* (New York: Pantheon, 1983). Murray used the words "power-hungry" rather than "energy-poor," but of course he meant power in the sense of electric rather than influential.

8. Lester Lave of the University of California, Irvine, finds strong statistical evidence to support this. See his article "Speeding, Coordination and the 55 m.p.h. Speed Limit," *American Economic Review* (December 1985).

9. Cyrus Chu, an economist at the National Taiwan University, develops this idea into a mathematical justification for the cyclic behavior of crackdowns followed by lax enforcement in his working paper "Justifying Short-lived Enthusiasm in Law Enforcement."

10. See his book *Micromotives and Macrobehavior* (New York: W. W. Norton, 1978), Chapter 4.

11. See his article "Stability in Competition," *Economic Journal* (March 1929).

12. *The General Theory*, vol. 7 (of Keynes' collected works) (New York: St. Martin's Press, 1973), p. 156.

13. For some amusing stories about the tulip bulb mania see Burt Malkiel's *Random Walk down Wall Street* (New York: W. W. Norton, 1975), pp. 27–29. Charles Kindleberger's *Manias, Panics and Crashes* (New York: Basic Books, 1978) is a highly instructive and entertaining examination of the history of booms and busts in a variety of markets.

10 THE STRATEGY OF VOTING

1. The story of Pliny the Younger is first told from the strategic viewpoint in Robin Farquharson's 1957 Oxford University doctoral thesis, which was later published as *Theory of Voting* (New Haven, Conn.: Yale University Press, 1969). William Riker's *The Art of Political Manipulation* (New Haven, Conn.: Yale University Press, 1986) provides much more detail and forms the basis for this modern retelling. Riker's book is filled with compelling historical examples of sophisticated voting strategies ranging from the Constitutional Convention to the recent attempts to pass the Equal Rights Amendment.

2. The arguments are presented in their book *Approval Voting* (Boston, Mass.: Birkhauser, 1983).

3. This topic is addressed in recent economics working papers by Princeton professor Douglas Bernheim and University of Michigan professor Hal Varian.

4. This history of the line-item veto and the empirical results are reported in Douglas Holtz-Eakin's paper "The Line Item Veto and Public Sector Budgets," *Journal of Public Economics* (1988): 269–92.

11 BARGAINING

1. The generalization to bargaining without procedures is based on recent work by economists Motty Perry and Philip Reny.

2. This case is discussed by Larry DeBrock and Alvin Roth in "Strike Two: Labor-Management Negotiations in Major League Baseball," *The Bell Journal of Economics* (Autumn 1981).

3. Howard Raiffa's book *The Art and Science of Negotiation* (Cambridge, Mass.: Harvard University Press, 1982) is an excellent source for strategy in multiple-issue bargaining.

13 CASE STUDIES

1. For more on this problem, including a historical perspective, see Paul Hoffman's informative and entertaining book *Archimedes' Revenge* (New York: W. W. Norton, 1988).

2. Columbia Business School professor Kathryn Harrigan expresses

this principle in her maxim "The last iceman always makes money." (See *Forbes*, "Endgame Strategy," July 13, 1987, pp. 81–204.)

3. The incentive for Saudi Arabia to cooperate also depends on the size of the market. As the market expands, cheating becomes more profitable, and the Saudis might not be above sneaking in a defection if they thought it safe to do so. The rewards to the leader of holding the cartel together are larger in adverse markets. This conclusion accords with the story of OPEC. It was when the market weakened in the early 1980s that the Saudis clearly committed themselves to the role of the "swing producer," promising to reduce their output so as to allow the smaller members bigger shares.

4. Garrett Harding, "The Tragedy of the Commons," *Science* 162 (December 13, 1968): 1243–48.

5. Martin Shubik, "The Dollar Auction Game: A Paradox in Noncooperative Behavior and Escalation," *Journal of Conflict Resolution* 15 (1971): 109–111.

6. This idea of using a fixed budget and then applying backward logic is based on research by political economist Barry O'Neill, which is forthcoming in the *Journal of Conflict Resolution*.

7. A summary of the arguments appears in F. M. Scherer, *Industrial Market Structure and Economic Performance* (Chicago: Rand McNally, 1980).

8. Bruce Ackerman's book *Social Justice in the Liberal State* (New Haven, Conn.: Yale University Press, 1980) provides several alternative definitions of liberalism in his defense of the principle.

9. Start with RR, and compare it with GR. The two differ only in the color of Rosencrantz's walls, and being the nonconformist, Rosencrantz prefers GR. So we accept GR. Now introduce GG. This differs from GR only in the color of Guildenstern's walls; Guildenstern is the conformist and prefers GG. Compare that in turn with RG; here Rosencrantz's preference for RG should be respected. Finally, bring back RR, which wins since it belongs to Guildenstern's realm of privacy. The cycle can continue indefinitely.

10. Alan Gibbard, "A Pareto-consistent Libertarian Claim," *Journal of Economic Theory* 7 (1974): 388–410.

Index